Understanding Economic Recovery in the 1930s

Understanding Economic Recovery in the 1930s

Endogenous Propagation in the
Great Depression

Frank G. Steindl

The University of Michigan Press

Ann Arbor

To David, Andrew, Peter, and Matthew

2007   2006   2005   2004   4   3   2   1

A CIP catalog record for this book is available from the British Library.

Library of Congress Cataloging-in-Publication Data

Steindl, Frank G. (Frank George), 1935–
    Understanding economic recovery in the 1930s : endogenous
propagation in the Great Depression / Frank G. Steindl.
        p.   cm.
    Includes bibliographical references and index.
    ISBN 0-472-11348-8 (Cloth : alk. paper)
        1. United States—Economic policy—To 1933. 2. United
States—Economic policy—1933–1945. 3. Depressions—United
States—1929. 4. Business cycles—United States. 5. United
States—Economic conditions—1918–1945. 6. United States—Politics
and government—1933–1945. I. Title.
HC106.3 .S7275   2003
330.973'0917—dc21   2003005020

Contents

Preface

The Great Depression continues to captivate scholars, and not only senior ones for whom reminiscing may be a most enjoyable, important activity. This book is concerned with the Great Depression, but in contrast to so much of the literature, its ambit is the economic recovery from the disastrous economic dive culminating in the spring of 1933. The particular focus is on the macroeconomic developments responsible for the move back to the trend rate of growth of output, to a high-employment economy more in keeping with its performance in the early half of 1929.

By far the dominant concern of those writing about the 1930s is with the three and a half year decline into early 1933, so much so that one hears frequently the term *Great Depression* assigned to those years of Contraction. In contrast, the recovery, which lasted more than twice as long as the slide, receives scant attention. That an economy could deteriorate so much and to such depths seemed inconceivable; it demanded an explanation. It thus captured the attention of scholars as it called out for analysis and understanding, and therefore explication, of its causes, processes, and likely options for recovery. This activity so consumed investigators in their quest for answers that it is only in the past decade or so that professional attention has shifted to the recovery.

Economists of course were not alone in writing about the 1930s. Certainly historians, political scientists, essayists, and the media devoted much energy and many words to those times, again however the bulk concentrating on the Contraction. To the extent that the recovery was considered, it was largely incidental to the many studies dealing with Franklin D. Roosevelt and the politics, policies, and programs spawned by his New Deal—these being largely microeconomic forays owing to belief that the capitalist system needed to be restructured. Much of the material that interests them is the same as that which absorbed the energies of the policymakers in that decade, namely, microeconomic restructuring actions, of which the National Industrial Recovery Act is a prototype.

In contrast, the present essay says virtually nothing about the 1929–33 cataclysm. It similarly does not deal in any detail with specific happenings that so fascinated Roosevelt scholars, except as any of them clearly affected the march to a high-employment economy, that is, as any one had a discernible macroeconomic impact.

Postwar studies have taken as their point of departure examination of macroeconomic impulses, which almost without exception are investigations of aggregate demand actions. And that is fully understandable given the attention devoted to the cyclical behavior of the aggregative economy. The present study proceeds likewise; it concentrates on the influences of four macroeconomic mechanisms, the first three of which are aggregate demand forces: monetary, as captured in the behavior of the quantity of money; fiscal as measured by federal government deficits; and the credit channel as supplementary to monetary actions affecting commercial bank lending. The last of the macroeconomic forces examined is what here is called endogenous propagation, a mechanism that underlies a mean-reversion propensity of the economy to move back to trend, an aggregate supply consideration.

The odyssey by which this book came to be written may be of interest. In my previous work, which culminated in *Monetary Interpretations of the Great Depression*, I was impressed by the extent to which some scholars identified the economy's collapse with the shrinkage of the quantity of money, a theme associated with the seminal work of Friedman and Schwartz (1963), which appeared three decades after the nadir of the Contraction. At the same time, no one writing in the 1930s had the main ingredients central to the Friedman and Schwartz analysis, their analytical core. That interpretation, controversial when it appeared, is now a central element, if not the canonical tale, in economists' turn-of-the-century understanding of the momentum of the Contraction.

It thus seemed natural to inquire into the extent to which the writers living during the recovery looked to the behavior of quantitative monetary measures as important. That is, were there economists who interpreted the recovery in terms of the growing stock of money? It was this that piqued an interest in the issue of what drove the recovery. A difficulty however was that there were no official series on the money stock available in the Depression decade. It thus became necessary to construct one, from the point of view of a series to which those living then would most likely have turned in their attempts to understand the recovery in terms of growth of the quantity of money.

Having thus been prodded into thinking about the recovery in terms of the behavior of the money stock, a direct carryover of its role in the Contraction, it was a natural step to look for evidence of the relationship between the two in the professional literature, and in the data. It was not hard in coming. If one were living then, how would one have proceeded? An obvious way would be to get each month's data on money, industrial production, and wholesale prices as it appeared and then plot them on scatter-diagrams, an approach favored by economists in the 1930s. Within two or so years of so doing, the interpretation would have become increasingly clear, and straightforward; it would have been, for the most part, singular in establishing the case for a money-led recovery. Postwar analyses of the recovery were based on more sophisticated empirical methods as well as on a wider array of data; their conclusions were similar, as they argued for an overarching role of the behavior of the money stock in the recovery.

Chapters 3 through 5 are concerned with presenting this evidence, where the latter two deal with economists who wrote in the post-1933 period. The results of the inquiry into economists' monetary analyses of the recovery appeared initially in the *Journal of Macroeconomics* (Steindl 1998) and the *Journal of the History of Economic Thought* (Steindl 1997).

Midway through the recovery, the sharp, severe depression of 1937–38 hit. Could it and the subsequent revival be understood in terms of the behavior of the quantity of money? This is the subject of the sixth chapter. Here again, the behavior of the stock of money is of consequence in understanding what induced that depression, though there was little discussion of it at that time. It is a bit surprising that the late-1930s depression and in particular the subsequent revival has received so little professional attention, and what it has received is in large part due to the fact that it was then that the notion of fiscal actions as a deliberate policy tool was born. The seventh chapter deals with the evidence of fiscal policy on the recovery. The following chapter considers the credit channel in conjunction with the monetary and fiscal forces; it stands as a summary chapter of the accumulating empirical evidence. The credit channel is considered as a logical extension of the influence that was found for it during the Contraction.

Discussions of the Great Depression, certainly those in the postwar era, are heavily conditioned on aggregate demand considerations—what caused demand to fall in the 1929–33 and 1937–38 contractions and what were the factors at play in causing it to increase relative to trend during the recovery. In discussions with many other economists of the general topic of the recovery, I would ask how they would go about studying the recovery. Without exception, each talked about one or more aggregate demand influences, generally with emphasis on one of them. And this is quite understandable. The rise in importance of macroeconomics is in large part the story of variations in aggregate demand and their influences on income, prices, unemployment, and the balance of payments. We have been conditioned to think in terms of the instability of aggregate demand relative to aggregate supply as the first line of inquiry, and I was no different.

It is of interest to note that this stands in contrast to the way in which many economists perceived the Depression in the 1930s. The observed surfeits of goods then were thought to be the result not of a deficiency of aggregate demand but of an excess of productive capacity, of which the farm situation was a patently clear case. The notion of production outrunning consumption was a common theme, and indeed was at the heart of the NIRA. Today, the orientation is on deficiency of aggregate demand.

It thus took some time and thought before I brought myself to view the economy's course during the recovery as having a strong, inherent tendency to move back to trend, that is, to think in terms other than aggregate demand phenomena. The key insight came when trying to understand the revival from the 1937–38 depression. For it was here that the monetary interpretation that seemed so robust was now unable to give a satisfactory explanation, though I tried. My initial attempt appeared in the *Cato Journal* (Steindl 2000), but I now believe it was flawed, the reason being that I was still caught up with an aggregate demand orientation as I tried to highlight the behavior of the money stock in the robust revival from that depression. The view to which I at last subscribed is detailed in the ninth chapter, one that may seem surprising to economists.

Acknowledgments

This book was written largely during the course of a sabbatical leave at the University of Iowa. The support of the College of Business Administration at Oklahoma State University was crucial to bringing the project to completion. I also thank the Ardmore Foundation whose professorship funds materially aided the research. I want to single out for special thanks Junhui (Grace) Yan for her outstanding assistance.

I wish also to acknowledge and thank Charles H. Whiteman who extended the invitation to visit at Iowa. Of more consequence, he also was an active participant in discussions of the book's material. It was in conversations with Chuck that the subtitle of the book emerged. Others who supplied informed and spirited comment were Thomas F. Pogue and Gerald P. Dwyer. Tom and I spent many hours over lunch discussing issues in the book. Gerry extended an invitation to present a seminar at the Federal Reserve Bank of Atlanta where the material in the book received its first public airing. His quizzical comments resulted in reorienting several chapters. Mark Snead was the source of much good econometric advice and economic sense.

The best is saved for last. Anyone who has been wrapped up in an extended intellectual enterprise knows the enormous contributions made by a spouse, some perhaps in material germane to the inquiry but of much more consequence mostly in all those things necessary for stability of family life. Those who have engaged in such research activity know well the sacrifices made and joys contributed by a spouse. I am indeed grateful to and lucky for Joyce. Because my earlier book was dedicated to her, she demurred from being so acknowledged in the present enterprise. And so, it is to our sons—David, Andrew, Peter, and Matthew—that the book is dedicated.

As part of this work, I have quoted extensively from several publications. I thank the following for permission to use their materials.

A Monetary History of the United States, 1867–1960 by Milton Friedman and Anna J. Schwartz (Princeton University Press, 1963), reprinted by permission of Princeton University Press. For permission to adapt and use material appearing in earlier articles of mine, I thank the History of Economics Society for "Was Fisher a Practicing Quantity Theorist?" *Journal of the History of Economic Thought* 19 (fall 1997): 241–60 as well as "Fisher's Last Stand on the Quantity Theory: The Role of Money in the Recovery," *Journal of the History of Economic Thought* 22 (December 2000): 493–98; Elsevier Science, B.V. for "The Decline of a Paradigm: The Quantity Theory and Economic Recovery in the 1930s," *Journal of Macroeconomics* 20 (fall 1998): 821–41; and the Cato Journal for "Does the Fed Abhor Inflation?" *Cato Journal* 20 (spring/summer 2000): 215–21.

CHAPTER 1

An Overview

The Great Depression. This fervid phrase, pregnant with emotions, evocative of a time few wish to repeat, has at least two meanings. For some, it is the horrendous debacle of 1929 into early 1933. For many others, it is the entire decade of the 1930s for which *The Grapes of Wrath* stands as a metaphor, with its Dust Bowl milieu where collective action among the downtrodden shielded them from being destroyed. Discussions with and reminiscences of those who lived through that decade illustrate this quite clearly. The oral histories in *Hard Times* (Terkel 1970) give particularly vivid examples.[1] Some deal with specific events, others concentrate on the years 1929–33, and many range over the entire decade, to the time when getting into the army at the beginning of the war was "the good life."[2] An illustrative posting in the Herbert Hoover Library captures that sense: what began as "a relatively minor downturn [in fall 1929 turned into a] decade long nightmare."[3]

Because of the likelihood of confusion as to the particular meaning of the term *the Great Depression,* some have chosen to label the experience of 1929–33 as *the Great Contraction,* reserving for the entire decade the Great Depression phrase. This convention is followed here; that is, the events of 1929–33 occur in the Great Contraction (or simply the Contraction). Then the severe depression of 1937–38 can be unambiguously referred to as a depression, or perhaps as the late-1930s depression, without confusing it with the Great Contraction.

However labeled, the Great Depression is surely one of the watershed events in the history of the United States and the world during the twentieth century, certainly *A* if not *The Defining Moment* (Bordo, Goldin, and White 1998, esp. 10–18). This comes through clearly when one talks with those who lived through that decade. Without doubt, it is the singular event in their lives, rivaled perhaps only by action in combat in World War II. Even decades later, they feel very passionately about the difficulties and anxieties of those times.

Much of course had been written about the unprecedented fall in economic activity in the Great Contraction, with questions about its causes and the reasons for its protracted decline especially prominent. But there indeed was a recovery, though long, tortuous, and uneven. That those living during the "decade long nightmare" did not realize recovery was under way may well have been due to a belief that any resurgence of economic activity was transitory, that the permanent condition of the economy was one of excess labor and output: to use a popular phrase of the times, a case of "production outstripping consumption."[4] This book is concerned with those recovery years. More to the point, the concern is with identifying the reasons, the prime causes, of the recovery. Since much postwar research has singled out the importance of the growth of the money stock as the most influential factor, it is of interest to inquire whether those living in the 1930s similarly looked to the behavior of the quantity of money in their attempts to understand the recovery.

A major difficulty in attempting after the fact to re-create the events of a turbulent time is that those who lived through it know the outcome, as do those who are witnesses to the recounting, and so the great uncertainties, apprehensions, and anxieties that were central to the earlier situation are absent. To try to re-create the experience decades later is even more difficult. This quite likely is the case when the events in question are particularly dire. The actual outcomes in many cases are not anywhere close to the ones thought most likely during the turbulent times in question. Hence it becomes impossible for people who did not actually experience those events to re-create the past feelings, thoughts, anxieties, and apprehensions, especially when they were traumatic, difficult times.

For instance, the servicemen who talk of combat action in World War II are the ones who survived. Further, they may well have had very satisfactory, rewarding lives afterward. When they speak of their combat experiences, listeners know that whatever is said, those "re-creating" the battles survived; they were not killed. Furthermore, those hearing the retelling know something of the later fortunes of those recounting their experiences, and the later circumstances may well have been relatively satisfactory, which further distances the reality of the "re-created" events to listeners.[5]

And so it is with those who lived through the Depression. The pervasive gloom and doom felt throughout the decade did not materialize.

True, the war showed that the economy was not stuck in a permanent depression. With the end of the war, the economy prospered, rather than sinking again into what many at the time believed would be a reversion to a permanent state of depressed activity, as was thought most likely in the 1930s.

Juxtaposed against the attention given the Contraction, professional interest in the subsequent recovery pales. Yet it is a fascinating episode, one the following chapters describe, discuss, and seek to understand as they consider the effects of various influences on the path of recovery. One of the principal fascinations comes from seeing an economy that was operating more than a third below its potential in 1933 move back to trend, to its full potential, nine years later. Real output and industrial production increased at what in normal conditions are extraordinarily high rates.

Correspondingly, the unemployment rate decreased from over 25 percent of the labor force in 1933 to just under 10 percent in 1941.[6] The following year's sharp decline to half that level is however quite understandable as a product of the command economy due to the United States' full involvement in World War II.

In the oral history of Studs Terkel (1970) and in listening to those who lived through the decade, the stock market crash is prominent, both as a shock to confidence and as a forerunner of things to come. One also reads about the crash as being of little consequence in small towns. A persistent theme is job loss and tensions faced by "eatin or not eatin," even to the point of wandering off "in despair because they couldn't support their families" (1970, 346). In the same vein, the notion appears that the economic system broke down—"that it quit" (1970, 309)—and was fundamentally in need of major restructuring. The understandable attraction of planning, indeed socialism or at least a third way, comes through in many of the thoughts.[7]

Interestingly, there seems to be little recognition of a recovery after spring 1933, though the presence of Roosevelt as a savior of the system is a recurring, even pervasive theme. However, that may be more hindsight than the actual perception of those living through those hard times. To see Roosevelt as fundamental to the recovery is a widespread view, one to which the vanquished Alf Landon, FDR's 1936 opponent, subscribes (1970, 336). Indeed, the economy did bottom in March 1933, having experienced more than a 50 percent decline in industrial production from August 1929. Wholesale prices were over a third lower.[8]

The realization that the economy was recovering must understandably have been long in coming, particularly the idea that the rebound was not transitory (except for those who followed such statistics). For many, the perception most likely was of continued gloom and doom. It certainly would not have been one of renewed optimism.

Even professional economists would have been somewhat leery about forecasting a recovery in spring 1933, or for that matter anytime that year. It was after all less than a year earlier that the economy appeared to have turned around, as industrial production increased 13 percent between July and October 1932, only to fall by March 1933 close to where it had been in July. Wholesale prices also exhibited a slight increase between July and September 1932.[9] The fact that the price decline to mid-1932 was arrested was perhaps reason for some optimism, particularly in light of the price behavior a decade earlier, during which the sharp 1920–21 depression saw prices fall over 40 percent as industrial production declined a third, after which output rose up to the dawn of the Great Contraction with prices remaining essentially stable.[10]

But the nascent recovery proved stillborn as the economy then deteriorated dramatically through spring 1933 when the recovery finally began. But the recovery was long, uneven, and painstakingly slow. This reflected adjustment to the depth of the Contraction's decline and importantly to the extremely sharp 1937–38 depression. From the nadir of the Contraction in the spring, the economy began recovering but only for a few months. By late summer 1933, industrial production was again declining, as was real GNP (gross national product). The following year, this roller coaster ride was repeated as the economy backed off its summer highs, retreating a bit before beginning in earnest a sustained recovery in the last months of 1934. With a record of dashed hopes—recovery becoming recession, recession seeming to turn into recovery, then again becoming recession—it is little wonder that the realization that recovery was under way was long in coming.[11]

The case of James Harvey Rogers, Sterling Professor of Economics at Yale and one of the most prominent monetary economists of the decade, is enlightening in this regard.[12] Though initially optimistic about recovery as a result of the mid-1932 turnabout in prices and industrial output, he soon became disillusioned. In his groping for an understanding of why there appeared to be no recovery, he hit on the idea of a "gap" between the distributors and the users of credit—

lenders and borrowers. In contemporary terms, the gap could be interpreted as a credit crunch. This gap was regarded as a failure of the capitalistic system. He maintained, as a result, "that at least temporarily our economic equilibrium is broken" (1933b, 127). This pessimism was to grow to the point where he foresaw "the capitalistic system which has been with us less than two hundred years" moving rapidly into "state capitalism . . . a system under which the economic powers, instead of remaining in the hands of private individuals, pass more and more completely into the hands of the government," this at the bottom of the 1937–38 depression (1938, 5–6).

From fall 1934, the economy continued its movement back toward trend until mid-1937, at which point it deteriorated sharply; for instance, industrial production fell 33 percent in twelve months.[13] Whether that 1937–38 depression was regarded at the time as an event unto itself or simply another manifestation of the terrible times is difficult to tell. Perhaps it was more a matter of personal situation as well as the selectivity of memory decades later. For instance, Robert E. Wood, the retired president and chairman of Sears, Roebuck, saw that "things began to pick up around '34 or '35 [but] it was '36 before they began to pick up strong . . . to recover on a big scale" (Terkel 1970, 442–43). For him, there apparently was no 1937–38 depression. Raymond Moley, of Roosevelt's Brains Trust, regarded that depression as a "slight recession" (251), whereas David Kennedy, later president of Continental Illinois National Bank and secretary of the Treasury under President Nixon, saw a "very, very serious recession in '37" (274).

As the depression bottomed in late spring 1938, the economy resumed its move back to trend. The prosperity that the 1920s saw as the economy's natural right was again coming. Whether the war was a return to prosperity, a manifestation of that natural right, is considered in the next chapter. By the usual measures of economic performance, the economy had returned to trend sometime in 1942. Yet this was a war economy, one in which shortages, conscription, and price controls were present. Various economic data and measures of aggregate performance during the recovery from the Great Contraction are considered in chapter 2, where monthly information on prices, interest rates, gold, bank assets, the quantity of money, the federal deficit, and Federal Reserve Credit, to name a few, are presented in graph form. The chapter also considers questions about returning to trend and the international experience.

There are two noteworthy features of the data. First is the use of information that was published and thus was available for analysis and discussion in the 1930s. To a large extent, these are essentially real-time data, that is, data that are not subjected to revision. This is the information on which economists living in that decade would have relied. Second, based on the data then available, a money supply series is constructed to link recovery to movements in the stock of money, a framework that employs the only extant macroeconomic model of that time, the quantity theory of money.

The third chapter arrays support for the view that the recovery was due to the growth of the money stock. This is done first by examining the burgeoning postwar evidence. The chapter then considers the relation between the money stock series, as it could have been constructed in the 1930s, and prices and output. The intent is to show that an analysis of recovery that relied on the behavior of the quantity of money would have concluded that the recovery and the late-1930s depression were due to movements in the money stock, as would be predicted on the basis of the quantity theory. In other words, the intent is to show that the conclusions of the postwar analyses could in large part have been anticipated in the 1930s.

A development of particular interest deals with the first two years of revival from the late-1930s depression. It is then that industrial production increased rapidly as the quantity of money grew. But, surprisingly, prices did not rise; they in fact fell. How is that to be understood, particularly in quantity theoretic terms, if a demand shock theory is the foundation on which an understanding of the recovery is based?

Given the ready availability of data for a quantity-theoretic interpretation, how did economists interpret the recovery, how long did it take before they were convinced that it was firmly under way, and who (and how many) looked to the behavior of the money stock as one of the main causes of the recovery? What was to be made of the 1937–38 depression, certainly a major unexpected disruption? For instance, it "was all it took to change [Alvin] Hansen's mind. The Great Depression was no mere business cycle. It was the end of an era" (Mehrling 1997, 119). Based on that, Hansen altered radically his orientation from skeptic to apostle/disciple of the Keynesian lack-of-aggregate-demand paradigm with its correlative emphasis on the requirements for and necessity of fiscal actions.

Chapter 4 considers whether economists living in the 1930s saw recovery as driven by increases in the stock of money. It looks at their investigations to try to understand how each viewed what was happening, and why. Before that examination, however, the recognition lag is addressed, as is the issue of the standing of the quantity theory in the 1930s. Attention is paid to those familiar with a monetary aggregate, either through compiling such a series individually or through use of publicly available data. One of the more interesting investigations relates to Milton Friedman's views in 1940, as reflected in a business cycles course he taught almost a decade before he and Anna Schwartz initiated their influential study of monetary forces (Hammond 1996, 46–58). The chapter also discusses the attention given to the rising amounts of excess reserves in the banking system and to gold, especially since the United States was not on the gold standard for virtually the entire recovery period.

Chapter 5 deals in detail with Irving Fisher, one of the most prominent contemporary observers of events, though his star had faded due to his turn-of-the-decade stock market predictions. He is rightfully regarded as the quintessential quantity theorist. Yet the advent of the Contraction persuaded him to rethink the role of the money stock in the movement of the economy. To that end, he formulated the debt-depression theory in which the stock of money was a passive entity subject to the whims of prospective borrowers. The "problem" of mounting excess reserves was to be dealt with by raising reserve requirements to 100 percent (Fisher 1936a). Nonetheless, through his business cycle institute he was a close follower of current developments (1930). In addition, his penchant for analysis and reform, indeed for crusades to improve the human and societal condition, makes him an understandable choice for consideration. His work is considered in light of the central question of whether he reverted to the quantity theory views he had held prior to the Contraction.

The late-1930s depression was surprisingly sharp, deep, and unexpected. It therefore was a fascinating event (making chapter 6 the longest in the book). It was characterized by dramatic declines in output and prices. At its trough a year later, interest rates were near-zero, prices were falling, Federal Reserve credit was declining as were loans by banks, and excess reserves in the banking system were extraordinarily high and mounting. The likely prognosis for the economy over the next term would certainly have been less than optimistic. Anyone viewing it at that point would have foreseen a continuation of the sharp slide that began the previous spring. Had there been a contest for the most pessimistic economic outlook, that period certainly would have been a finalist. Yet output rebounded along with an expanding stock of money, but prices continued falling, for more than two years. Excess reserves continued growing. Interest rates remained low; the rate on short-term treasury bills averaged less than 5 basis points—that is, less than five-hundredths of a percentage point—for the next three years.

The discussion deals with economists' explanations for the rebound as well as those likely responsible for the depression. It is somewhat curious, indeed ironic, that the professional literature has little to say about the revival from that deep depression, except to attribute it to fiscal policy due perhaps to the gathering war clouds or more likely to Roosevelt's conscious acceptance of it—the "critical decision to turn to spending 'for its own sake' as the main road out of the recession" (Stein 1969, 109). It, however, is this revival episode that calls into question the importance of the growth of the quantity of money, as well as fiscal actions, as the driving force(s) in the recovery. If the increasing money stock and fiscal spending were the driving forces, then prices should have increased, along with output. But prices fell, for more than two years. How is this to be interpreted? A demand shock orientation, such as is integral to monetary and fiscal impulse mechanisms, could not have prices falling and output rising. This question and the resolution of the apparent conundrum are taken up in the penultimate chapter.

Before turning to that issue, two additional recovery mechanisms are considered. One that came to be discussed at length is the influence of fiscal policy. Its role is the principal concern of chapter 7. The interest is in large part due to economists' increasing attention to Keynes's policy prescriptions, and so it is not surprising that much of the literature dates from the late 1930s.

There was a *post hoc, ergo propter hoc* element at that time. In the face of general disillusionment about the effectiveness of monetary actions stimulating recovery, it was understandable that the recovery would be associated with increasing budget deficits as a matter of cause and effect. To a large extent, the subsequent theoretical and policy literature looked favorably upon fiscal actions as the recovery vehicle. One of the authoritative assessments of fiscal policy in the 1930s was made by E. Cary Brown (1956). His findings essentially did not identify a meaningful role for fiscal actions. Interestingly though, in a testament to the times he argued that this was not because it had been tried and found wanting but rather because it had not been tried. Subsequently, others addressed the question of the effectiveness of fiscal actions. Those results largely confirmed his.

One of the difficulties in assessing fiscal policy is the low frequency of the data collection on which the associated empirical work necessarily relies. With one exception, they are annual, which obscures timing relations. The exception is John Firestone's (1960) monthly federal budget estimates. The influences of monetary and fiscal actions are evaluated here in a model of monetary and fiscal effects on industrial production. The results provide further support for Brown's skepticism about the importance of fiscal policy in promoting recovery. They also underscore the seeming importance of the growth of the money stock.

Another recovery avenue is the credit channel, as initially hypothesized by Irving Fisher (1932) and subsequently developed by Ben Bernanke (1983). Chapter 8 discusses this along with the important role of bank examination regulators in striving not to repeat the banking debacle of the early 1930s. The likely effect of those actions is to discourage banks from lending, which was widely perceived to have occurred. The actions of bank examiners would have added regulatory weight to the banks' rising "cost of credit intermediation," which is "the cost of channeling funds from the ultimate savers/lenders into the hands of good borrowers" (Bernanke 1983, 263). Among those costs are screening and monitoring, as well as expected losses.

Chapter 8 ends with an extensive empirical analysis assessing the separate contributions of the quantity of money, the credit channel, fiscal policy, and interest rates on the recovery. The credit channel is addressed through the medium of a lending series constructed from available Federal Reserve data. The series represents bank lending for commercial and industrial loans, the loan category most aligned with the credit channel because it does not include lending for purely financial purposes. One conclusion is that the growth of the quantity of money stands out as a main vehicle promoting recovery. Interestingly, the movement of real interest rates, which is largely due to changes in the price level, is also of importance.

To this point, the evidence from the research reported in the professional literature and that adduced here strongly supports the view that the recovery was principally due to the growing money stock, so much so that it seems incontrovertible. That evidence derives from a variety of investigations, some dealing with data available in the recovery period, while other inquiries employed tabular, graphic, literary, and empirical modes. As such, it appears quite robust. Yet, there are a few caveats to unequivocal acceptance.

One is that the money stock's growth was not due to actions by the Federal Reserve. In fact, the credit it extended to banks was essentially unchanged for much of the period. The two principal factors that "financed" the growth of money were the devaluation of the dollar in the recovery's first nine months and then the continued inflow of gold due to the growing uncertainties in the world, principally Europe. Would the pace of recovery have been much slower had neither of those fortuitous events occurred?

Of more consequence is the conundrum raised by the two-plus years of revival from the late-1930s depression. The stock of money increased rapidly, as did output, but prices fell. How can we explain that? This is addressed in the penultimate chapter. In brief, the resolution relies on two mechanisms, separate but operating simultaneously. One is the quantity theory of money in which the demand-for-money dimension has the place of prominence, in contrast to the usual emphasis on the behavior of the money stock. The other mechanism is what is called endogenous propagation, the notion that inherent in the economic system are mechanisms that move the economy toward its trend level of growth. An approximate synonym for endogenous propagation is mean-reversion, though the latter is the result of the operation of the former. It is the forces of endogenous propagation—the mechanisms, incentives, opportunities, and apprehensions of a market system operating below its trend rate—that underlie mean-reversion.

The argument developed in chapter 9 relies on some earlier suggestions of a natural tendency to rebound, principally econometric work. The argument then concentrates on the particulars of the seemingly anomalous behavior of prices, output, and the stock of money in the revival from the late-1930s depression, a period that occupies almost a fourth of the entire recovery time.

One of the attractions of studying the 1930s is that it was far from normal; it truly is an outlier, and this pathology is one of its fascinations. Such times are opportune for observing behavior and developments that are masked in normal times when the range of variation is quite small. The typical strategy of conventional theory stresses the role of policy variables and their influences on the direction of the economy's target variables. The influence of seemingly exogenous develop-ments, though not ignored, tends to be treated by the use of a port-manteau variable, such as a "food and fuel" shock. The analysis then typically turns to the role of policy actions that seem most suitable for dealing with such a shock.

The revival represents an exceptional opportunity to study an out-lier. The evolution of output with falling prices provides evidence on the importance of endogenous propagation as a mechanism of recov-ery. It is impossible to say whether it is the principal one, since it is characteristically masked by the behavior of policy variables, but there is little doubt as to its importance. That is the main theme of this book's penultimate chapter.

The final chapter steps back and discusses the findings on this extra-ordinary period in the economic life of the United States. Its emphasis is on the economics of the decade. In what may be a surprising turn, virtually nothing is said about the political environment and the impor-tance of the New Deal, the stock-in-trade of so much of the writing about the recovery. The book is an essay on the economics of the recov-ery, not a history of the social and political evolution of the decade. It deals with the macroeconomic forces that were at play in returning an economy that was over a third below its capacity rate to its trend out-put level over the course of nine and a quarter years, a period of 111 months during which output and prices increased and declined, some-times in concert and other times along antithetical trajectories.

The next chapter presents graphical depictions of the evolution of the various economic variables of interest, and it is to that material that the essay now turns.

CHAPTER 2

————◄O►————

The Facts of Recovery

There is little debate about when the slide that was the Great Contraction ended: the low point was in March 1933. The beginning of the recovery can simply be dated from then. The recovery, however, was far from evident in the months immediately following the trough. The more interesting question relates to when the recovery began in earnest (see the next section). Similarly, it is of some interest to date the return to the trend rate of growth of output, that is, to a high-level economy, and this is done following the discussion of prices and the international experience. The main focus of this chapter is the presentation in the form of graphs of the relevant economic data in the recovery, which began in April 1933. With few exceptions, all data are monthly.

Output

Figure 2.1 presents the quarterly behavior of real output (measured as the real GNP) and industrial production for the entire decade of the Great Depression, from its beginning in the third quarter 1929 through the trough in early 1933 on to the second quarter 1942. Real output is measured by the series on real GNP constructed by Nathan Balke and Robert J. Gordon (1986). The index of industrial production is a monthly series converted to quarterly observations. It is shown for comparison against the behavior of real output. As can readily be seen, the two are highly related, with the correlation between them being 98 percent for the entire period, as well as for the two subperiods, the 1929–33 Contraction and the 1933–42 recovery. In order to appreciate better the timing of various aspects of the recovery, much of the subsequent discussion deals with monthly data. The high degree of correla-

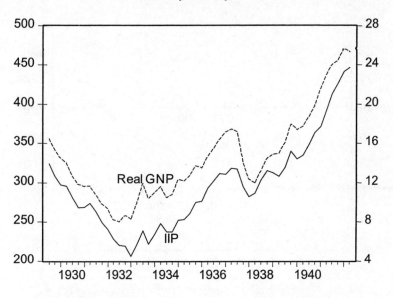

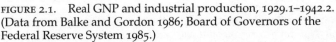

FIGURE 2.1.   Real GNP and industrial production, 1929.1–1942.2.
(Data from Balke and Gordon 1986; Board of Governors of the
Federal Reserve System 1985.)

tion between the quarterly and monthly averaged observations suggests that little would be lost in using higher frequency data. At the
same time much is to be gained in terms of detail.

The graph of the monthly industrial production data is shown in figure 2.2. There are two such series. The lower (dashed) one is the index
of industrial production as it was available in the 1930s. This is a real-
time series in that it is taken from each month's *Federal Reserve Bulletin;*
the index base, measured on the left-hand axis, is 1923–25 = 100. The
solid-line industrial production series is a 1985 revision, with an index
base of 1977 = 100, shown on the right-hand axis. Real-time data are
those that are first reported after they are collected and published
monthly in the 1930s; they subsequently were revised, several times in
fact.[1] The extent of the revisions is captured in the figure. The earlier
data, available to those living in the Depression, have greater amplitude. One reason is that they were rounded so that an index reading of
93.4 became 93 and one of 93.6 became 94.

Each series exhibits what may be regarded as implausibly large
monthly movements. In the first four months of the recovery, for

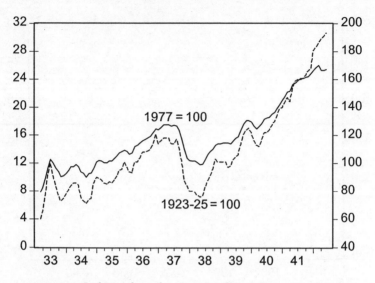

FIGURE 2.2.   Industrial production, April 1933–June 1942 (1977 =
100, solid line; 1923–25 = 100, dashed line).
(Data from Board of Governors of the Federal Reserve System
1985; *Federal Reserve Bulletin*, various issues.)

instance, the real-time series has monthly rates of increase of 10, 18, 18,
and 9 percent, which translates into an annualized rate of increase of
363 percent over those four months! The revised data have somewhat
smaller, but still implausibly large changes, an annual rate of increase
of 296 percent in the same April–July 1933 period. Thereafter, industrial
production fell across the July–November 1933 period at annual rates
of 61 and 47 percent for the real-time and revised data, respectively.
Thus by November, industrial production was higher than in March by
a 28 percent annual rate for the revised data and 30 percent for the real-
time 1930s series—rates that strain one's credulity. These large, sharp
changes would have made the difficult problem of trying to understand the recovery even thornier than normal.

Although these are some of the most egregious examples, there are
others in which dubiously large movements occurred. A comparison
between the two industrial production series shows several sharp differences. In May 1935, the original series indicates no change, whereas
the revised series has industrial production increasing at a 36 percent
annual rate. In December of that year, the original series shows a 14.7
percent (417 percent annual rate!) increase, whereas the revised series

has a 6.6 percent (115 percent annual rate) increase. Such substantial movements are the result of the data collection methods of the time, which is the basis for Christina Romer (1986a, 1986b) asking whether the seeming postwar stability is more a product of the data than of the reality.[2]

Though the correlation between the two is very high, there are some noticeable differences. The real-time data indicate that the initial recovery months exhibited a somewhat more robust rebound and then a sharper reversion, with fits and starts until September 1934, a year and a half after the bottom of the 1929–33 Contraction.[3]

One of the more striking differences between the two series relates to the 1937–38 depression. The real-time data indicate that it begins in January; they also show a steeper decline, 37 rather than the 33 percent in the postwar revisions.

The recovery began in earnest a year and a half after the Contraction's low point. Thereafter, economic activity continued to move toward trend, reaching in December 1936 the level at which it had been when the Depression began. It continued rising until the following May at which time it was 4 percent higher than in December. In that month, there began a fall in production greater than in any twelve-month period during the 1930s, a decline of 33 percent. After that, the economy moved progressively back to trend, with industrial production increasing at a 22 percent annual rate, thereby more than doubling by mid-1942.[4] Interestingly, it was in September 1939 that industrial production again reached the level where it had been when the Contraction began, almost to the month a decade earlier.

The annualized rate of recovery of industrial production was 13.5 percent, a remarkable rate by the standards of an economy operating close to trend. But the fact that it took over nine years to return to trend, that the economy moved in fits and starts, sinking into an exceptionally deep depression halfway through the tortuous adjustment period, indicates that the recovery was far from rapid and smooth. As Friedman and Schwartz argued, "the most notable feature of the revival after 1933 was not its rapidity but its incompleteness" (1963, 493).

Prices

The behavior of prices was also of considerable interest.[5] Peter Temin and Barrie Wigmore, using the intellectual framework of Thomas Sargent (1986), highlighted the rise in prices that began in March 1933 as basic to the turnaround that month. This was based on the belief that rising prices would be confirmation of "the establishment of a new policy regime" (1990, 484). Figure 2.3 shows the movement of wholesale prices during the recovery.

This series is the only comprehensive price index that was available then. As with industrial production, the early recovery months saw implausibly large gyrations. Wholesale prices increased in May, June, and July at annual rates of 57, 54, and 101 percent! In fact, both increases and decreases in excess of annual rates of 20 percent occurred in almost a fourth of the 111 months of the recovery.

From the low point in 1933, wholesale prices increased almost continually until April 1937 at an average annual rate of 10 percent. Thereafter, they declined 15 percent—an annual rate of 6.6 percent—over the next twenty-eight months, to August 1939. Then followed a sharp two-month rise (a 41 percent annual rate) associated with panic buying deriving from the German invasion of Poland, the beginning of the European phase of World War II. Thereafter, they declined a further 2.5 percent over the next ten months, into August 1940. From then through

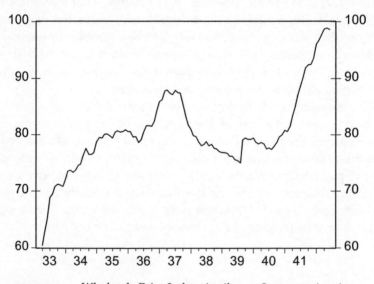

FIGURE 2.3.   Wholesale Price Index, April 1933–June 1942 (1926 = 100).
(Data from *Federal Reserve Bulletin*, various issues.)

the remainder of the recovery, prices rose 27.4 percent, an annual rate of 14 percent. The extended deflation of three and a third years associated with the 1937–38 depression, particularly the more than two years of revival from it, stands in marked contrast to the price experience in the recovery from the 1929–33 Contraction. How were rising prices in the 1933 turnaround fundamental to recovery but not in the more vigorous later recovery? Prices in the 1930s were never above their level at the beginning of the Great Contraction. In fact, it was only in February 1942 that they rose to their pre-Contraction 1929 levels.

International Dimension

The Depression experienced by the United States was not unique. It was, to use Charles Kindleberger's felicitous title, part of "the world in depression" (1973). With the exception of the 1937–38 depression, the economic experience of advanced countries in many ways paralleled that of the United States. Figure 2.4 depicts the behavior of industrial production in four leading European countries, plus the United States. The data are normalized to 1929 = 100. With the start of World War II in

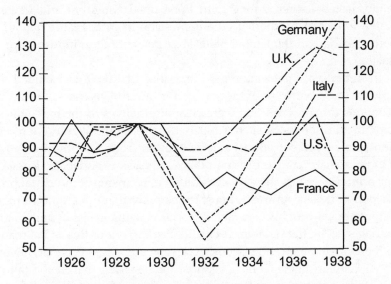

FIGURE 2.4.   International industrial production (1929 = 100). (Data from Mitchell 1998.)

September 1939, data beyond 1938 were not collected in many countries. In addition, even if they were, they would have reflected not those of markets but of a planned economy.

The United States and Germany clearly experienced the most severe contractions, with the United States about 15 percent worse than Germany. That occurred in 1932, based on annual data. By 1935, Germany's production was back to its 1929 level. The United States having slightly passed its pre-Contraction level in 1937 had a serious setback in 1937–38. By 1938, Germany's production was almost 40 percent above its 1929 level, whereas the United States was almost 19 percent below. The United Kingdom saw economic activity declining 10 percent by 1931, after which it leveled off and then began increasing. By 1934, its production exceeded its 1929 level, and it continued rising until it experienced a mild slump in 1938, when industrial production fell 2.7 percent. Its Great Contraction slump thus was relatively minor compared to those of Germany and the United States. France's depression began a year later than the rest and basically continued through the entire period. By 1935, production was almost 30 percent lower than in 1929. Thereafter, it bounced around so that in 1938, it was back to its 1932 level, which was approximately 25 percent below its 1929 level. Its depression, though not as severe as that in the United States and Germany, lasted longer. Along with the United Kingdom and United States, France also experienced a depression in 1938: France had an 8 percent drop and the United States a 21 percent fall in industrial production.

In figure 2.5, the economic performance of Russia is included, in order to underscore one of the reasons for the attractiveness of forms of economic organization that were clear alternatives to the market system.[6] In addition to Russia not experiencing even the slightest of recessions, its 19 percent annual rate of growth from 1925 through 1938 stands in sharp contrast to the other countries' experiences. Russia's performance dwarfs the very substantial movements of industrial production in those countries, almost to the point that the graphs of their output appear roughly constant. Associated with the loss of faith in the market system, the economic evidence issuing out of Russia led many in the United States and elsewhere to view a planned economy favorably.[7] William Leuchtenburg reports, for instance, that in the fall of 1931 there were "100,000 applications for jobs in Soviet Russia" (1963, 28). Though it is now recognized that the Russian data were overstated,

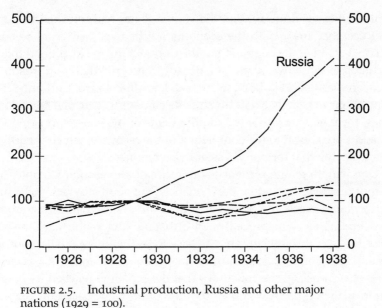

FIGURE 2.5.   Industrial production, Russia and other major
nations (1929 = 100).
(Data from Mitchell 1998.)

and grossly so, this was not obvious in the 1930s. A part of the reason
for the overstatement of output is due to the difficulty of attempting to
arrive at satisfactory economic valuations in a system in which there
are no markets.[8] This is a particular case of attempting to value government output when there are no market prices on which to base such
valuations. As discussed in the next section, this is especially relevant
to the question of when the United States fully recovered.

The End of the Recovery

There is little meaningful dispute about when the recovery began.
When the economy was fully recovered is a more difficult issue. Many
understandably take December 1941 with the entry of the United States
into World War II as the point at which to shift emphasis (Bernanke
1983; Friedman and Schwartz 1963). Others (Cole and Ohanian 1999)
end their recovery analysis in 1939, because of the outbreak of the
actual European conflict. Yet, it is doubtful whether analyses of the
recovery should end then.

It similarly is doubtful that the United States had returned to trend by December 1941. With the economy a little over two years beyond where it stood at the beginning of the Contraction, the likelihood that it made up in those two years for a decade of no growth, that it was fully recovered as Pearl Harbor was attacked, is almost zero. Certainly, it is convenient to use that date to shift discussion to wartime considerations, for it was then that the requirements of the war effort provided an additional boost to the completion of the recovery, which is equivalent to saying that recovery was not yet complete.

One way to gauge recovery is to estimate the economy's potential output relative to its actual performance. The point at which the actual performance meets the potential is then the point when the economy recovered. This is the procedure of Christina Romer. She takes the real GNP for 1923 through 1927 as the base for estimating potential output because "they are the four most normal years of the 1920s" (1992, 760). With that measure, she concludes that the economy reached its potential in 1942 because it was then that the trend value based on 1923–27 equated with the actual level of output.

Harold Cole and Lee Ohanian take a similar but more sophisticated approach. They use as their framework data filtered "through the lens of [neoclassical growth] theory" (1999, 4). The relevant data are real per capita output adjusted for trend. The economy's long-run trend of 1.9 percent is obtained by calculating the average annual growth of real per capita output between 1929 and 1997. The data on real per capita GNP are then detrended and normalized by taking 1929 as the base. Their analysis ends in 1939, at which point they find that the economy is still 27 percent below trend. The real (GNP) output data they employed were based on 1972 prices. Those have been revised based on a chained price index in 1996 dollars (U.S. Department of Commerce 2001). It is these estimates that are used in what follows.

On the basis of that data, figure 2.6 reports the results of duplicating their procedure.[9] The calculations are carried through 1950. The figure shows the economy attaining its trend level in 1942. Of interest are the subsequent three years of maximum war effort in which the economy operated well above trend, rising to 25 percent above in 1944. That the economy could operate so much in excess of its long-run capacity strains one's credulity, in part because of the use of labor—teenagers, older workers, and housewives—whose labor market skills were lower. The subsequent reversion to trend in the years following 1944

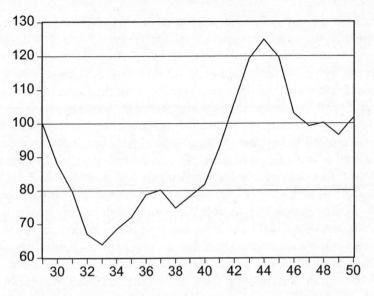

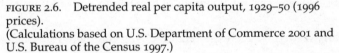

FIGURE 2.6.   Detrended real per capita output, 1929–50 (1996 prices).
(Calculations based on U.S. Department of Commerce 2001 and U.S. Bureau of the Census 1997.)

implies a recession, and a sharp one at that, and that is what the official National Income and Product Account data also show. The years 1945 through 1947 are ones of falling real output, with 1946 exhibiting the largest drop, over 11 percent. The Cole-Ohanian procedure shows a sharp fall (20 percent) in economic activity as the postwar economy again was operating at its long-run capacity.

This evidence supports the position of Robert Higgs (1992, 1997, 1999), who argues that the transition back to normalcy did not occur until the immediate postwar years. It is only then that the economy could meaningfully be viewed as having fully recovered. He argues that the dominance of wartime government expenditures distorted the official data because of the difficulty of measuring output in the absence of market prices. One important piece of evidence is shown in figure 2.7 in which real GNP and consumption are graphed relative to their 1929–46 trends. Use of the NIPA data indicates that the economy operated 23 percent above trend in 1944, which is almost the same as estimated by Cole-Ohanian who used a very different procedure. Thereafter, the economy experienced a three-year contraction through 1947. "In 1946, the bottom fell out: real GDP dropped more than 20.6 percent, by far the largest annual fall ever in U.S. economic history, exceeding even that of the worst year (1932) of the Great Depression" (1999, 602).[10] The key to the explanation lies in the difficulty of having satisfactory data on real output in an economy in which the dominant part is outside the market. According to Higgs (1999, 606), 40 percent consisted of war-related materiel. The corollary is that the actual inflation of prices captured by the implicit price deflator used to calculate real GNP was evidently greater than that recorded in official price indexes (Higgs 1999, 611). With the actual inflation rate greater than officially reported, real output was less than the measured output. With the end of the war and the rapid dismantling of price controls, the officially measured postwar data more satisfactorily track the reality of production. In other words, the data on output during the war overstate actual levels, and the behavior of the data in figure 2.7 is evidence of this.

The answer as to when the recovery was complete must be some-

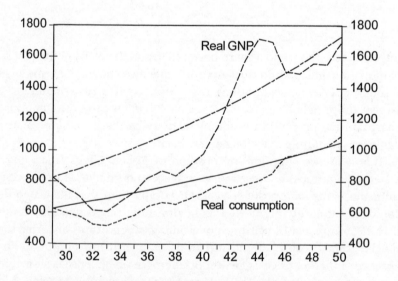

FIGURE 2.7.   Real GNP (large dashes) and consumption (small dashes) around respective 1929–46 trends, 1929–50. (Data from Department of Commerce 2001.)

what uncertain. The likelihood that the economy hit full stride in December 1941 is almost nil. The Romer and Cole-Ohanian approaches indicate that as they point to 1942 as the appropriate date. Higgs's evidence also calls for rejecting 1941. Though it may well be that the normal full-employment peacetime economy did not occur until after the war, it nonetheless is true that the economy was moving strongly toward full recovery in the early 1940s. It is those considerations that are basic to taking mid-1942 as the point at which to regard as complete the roller coaster ride that began almost thirteen years earlier with the onslaught of the devastating Depression.

Stock Prices

The stock market, so much in evidence in discussions of the Contraction, evoked little comment during the recovery. The behavior of the Standard and Poor's stock price index is shown in figure 2.8. The data are taken from the Federal Reserve's *Banking and Monetary Statistics* and therefore are not real-time data. From its 1929 high of 31.3 in September, the index plunged 85 percent to 4.77 in June 1932. It then recovered 31 percent to 6.23 by March 1933. The following month, the first one shown in the figure, it rose 11 percent. After moving somewhat erratically, though downward for the next two years, it began in April 1935 an upward move until February 1937, at which point it was almost three times its Contraction low but still 42 percent below its pre-Depression peak. Thereafter, it moved downward until the end of the recovery, falling to 8.77 by June 1942, almost three-quarters below its previous high. It was not until September 1954, exactly twenty-five years to the month, that the index reached its previous high.

Interest Rates

The behavior of interest rates is shown in figure 2.9. The data are taken from the Board of Governors (1943, 1976). The yield on U.S. government bonds does not extend past December 1941 due to a reclassification of the series, the effect of which is to show a marked upward jump in the rate. One of the things that is clear is the downward drift in all rates, with the three long-term rates showing marked declines. The

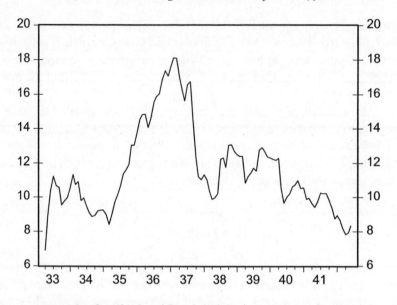

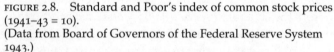

FIGURE 2.8.   Standard and Poor's index of common stock prices
(1941–43 = 10).
(Data from Board of Governors of the Federal Reserve System
1943.)

respective Baa and Aaa rates fell from about 8 to 4.33 percent and from
4.62 to 2.85 percent by June 1942. The rate on U.S. bonds was slightly
less than 2 percent by December 1941.

The commercial paper rate declined from 2.5 percent at the recovery's start to about 1 percent and then to 75 basis points a year later. It
remained there until a month before the 1937–38 depression, when it
moved up 25 basis points to 1 percent through February 1938. Thereafter, it began a descent to nine-sixteenths of a percent by January 1939,
at which level it remained throughout the remainder of the recovery.
The series for U.S. treasury bills was based on quotations from government security dealers and thus were auction yields.[11] In only three
months during the entire recovery did the rate exceed one-half of a percent, and from October 1937 it was generally less than 10 basis points.
As indicated in the figure, the treasury bill rate was close to zero, many
times being less than 10, even 5, basis points. This was particularly true
during 1938 through 1940, when the economy rebounded robustly
from the 1937–38 depression. From 2 basis points in January 1941, the

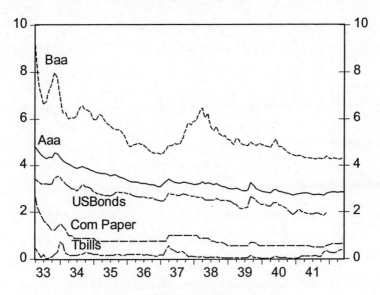

FIGURE 2.9.   Interest rates, April 1933–June 1942.
(Data from Board of Governors of the Federal Reserve System
1943.)

yield on treasury bills rose to three-eighths of a percent by the end of the recovery.

It was those low levels of interest rates and their continuing slide during the Contraction that reinforced the disillusionment of economists and policymakers with monetary actions as a credible recovery policy. The corollary was a search for an alternative recovery vehicle, whether structural realignment of the economy as envisioned initially by Roosevelt's Brains Trust or fiscal actions, as evolved later (Stein 1969, esp. 91–130).

Bank Assets

The following two figures relate to the assets of commercial banks. Figure 2.10 shows the behavior of the earning assets, loans, and investments, including U.S. government securities, of commercial banks.[12] Figure 2.11 charts the holdings of the excess reserves of member banks,

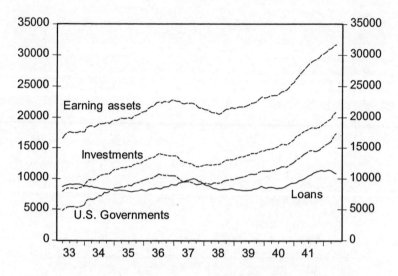

FIGURE 2.10.   Earning assets, loans, investments, and U.S. government securities, commercial banks (millions), April 1933–June 1942.
(Data from Board of Governors of the Federal Reserve System 1943.)

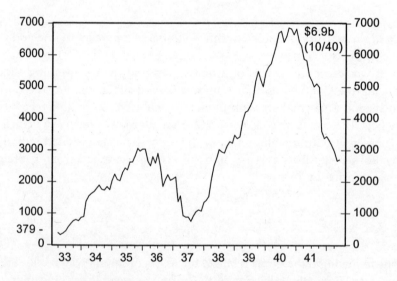

FIGURE 2.11.   Excess reserves of commercial banks (millions), April 1933–June 1942.
(Data from *Federal Reserve Bulletin*, various issues.)

a variable about which there was growing policy concern as the nascent recovery developed more vigorously in the mid-1930s.

Earning assets are the sum of bank loans and investments, where the latter consists principally of U.S. government securities. Two things stand out. First, the rise in earning assets is principally due to bank purchases of U.S. government securities. The correlation between earning assets and U.S. governments is 98 percent, reflecting a 98 percent correlation between earning assets and investments and one in excess of 99 percent between investments and U.S. governments. Second, bank lending (the solid line) lagged behind the pace of recovery. It was only in the last quarter of 1940 that it exceeded permanently its levels in the first three months of recovery. It initially was 9 percent larger than bank investments. By the recovery's end, it was 48 percent lower, only about half as large.

After a modest rise in the first half-year of the recovery, loans fell 13 percent across the next two years. In October 1935, they began to increase, rising by the following October to a level above where they were when the recovery began. They then increased 15 percent by the following September, four months into the 1937–38 depression, after which they declined over the subsequent twenty-one months, until June 1939. Thereafter they rose, surpassing in May 1941 their previous high (September 1937). At that point, they were only 31 percent higher than at the beginning of the recovery. In real terms, however, they were still 15 percent below that beginning level. Real loans were higher at the recovery's start than any time after.

This is cause for pause for analyses concerned with the role of bank lending in economic recovery and growth, in brief for those that look to the credit channel as an important transmission mechanism.[13] The correlation between real loans and industrial production is inconsequential, only 7 percent. To the extent that bank lending is regarded as an important factor promoting continuing recovery, the behavior shown in the loans data is a call for the need to reconsider that view.

The importance of U.S. government security holdings can be seen in the increasing proportion of banks' earning assets in that form. The corollary to the increased acquisition of governments was an expanding stock of deposit liabilities, and therefore of money. At that time, however, there were no money stock data, though there was information on deposits from which a money stock series could be constructed.

From a base ratio of 29 percent U.S. governments to total earning assets in April 1933, commercial bank holdings increased to 55 percent in June 1942, due not to a shrinkage of earning assets but to a 262 percent increase in their net purchases. Banks were adding to their U.S. government security holdings at the rate of 15 percent per annum. Their holdings of other securities hardly increased, rising only 13 percent during the entire recovery.

Another asset of consequence, particularly to the monetary authority, is the excess reserves of banks. This is a statistical construct, obtained by subtracting from total reserves those mandated by reserve requirements. That such reserves are arithmetically calculable as excess does not imply that they are surplus reserves. For banks, excess reserves may be desired as a form of insurance against any of several possible contingencies. This series is shown in figure 2.11. In the quarter in which recovery began, they averaged $353 million.[14] Thereafter, they steadily increased to over $3 billion in early 1936. On August 16 of that year, the Board of Governors, using its newly approved authority granted by the Banking Act of 1935, instituted the first of a three-step (August 1936, March 1937, May 1937) doubling of reserve requirements. Excess reserves subsequently fell almost 70 percent to $750 million by August 1937. Thereafter, banks began rebuilding their excess reserves, assisted in part by the Board's April 1938 reduction that moved requirements to about where they had been at the time of the second increase. Excess reserves reached a high of $6.9 billion in October 1940, after which they fell 65 percent to $2.4 billion in June 1942. This was approximately the level at which they had been when the first of the reserve requirement increases was enacted in August 1936.

Federal Reserve Credit and Gold Influences

The respective contributions of gold and Federal Reserve credit to movements in the monetary base are shown in figure 2.12. Federal Reserve credit reflects the role of the Federal Reserve as it provides reserves to banks through open market purchases and lending through the discount window at what then was known as the rediscount rate.[15] Federal Reserve credit is the major policy variable determining the reserve base of the banking system. The monetary base—government "printed" money—is the sum of bank reserves plus the currency holdings of the public. It represents the direct monetary liabilities of the government, as construed by the Constitution. As such, it is one of the important influences on the size of the money stock. The monetary base is in fact the base for a money stock that is a multiple of it, hence the term *monetary base*. Earlier writers, of whom the most prominent are Friedman and Schwartz (1963), use the term *high-powered money* as a synonym, which itself connotes the idea of it being the base on which a much larger stock of money can be maintained.[16]

With few exceptions, the base grew continually—at a 13.8 percent annual rate—through April 1937, a month prior to the start of the depression. It then leveled off before declining slightly, falling 2.4 percent (annual rate) over the next six months. It then resumed its earlier climb, rising at a somewhat higher rate—14.6 percent—through the remainder of the recovery. Had the monetary base not shrunk, it would have been $1.1 billion larger in October 1937, when it ceased falling, enough to have moderated decline.

The monetary gold stock is another factor determining reserves and the monetary base. As a result of the progressive devaluation of the dollar culminating in January 1934, the gold stock, which is valued at the official gold price, shot up as the price moved to $35 a troy ounce. Thereafter U.S. gold holdings continued increasing due to gold inflows,

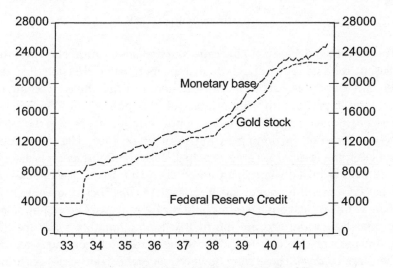

FIGURE 2.12.   Monetary base, gold stock, and Federal Reserve credit (millions), April 1933–June 1942.
(Data from Board of Governors of the Federal Reserve System 1943.)

principally from Europe. In all, it increased 466 percent over the remaining months of the recovery, an annual rate of 23 percent. It is clear that increases in the gold stock were the principal driving force behind the increase in the monetary base, which itself increased at a 15 percent annual rate. The two are correlated at 99 percent.

As is readily apparent, Federal Reserve credit contributed almost nothing to the growth of the base. For the entire recovery, it is negatively correlated with the base, at 14 percent. It was $2.5 billion at the start of the recovery. By the beginning of the next depression, it had increased only $62 million, an annual rate of six-tenths of a percent. Federal Reserve credit increased slightly until the end of 1937, after which it fell over the next twenty-six months, at which point it was a bit more than $250 million lower than at the beginning of the recovery almost eight years earlier. In March 1941, it began once again to increase, this time rather briskly, so that it was approximately $250 million higher at the end of the recovery relative to its level at the beginning, with the rise above its beginning level coming only in the last two months of the recovery. For the entire recovery the annual rate at which Federal Reserve credit increased was 1.1 percent.

Money Stock

There is much debate as to the causes of the Great Contraction and the reasons for its depth. Though there appears to be no rejection of virtually any hypothesis about its causes, there is a definite converging of thinking regarding the importance of the policies of the Federal Reserve as a factor perhaps initiating but certainly deepening the business contraction beginning in the summer of 1929. The hypothesis indicting the Federal Reserve as culpable for the Contraction is associated primarily with Friedman and Schwartz (1963).[17] Their analysis relies on a monthly money stock series they constructed, inasmuch as there were no such official series until the early 1940s. The money stock estimates they derived are the first to report monthly totals for the entire recovery period; much subsequent research continues to use their money data. There were however several private series covering the Contraction years, in particular those of Lauchlin Currie (1933, 1934b), which was annual, and James W. Angell (1936), which was both annual and monthly. The first official series—"something of a patchwork job" (Friedman and Schwartz 1970, 272)—appeared in the Board's *Banking Studies* (1941).[18]

Figure 2.13 graphs the quantity of money series developed by Friedman and Schwartz (1963, 712–16).[19] They are for the M1 and M2 definitions, denoted respectively as *M1FS* and *M2FS*. The other two money series are ones constructed for this book using real-time data taken from monthly issues of the *Federal Reserve Bulletin*. These two series correspond to the traditional medium-of-exchange and store-of-value notions and are denoted *M1FRB* and *M2FRB*, respectively. The two series are useful because they employ data that were available to economists living during the 1930s, data that could be used to try to understand the recovery in terms of the money stock, a framework quite in keeping with the canonical monetary theory of the time, the quantity theory of money.

The desired data for *M1FRB* and *M2FRB* were assembled by aggregating information appearing in different tables in the *Bulletin*. One was labeled the *Money in Circulation* series, which includes the currency component of the money stock as well as currency held as vault cash by

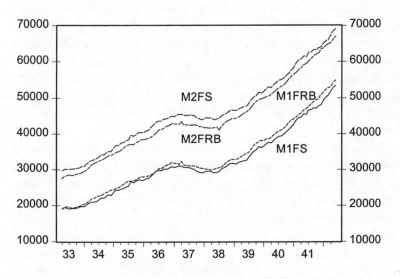

FIGURE 2.13. Money supply: Friedman and Schwartz, *M1FS* and *M2FS*; Federal Reserve Board constructed *M1FRB* and *M2FRB* (millions), April 1933–June 1942.
(Data from Friedman and Schwartz 1963, and *Federal Reserve Bulletin*, various issues.)

commercial banks. Today it is known as Currency in Circulation. Earlier it was Money in Circulation, reflecting the debate about the grouping of liquid assets constituting money. The requisite deposit data, taken from another table, were *net deposits* and its subset *net demand deposits* at member banks.[20]

Quite understandably, these data seem deficient a priori as fully satisfactory measures of the money stock, for various reasons. They do not include deposits at nonmember banks. Sometimes the data are monthly averages of daily figures, and other times, end-of-month figures. In addition, the data are not seasonally adjusted, as would be expected of a monthly series.[21] Another shortcoming is that currency, coming as it does from the Money in Circulation table, includes vault cash.

In relation to Friedman and Schwartz's carefully estimated data series, $M1FRB$ is systematically larger than $M1FS$, approximately 3.25 percent, whereas the constructed $M2FRB$ series is approximately 4.4 percent smaller than $M2FS$. Of most interest, however, are the correlations between the constructed and the Friedman and Schwartz series. For the narrow money measures, the simple correlation coefficient is 0.999. And for the broader money series, it is the same![22]

Each series showed double-digit annual rates of increase from the start of the recovery until just prior to the onslaught of the depression. The rate of increase for $M1FS$ was 62.7 percent (an annual rate of 12.9 percent), whereas $M2FS$ had an annual rate of increase of 11.1 percent. Each then fell the remainder of the year—$M1FS$ by 6.1 percent and $M2FS$ by 3.3 percent. Thereafter, each rose rapidly through the remainder of the recovery: $M1FS$ at a 14.4 percent and $M2FS$ at a 10.5 percent annual rate.

With the exception of GNP, the monetary base, and the Friedman and Schwartz money stocks, each of the series discussed was available during the recovery. The interesting question relates to the uses to which the data were put as economists of the 1930s attempted to understand the recovery.

Government Receipts
and Expenditures

Analyses of the recovery did not emphasize fiscal policy as a recovery vehicle until the late 1930s, though the effects of particular expenditure programs, to be sure, were noted. However, the general matter of run-

ning deficits was an issue more on a political plane than on the technical economic effects. It was in later analyses that the economic consequences of the federal budget came to be emphasized, due in large part
to the framework deriving from Keynes and its further development by
his coterie. It was then that the economic consequences of the fiscal
actions came to the fore.

Federal fiscal data are available from several governmental
sources.[23] Each however is an annual series. The only published
monthly series is that of John Firestone (1960). Figure 2.14 depicts the
seasonally adjusted data for federal government receipts, expenditures,
and the deficit. Deficits occur in all but one (December 1937) of the
recovery's 111 months. The data are seasonally adjusted using the
National Bureau of Economic Research's "ratio-to-twelve-month-moving-average method" (1960, 3). Even with the seasonal adjustment, the
three series exhibit a considerable amount of random fluctuation. This
is due to the short-term vagaries of factors affecting government
finances. If the data are aggregated into quarterly observations, the
series are considerably smoother. Greater noise is to be expected of
higher frequency data.

There are several things to note. One is the growing size of the
deficits after December 1937, the one surplus month. In fall 1940, a year

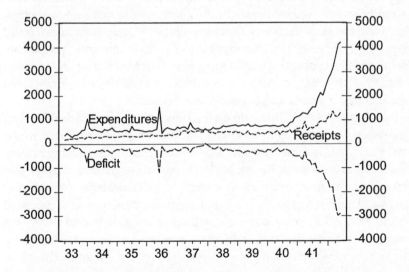

FIGURE 2.14. Federal deficit, expenditures, and receipts (millions), April 1933–June 1942.
(Data from Firestone 1960.)

after the beginning of World War II in Europe, the deficit began rising sharply. From a level of $300 million in October 1940, it increased to half a billion three months later and then to $1.1 billion by September 1941. A second feature is the two sharp one-month increases in spending, the first in January 1934 and the other in June 1936. The first represents a $450 million and the latter a $924 million increase, changes of 75 and 150 percent, respectively.[24] A third point, about which much has been made, is the shrinking of the deficit beginning in mid-1937 and running through the end of that year. From deficits in excess of $200 million during the first half, indeed the previous twelve months, the deficit fell to an average of $80 million in the last six months, with a surplus (of $14 million) in December 1937.

Concluding Observations

This chapter presented and discussed various economic data, much of which was available in the 1930s. The evidence substantiated that the recovery was indeed a long process, that it was characterized by fits and starts. The financial data on stocks, interest rates, bank lending, and Federal Reserve credit, so visible, so immediate, so ostensibly relevant, appeared to give little hope for optimism that somehow the economy would recover. Rather, it was in the charts of the monetary variables, gold and the stock of money, that signs of the recovery mechanism could be seen. To the extent that the experiences of other countries were of consequence, the conclusion would seem to be that forms of social organization other than the market were desirable, or at the very least that some form of management and planning was in order.

The next chapter follows up on the suggestive evidence dealing with monetary variables as it considers the role of monetary forces in the recovery. This is done by examining the burgeoning postwar evidence on the macroeconomic forces that promoted recovery. The chapter also considers the intellectual environment of economists as the recovery began. The discussion then turns to a presentation of evidence that could be exploited by economists in that decade. It deals with the behavior of prices and output in relation to the movements of the quantity of money, a framework encapsulated in the quantity theory of money. Whether any did in fact pursue such an approach is the subject of the subsequent chapters.

CHAPTER 3

Money and Recovery

The principal concern of this chapter is an examination of the role of the money stock in promoting recovery. Its perspective is a macroeconomic aggregate demand orientation, which was the preferred framework in postwar analyses of the economy. This stands in contrast to the microeconomic approach favored by the political and institutionalist economists in the Depression, the structuralists (Hawley 1966; Barber 1996, 5–10), who dominated policy-making in the political arena in the first several years of the recovery.[1] For them, the road to recovery lay in planning as the vehicle to "rationalize" industry, to restructure, in order to avoid what was widely regarded as the ruinous consequences of competition.[2] The problem was viewed as economy wide excess supply—the idea of want among plenty—which was believed due to excessive efficiency and not to deficient aggregate demand. Hence the solution emphasized reducing supply; the archetypal example of this in agriculture was the infamous plowing up "some ten million acres of sprouting cotton and [slaughtering] some six million squealing piglets" (Kennedy 1999, 205). It was also the belief of the structuralists that business concentration was the problem, hence the need to restructure that sector. To that end, the National Industrial Recovery Act (NIRA) with its implementation arm, the National Recovery Administration (NRA), was to be the chief instrument of execution.

One of the central focuses of the NIRA was to raise prices and wages: "The President's hope was that the N.R.A. would promote recovery in two ways; by raising prices, and so dissipating the gloom of business men and encouraging investment; and by raising wages, and so increasing purchasing power" (Lewis 1949, 107). The inconsistency of having at the same time higher profits due to higher prices and lower profits due to higher wages evidently was not a concern (107–8). What is interesting is that the route to higher prices and wages was not to be monetary expansion.

At the time of the Great Depression, macroeconomics was not an acknowledged specialized field of economics.[3] There of course was the monetary theory field with its focus on the purchasing power of money, that is, the price level. To the extent there was concern with the aggregative economy, there were two principal approaches: the quantity theory with its emphasis on the role of changes in the stock of money (Fisher 1925) and the banking school–real-bills framework with its orientation on credit conditions, particularly in relation to international monetary policy under the gold standard (Wheelock 1991). As such, policymakers at the Federal Reserve favored the latter. Academic economists were more disposed to the quantity theory with its modus operandus of changes in the money stock inducing changes in economic activity. This does not imply the approaches were disjoint; there were academic economists who consistently employed a banking school view (H. Parker Willis of Columbia and O. M. W. Sprague of Harvard, for instance) as well as some who wrote quantity theory tracts but practiced real-bills in their policy prescriptions (Edwin W. Kemmerer, the "money doctor" of Princeton, for example). To the extent there was a prevailing macroeconomic paradigm, it was the quantity theory, though there indeed was considerable skepticism in many quarters regarding it, as attested by the underconsumptionists, Wesley Mitchell's eclectic National Bureau approach, and the Institutionalist school in general. It would, however, be difficult to argue that any of these in fact constituted a macroeconomic framework. Although the quantity theory was the main macroeconomic framework, it likely was the case that a minority of economists subscribed to it.[4]

That the quantity theory may be regarded as such a paradigm in the early years of the 1930s can be regarded as an understandable, natural outcome of its post-1870 evolution through considerable theoretical advances and policy debates, as analyzed by David Laidler (1991). As he demonstrated, the analytical input undergirding the theory was developed in the 1870–1914 "golden age." Thus, by the beginning of the Great War, well in time for the economic debacle of the 1930s, the theory in its logical, theoretical form and in its applicability to policy issues was in place. George Tavlas (1997, 154–57) discussed some of the profession's quantity theory forays in the Depression, capturing the flavor of Friedman's oft-quoted introductory comments (1956, 3).[5] In those times, the quantity theory was employed less formally than now, particularly as an empirical proposition. Nonetheless, as Lauchlin Currie emphasized, "the logic of practically all monetary theories of the business cycle called for an energetic expansion of money in 1930–33" (1934b, 4), a clear quantity theory orientation in that it presupposes that the quantity of money is essentially under the control of the central bank and therefore is not endogenous in the real-bills sense. Accordingly, increases in it could be expected to lead to increased economic activity via an expansion of aggregate demand, hence to higher prices and output.[6]

Evidence

One of the earliest hints on the role of the money stock in the recovery were in Gardiner Means's comments (1946) on a paper by Arthur Smithies (1946). In his prefatory remarks to the latter's "fiscal interpretation of history," he pointed out that money stock, evidently $M1$, fell 25 percent between 1929 and 1933. "In contrast the New Deal adopted a policy of monetary expansion, bringing about an increase in the stock of money of . . . over 50 per cent. In our economy, which functions on the basis of money, you cannot increase the money supply by over 50 per cent and have no significant effect" (1946, 32). That, however, was the extent of his remarks on the role of money; he did not follow up by a more detailed examination of the influence of the money stock. A more detailed linking of the money stock and its influence on the recovery came almost two decades later.

Milton Friedman and Anna J. Schwartz

The earliest, most cogent, generally accepted analysis of the role of money in the recovery is that of Milton Friedman and Anna J. Schwartz (1963, 493–545). The preferred method is narrative, with heavy stress on timing relations based on charts.[7] The data are generally monthly observations. The analysis carries into 1941, but the bulk of their investigation deals with events through the onset of the late-1930s depression.

Their summary view was that "the most notable feature of the revival after 1933 was not its rapidity but its incompleteness" beginning with the "initially erratic and uneven" early months (1963, 493). In their subsequent analysis, four principal themes were developed. The first was that the recovery to mid-1937 had associated with it a sharp increase in the stock of money—"the broad movements in the stock of money correspond with those in income. From its trough in April 1933, the recorded stock of money rose 53 per cent to its subsequent peak in March 1937 . . . an annual rate of nearly 11 per cent per year" (1963, 497). Further, those double-digit annual rates were a result of increases in the stock of gold. Thus "the rapid rate of rise in the money stock certainly promoted and facilitated the concurrent economic expansion" (1963, 544).

Second, "despite a probably higher fraction of the labor force unemployed and of physical capacity unused than in . . . earlier expansions," the recovery raised wholesale prices by more than was typical of recoveries (1963, 498). As a consequence of this and of the dramatic rise in excess reserves, the Federal Reserve raised reserve requirements, doubling them between August 1936 and May 1937. This reduced the growth rate of the money stock and was an important factor responsible for the severity of the 1937–38 depression: reserve requirement policy "is an extremely potent control and was used in what seems retrospectively a drastic fashion" (1963, 517).[8] The effect of those increases was to reduce the growth of the money stock, as banks "sought to restore their excess reserve position" (1963, 526). The "impact of the rise in reserve requirements . . . first sharply reduced the rate of increase in the money stock and then converted it into a decline, [which] must surely have been a factor curbing expansion, and the absolute decline, a factor intensifying contraction" (1963, 544–45). They thus concluded, "consideration of the effects of monetary policy [the rise in reserve requirements in particular] certainly strengthens the case for attributing an important role to monetary changes as a factor that significantly intensified the severity of the decline, and also probably caused it to occur earlier than otherwise" (1963, 544).

The third important point made was that, with the exception of the increases in reserve requirements, the Federal Reserve was essentially passive during much of the recovery. Lending to banks essentially vanished, falling from $429 million in April 1933 to a fourth of that at the end of the year and then to $28 million in June 1934. It never again reached that level during the remainder of the recovery. In many of those months, it was less than $10 million.[9] The Federal Reserve's holdings of U.S. government securities, the medium through which open market operations were conducted, remained essentially constant, varying with two exceptions between $2.4 and $2.6 billion between

October 1933 and October 1940, after which it drifted downward about $200 million to $2.2 billion through March 1942.[10] Because of the near constancy of Federal Reserve credit, the central bank was not offsetting seasonal movements affecting the reserve balances of its member banks, in contrast to its actions in the previous decade. This was "a radical change in Federal Reserve policy" (1963, 515), the effect of which was that commercial banks desired somewhat larger reserve balances, which they held in the form of excess reserves. On the basis of their reading of the evidence, Friedman and Schwartz concluded, "Federal Reserve credit outstanding was almost perfectly constant from 1934 to mid-1940" (1963, 512); its coefficient of variation was only 3 percent for January 1934 through June 1940, whereas it was ten times that size in the 1920s.

Fourth, the increases in the money stock were primarily attributable to expansion of the monetary base, which in turn was the result of increases in the stock of gold. The increased gold stock was due initially to devaluation culminating in the January 1934 Gold Reserve Act. In the subsequent three months, the official dollar value of the gold stock increased 91 percent. The second factor increasing the gold stock was the increased capital imports arising from the growing uncertainties in Europe.

The actual behavior of the money stock is the result of the joint interaction between the monetary base and the money multiplier. This is typically captured in the expression $M = mB$, where M is the quantity of money, which they took as the $M2$ measure, m is the money multiplier, and B is the monetary base. Figure 3.1 illustrates the behavior of the $M2$ money multiplier, calculated by dividing Friedman and Schwartz's $M2$ by the monetary base. From a value of 3.8 at the beginning of the recovery, it falls almost continually to 2.5 by mid-1940. It then increases to 2.7 during the following two years. Simply as an algebraic matter, the monetary base has to increase all the more to keep the stock of money rising when the money multiplier is falling.[11]

The increase in the monetary base in turn resulted from increases in the gold stock arising initially from the devaluation and then from the continuing flight of capital. The process by which gold inflows became encapsulated in the base was that the Treasury bought gold, since the public could not hold monetary gold because of the Gold Reserve Act.[12] The Treasury paid for the gold from its deposit account at the Federal Reserve. The result was an increase in the reserve base of banks and

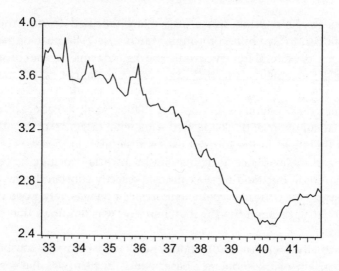

FIGURE 3.1.   Friedman and Schwartz *M2* money multiplier, 1933.2–1942.2.
(Data from Friedman and Schwartz 1963.)

therefore in the monetary base. With Federal Reserve credit essentially constant, "changes in high-powered money reflected mainly movements in the gold stock" (Friedman and Schwartz 1963, 505). For February 1934 through December 1941, the period of concern to them, the correlation coefficient between the two is 0.997, and for the entire recovery, it is similar, 0.991.[13]

That the inflows of gold were not sterilized during most of the recovery, as had been done in the 1920s, was due principally to the Roosevelt administration's desire to raise prices and secondarily to the System's passivity. There was however one period when the gold inflows were sterilized, December 1936 to September 1937.[14] In this, the Treasury rather than the Federal Reserve carried out the sterilization operation. It occurred through the Treasury borrowing funds to acquire the inflowing gold. It was Treasury actions of this sort that led Edward Simmons (1940) to argue that by altering its deposit account at the Federal Reserve, it effectively controlled bank reserve positions.

This last of Friedman and Schwartz's four points is important because it isolates a historical state in which the behavior of the money stock was effectively exogenous, providing a type of natural experiment. The movements of the money stock could not be attributed to the Federal Reserve increasing bank reserves by accommodating increased demands for loans owing to an improving economy; the observed increases in the quantity of money were "in no way a consequence of the contemporaneous business expansion" (1963, 544). Rather they were due to the expansion of the base owing to the increasing stock of gold.

Christina D. Romer

Friedman and Schwartz's presentation is narrative. Christina Romer (1992) employs a complementary empirical approach in the form of a simulation study that also allows her to assess the importance of fiscal actions. Her data are annual; she uses the Friedman and Schwartz *M1* money stock data. The procedure relies on estimates of monetary and fiscal responses that occurred during the deep 1921 and 1938 depressions. These become the basis for calculating "normal" expansionary policy effects on output. The policy influence on prices is not considered. The actual output effects are compared to the baseline "normal policy" effects. If for instance output under the actual and the "normal" policy paths are coincident, then policy does not add anything to the post-1933 recovery. In a similar manner, if the actual output path is well above that for "normal" stimulative policy, then that particular policy is in large part responsible for the recovery.

The method for gauging monetary actions uses deviations of the annual growth of *M1* from its trend, based on 1923 through 1927 "because they are the four most normal years of the 1920s" (1992, 760). Recovery is measured as the deviation of real GNP from its annual growth rate.

The principal concern is the role of the monetary and fiscal forces in the recovery relative to adventitious developments, events "affecting growth other than policy" (Romer 1992, 762). Fiscal policy is measured by the annual change in the ratio of federal deficit to GNP. The strategy revolves around calculating values of the policy multipliers β_m and β_f in the equation

$$\text{output change} = \beta_m(\text{monetary change}) + \beta_f(\text{fiscal change}) + \varepsilon_t.$$

The ε_t term captures all influences on output movements due neither to the monetary nor the fiscal influences, for instance, "supply shocks and changes in animal spirits" (1992, 761). To find the influence of forces captured in ε_t, it is necessary to obtain estimates of the policy multipliers, β_m and β_f. This is done by using data for the years 1921 and 1938 respectively, because in neither of those severe depression years was there an identifiable, meaningful influence other than monetary and fiscal factors, that is ε_t, is taken as equal to zero in each of those years (1992, 763). Since there are two expressions in the two policy multiplier unknowns, the value of each of the multipliers can easily be obtained.

The procedure is then straightforward. The actual path of the economy in terms of the real GNP is contrasted with what it would have been under "normal" policy, the policy that follows according to the monetary and fiscal actions of 1921 and 1938. Her conclusion for monetary policy is unambiguously strong: the behavior of the money stock was "crucial to the recovery. If money growth had been held to its normal level, the U.S. economy in 1942 would have been 50 percent below its pre-Depression trend path, rather than back to its normal level" (1992, 768–69). She follows by pointing out that the reason for the "large estimated effect of monetary developments is not hard to find[:] the extraordinarily high rates of money growth in the mid- and late 1930s" (1992, 769). Further, the source of "the huge increases in the U.S. money supply during the recovery was the tremendous gold inflow that began in 1933" (1992, 773). In this, she relies on Friedman and Schwartz, citing their concluding observation concerning the gold inflows: "Munich and the outbreak of war in Europe . . . in those [mid- and late 1930s] years, as Hitler and the gold miners had been . . . in 1934 to 1936" (1963, 545; Romer 1992, 773).

Though she does not consider in detail whether the recovery was primarily due to strong self-corrective forces, that is, endogenous propagation forces leading to mean-reversion, she concludes that not only were increases in the money stock the paramount cause of the recovery, they also were of sufficient strength to rule out analyses that give primary emphasis to any other forces, as for instance, the contention of J. Bradford DeLong and Lawrence H. Summers that "the substantial degree of mean reversion . . . is evidence that shocks to output are transitory" (1988, 467).

As for fiscal policy, her simulation has the actual and normal growth paths of fiscal actions essentially coincident. Fiscal policy accordingly "contributed almost nothing to the recovery from the Great [Contraction]. Only in 1942 is there a noticeable [influence] and even in this year

[it] is small" (1992, 767). In brief, she finds "that monetary developments were crucial [and] fiscal policy contributed little to the recovery" (1992, 782). Her conclusions echo those of Friedman and Schwartz on monetary influences and E. Cary Brown (1956) on the unimportance of the fiscal impulse.

Ben S. Bernanke

The previous two sections dealing with the role of the quantity of money focused solely on the United States. In a comparative study involving at times twenty-six countries, Ben S. Bernanke (1995) investigated the role of the money stock as it was linked to gold, in particular to the gold standard. For the United States, he used annual data on $M1$, based on Friedman and Schwartz's money stock estimates. His was not a study of the forces of recovery in the entire decade. Rather, he concentrated on the 1929–36 period because it was in the early years that the world economy spun down and then began to recover, with different countries initiating their respective movements back to trend at different times. The paper focused on the behavior of the quantity of money as responsible for the decline and recovery, with an emphasis on the gold standard as the vehicle underlaying the action.[15] This orientation served to view the gold standard as a restraint on independent monetary measures: "In particular, the evidence that monetary shocks played a major role in the Great Contraction, and that these shocks were transmitted around the world primarily through the workings of the gold standard, is quite compelling" (1995, 2).[16] As countries severed their ties to gold during his sample period, recovery commenced; "the evidence is that countries leaving the gold standard recovered substantially more rapidly and vigorously than those who did not" (1995, 12). The reason "this divergence arose [was] because countries leaving the gold standard had greater freedom to initiate expansionary monetary policies" (1995, 15).[17]

As a historical matter, the Brookings Institution in a comprehensive review of the Contraction and the subsequent early stages of recovery had articulated the linking of recovery to the abandonment of the gold standard. One of its conclusions was: "*Countries which remained on the gold standard show as a rule a considerably smaller degree of recovery than do those which abandoned or modified that standard*" (Brookings Institution 1936, 109, emphasis in original).

In exploring the role of the money stock, Bernanke dealt specifically with two issues. The first was an aggregate demand channel: in particular, the link between the economic experience of a country and the *M1* measure of its money stock in relation to its gold holdings. Here he found "that *monetary factors played an important causal role,* both in the worldwide decline in prices and output and in their eventual recovery" (1995, 3).

Having established the importance of monetary factors in the slide and subsequent recovery, he went on to explore a pair of aggregate supply mechanisms through which movements of the nominal money stock had real effects. The first of these was deflation and its effect on financial institutions, in which the Fisher (1932, 1933a) debt-deflation hypothesis was prominent. To this, Bernanke brought his earlier work to bear (1983). Relying on recent theoretical considerations, he concluded that principal-agent incentives and monitoring difficulties as related to financial institutions and borrowers were important factors that led to reduced lending by banks (or, to use his preferred phrase, a rising Cost of Credit Intermediation). The implication was that there was a breakdown in normal borrower-lender relations. The other aggregate supply factor was the inertia of nominal wages in that they did not move freely enough to bring real wages to market clearing levels.

The strategy employed to calculate growths of money stocks of countries was to link via an identity the stock of money to the value of a country's gold holdings, this in keeping with the workings of the gold standard. Through that expression, he followed the evolution of a country's money stock, attributing its movements to specific factors. Among the elements in the identity were the money multiplier and the gold backing requirement, which represented the minimum gold reserve relative to each unit of the monetary base, this determining the amount of gold that a central bank had to have for a given monetary base. During the decade under study, for instance, that minimum required ratio was 40 percent for the United States.

The gold standard is international in character. It acts as a link between the economies of countries, whereby each one's stock of money is determined by its gold holdings. No country can therefore pursue an independent monetary policy. Should one attempt to increase its money stock to combat deflationary conditions, it experiences a balance of payments deficit, which is financed by a loss of gold and a consequent induced shrinkage of its money stock.

On the basis of an examination of the behavior of the various elements in the identity, Bernanke identified the reason(s) for the actual movement of the quantity of money. In general, countries on the gold standard saw their money stocks decline after 1929. Those that left the gold standard, Sweden and the United Kingdom in 1931, the United States in 1933, experienced increases in their respective monetary stocks. The response to the money stock changes was in accordance with the quantity theory. Falling quantities of money brought deflation and declining output. Rising ones produced recovery.

This was apparent from a comparison of money movements and the course of prices and output before and after the times at which each of the countries ceased operating under the gold standard. He examined the behavior of up to twenty-six economies and their stocks of money as they were on or off the gold standard, from which he concluded that "countries adhering to the international gold standard suffered largely unintended and unanticipated declines in their . . . money stocks" (1995, 10). Further, "it seems reasonable to characterize these monetary shocks as exogenous . . . suggesting a significant causal role for monetary forces in the world depression" (1995, 10). As to the recovery, "the evidence is that countries leaving gold recovered substantially more rapidly and vigorously than those who did not" (1995, 12), as previously mentioned. Those countries that continued to adhere to gold experienced deflation and stagnant output growth (here France is a prime example), as a result of a failure of their money stocks to grow. It was only after leaving gold and therefore being able to experience monetary growth that the economies of those countries began recovering.

The results from the postwar research show that the economic recovery from the nadir of the Great Contraction in the United States (and in other countries) was principally due to increases in the stock of money, whatever the causes of those increases were. We now turn to an investigation of whether data available during the recovery would similarly have shown this result, namely, if a quantity theory approach could have been used to understand the recovery in output and prices.

The 1930s

It would seem natural that economists in that economically dismal but intellectually exciting, challenging decade would try to understand the causes of the slide and of the subsequent recovery. One macroeconomic framework for doing so was the quantity theory of money. A major difficulty, however, was that there were no official data on the quantity of money at the time.[18] There were, however, two privately produced estimates, those of Lauchlin Currie (1934b) who reported an essentially $M1$ series and James W. Angell (1936) who estimated both an $M1$ (circulating money) and an $M2$ (total money) series.[19] In what amounted to a comment on Currie's 100 percent reserves plan for demand deposits (1934b, 151–56), Lin Lin (1937) argued that time deposits were money, contrasting his evidence with Currie's. Lin used annual data as of June 30 for the period 1921 through 1933,[20] and Currie's final estimates extended only through 1934 and therefore could not be used to understand the entire recovery. Because Lin's only went through 1933, they were of no use for the recovery. Angell's estimates carried through 1934 and so were limited for purposes of trying to understand the entire period. In a subsequent largely theoretical tract linking the business cycle to changes in investment deriving from changes in anticipations, he extended his annual $M2$ monetary data through 1939 (Angell 1941). Though he was not principally concerned with an analysis of the recovery, his data are of interest in tracing how the influence of money could have been viewed by economists living in that time. His interpretation of the influence of the growth of the money stock is treated in the next chapter.

The strong monetary element in the Bernanke, Romer, and Friedman and Schwartz studies all employed the latter's money stock estimates, these appearing three decades after the nadir of the Contraction. For those living during the recovery, $M1$ and $M2$ type series could be constructed on the basis of data reported in the *Federal Reserve Bulletin*.[21] This in fact was what Fisher (1932, 93–95; 1933a, 356) did for his preferred monetary aggregate, net demand deposits. His procedure followed from his early, fundamental work (1911). In developing the equation of exchange in *The Purchasing Power of Money*, he dealt with the perennial question, What is money? To that end, currency was money, hence M, and its velocity was V. "Bank deposits transferable by check," though a form of "circulating media" (1911, 10–11), were not money; they were "deposit currency," which he denoted as M' for which the relevant velocity was V'.[22] In all of his subsequent work, he never combined the two.

Would use of a (real time) series garnered from issues of the *Federal*

Reserve Bulletin, with all the shortcomings discussed in the previous chapter's presentation of the two series *M1FRB* and *M2FRB*, have been useful for understanding the recovery and its robustness? How satisfactory would such a series have been? That is, could economists living during the 1930s have used a quantity theory framework to understand the monetary dimensions of the recovery? Recall that there is the very significant correlation between the *M1FRB* and *M2FRB* money stock series constructed from the *Federal Reserve Bulletin* and the Friedman and Schwartz series—99.9 percent for each pair. In the following discussion, the analysis proceeds for the most part on the basis of an *M1FRB* data series, the implicit assumption being that such was in fact constructed and used by economists trying to understand the recovery, specifically the movement of output and prices. Similarly, the output series is that of industrial production as it appeared in those times, that is, with a base of 1923–25 = 100. Likewise, the price series is for the Wholesale Price Index, whose base is 1926 = 100.

Money and Output

The data relating to the money stock, industrial production, and wholesale prices necessary to identify the strong monetary impulse in the recovery were readily available. The emphasis in this section is on the behavior of output. Figure 3.2 presents a scatter diagram graph for the entire recovery period. It shows the relationship between industrial production and the money stock, where each series is as it could have been observed from adding sequentially monthly observations from issues of the *Federal Reserve Bulletin.*

The respective notation is *IIP30s* for industrial production and *M1FRB* for the narrow money stock. In the figure, a line connects the monthly observations to allow the evolving time series to be seen more cleanly. The close relationship between the two variables is apparent. Inspection of that relationship makes it clear that a quantity theory orientation linking monthly observations on industrial production to movements of the money stock would have the recovery understood as a response to increases in the money stock. As to econometric sophistication, economists in that decade, with few exceptions, would have relied on evidence seen from a graph, such as from a scatter diagram as in figure 3.2. Correlation analysis was not a widely used empirical tool in economics. Rather, a scatter diagram would probably have been uti-

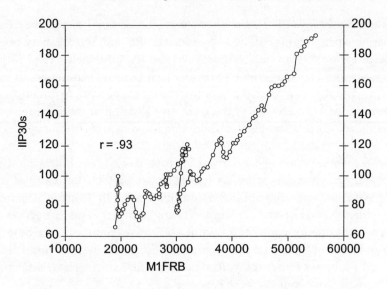

FIGURE 3.2.   Industrial production and constructed money stock,
April 1933–June 1942.
(Data from *Federal Reserve Bulletin*, various issues.)

lized, in which each evolving month's data could easily be added in
order to detect a pattern.

The simple correlation coefficient between *IIP30s* and *M1FRB* is 0.93,
as shown in the figure. If industrial production had been plotted
against the previous month's *M1FRB*, a one-month lag, the correlation
would also have been 0.93. If instead, the measure of the money stock
was *M2FRB*, the relation is similar, the correlation being 0.92. For the
Friedman and Schwartz series, the correlation coefficients for contemporaneous and one-month lagged *M1* are also 0.93. The correlation
between industrial production and the contemporaneous as well as
one-month lagged *M2* is 0.91.

However, the relationship depicted in the figure was not clear from
the outset. In part, this was due to the extremely large, virtually erratic,
movements in industrial production. For instance, in the first two
years, the relationship not only was quite weak—a correlation of about
6 percent—it at times was *negative*.[23] It was only in February 1936,
almost three years into the recovery, that the correlation rose above 50
percent. Had the industrial production data been collected and
reported as the revised series, the emerging link between the money

stock and recovery would have been clearer, for by July 1935 the correlation was in excess of 50 percent, testimony again to the benefits of
higher quality data. The sharp movements in industrial production had
the effect of extending the time before economists could feel confident
that recovery was in fact under way. That is, the recognition lag certainly seemed to be at least a year and a half to two years, and more
likely longer.

By the start of the subsequent depression in May 1937, the relationship was quite strong, the correlation being 84 percent. Beginning at that
time, there appeared very large, sharp downward changes in industrial
production, to the point where it looked as though it was changing
along a near vertical line. The money stock began falling in May and
continued to do so for a year, declining 7 percent. During that period,
industrial production (as measured by the 1930s index) fell 36 percent,
hence the near verticality of the graph during that year.[24] The deterioration of the economy in light of a decline in the money stock could hardly
be written off as happenstance, although other factors would most likely
be invoked as contributing to the depth of the decline.

Two periods of such a near vertical relationship are depicted on figure 3.3: April 1933 through the end of the year and, more to the point of

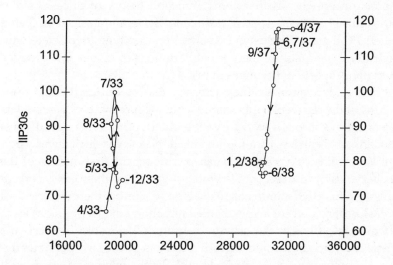

FIGURE 3.3.   Highly variable industrial production, April 1933–
December 1933 and April 1937–June 1938.
(Data from *Federal Reserve Bulletin*, various issues.)

the present discussion, April 1937 through June 1938 (the depression plus the months immediately preceding the peak and following the trough). A line with arrows between selected dates connects the points in each period. If the months in figure 3.3 are considered outliers and therefore removed, the relationship between industrial production and the money stock is very tight, the correlation coefficient being 0.96. Of course, economists of the time would not simply discard data in so cavalier a fashion, particularly in light of the anxieties attendant on the Contraction, indeed the Depression. To the extent they were trying to understand the recovery and depression using a quantity theory framework, the relevant graph is figure 3.2, and by that standard, the recovery could have been seen as due to increases in the money stock.

The evidence on the role of the quantity of money in promoting the recovery, which those living during that time could have used, is even a bit stronger when more satisfactory data are examined. The relationship between the revised measure of industrial production and $M1FS$ has a correlation coefficient of 0.96, slightly higher than the 0.93 for the data available in the 1930s.

Money and Prices

The quantity theory is first and foremost a theory of prices (Laidler 1991). This is particularly so in normal times, as emphasized by Irving Fisher: "The main conclusion is that we find nothing to interfere with the truth of the quantity theory that variations in money (M) produce normally proportional changes in prices" (1911, 183).[25]

Prices and the money stock increased sharply during the first three months of the recovery. After falling a bit, the money stock resumed its upward move through April 1937, the month prior to the next depression. It then began a twelve-month fall, at the end of which it was 7 percent lower. Wholesale prices began increasing the first months of the recovery, rising a third by December 1935. They then fell 3 percent across the first five months of 1936 before resuming their increase to a level almost 50 percent above their Contraction (and Depression) low.

Figure 3.4 depicts the scatter diagram relationship between the Wholesale Price Index and $M1FRB$. Here, as in the two previous figures, the points are connected to highlight the evolving record, with several key months indicated. In addition to the April 1933 initial

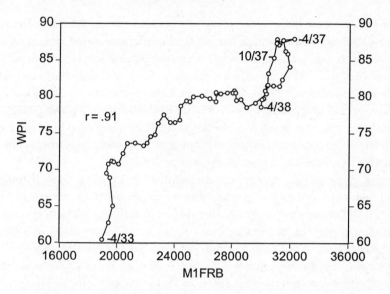

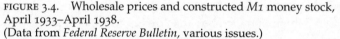

FIGURE 3.4. Wholesale prices and constructed M_1 money stock, April 1933–April 1938.
(Data from *Federal Reserve Bulletin*, various issues.)

month of the recovery, the graph identifies the Aprils prior to the beginning and end of the depression, as well as October 1937, the month in which prices dropped dramatically. The overall correlation is 0.91, as indicated in the figure. It is evident from the diagram that the general quantity theory proposition that has prices changing in the same direction as the money stock is operative. With few exceptions, the increases in the money stock through April 1937 have prices rising. Price movements correspond to those in the money stock. Similarly, the twelve-month contraction in the money stock that began in May 1937 results in falling prices, they being 11 percent lower by the following May.

As the recovery resumed, prices again began rising, though briefly, two months in fact. Economists of that time would then have been reassured that the price movements they observed were due to corresponding changes in their constructed money stock series. And then a surprising thing happened. The price decline that began with the depression a bit more than a year earlier continued through August 1940, allowing for the one-time price spike (at a 40.1 percent annual rate) in September–October 1939, of which the September increase alone was at an 89 percent annual rate, all the while with the money stock continuing to increase.[26] The *Federal Reserve Bulletin* in its Review of the Month did single out for comment that the "war in Europe resulted in abrupt price changes and sharp increases in activity in the commodity and financial markets" (October 1939, 839). In the same issue's National Summary of Business Conditions, it noted without comment the 4-percentage-point change in wholesale prices, from 75 to 79.

For a period of twenty-seven months, from May 1938 through August 1940, prices and money moved in opposite directions. In all, prices fell about 5 percent between May 1938 and August 1939 and then another 2 percent in the October 1939–August 1940 period. All told, wholesale prices fell about 15 percent from the start of the depression, not counting the September–October 1939 blip. Figure 3.5 shows the postdepression deflation in relation to the money stock. The break between the two deflation lines indicates the abrupt, sharp price increase in September–October 1939 owing to "speculative" demands

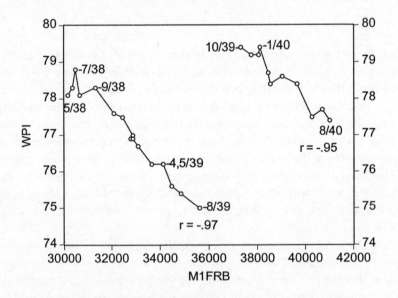

FIGURE 3.5.   Negative money stock-prices relations, May 1938–August 1939 and October 1939–August 1940.
(Data from *Federal Reserve Bulletin*, various issues.)

associated with the beginning of World War II. The correlation between the constructed quantity of money series and that of wholesale prices is negative: 0.97 for the May 1938–August 1939 period and 0.95 for the October 1939–August 1940 phase.

In the face of an expanding money stock, the continued deflation following the depression is a situation on which there was a seeming absence of comment, perhaps even notice. Neither Friedman and Schwartz, whose data appear on a chart (1963, 494), nor Romer (1999, 168), nor others—Chandler (1970, 129), for instance—mentioned this seeming anomaly, though each's data indicated the postdepression price fall.[27] Here is a situation of rapid monetary expansion (14.5 percent annual rate) apparently fostering robust increases in output, with industrial production increasing at a 22 percent annual rate, while at the same time prices are falling! And yet there was no marked comment, nor even passing acknowledgment, of the seemingly perverse evolution of the economy, particularly among those for whom money stock data were available. An analysis of the period in which this puzzling, anomalous situation occurred is presented in chapter 6, which deals with that depression.

After the extended decline, prices began increasing in September 1940 along with the money stock. They rose somewhat over 25 percent by June 1942. The constructed money series *M1FRB* increased a third (fig. 3.6).[28] The tailing off of the price rise, indeed a decline in prices, in the last two months is most likely due to the actions of the Office of Price Administration, which issued a general price freeze in April (Rockoff 1984, 93). The correlation for the period August 1940 through June 1942 is 0.99.

Here again in the almost two years preceding full recovery, there is affirmation of the quantity theory proposition that movements in the stock of money generate likewise movements in prices, as could have been seen by those who availed themselves of accessible information.

It is doubtful that anyone would have used the data in quite the detail found here. Regardless of whether anyone did, this chapter underscores the fact that a quantity theory approach would have identified as a principal source of the recovery an expanding stock of money. This judgment would have anticipated the robust findings of the mushrooming postwar research, which similarly had as basic to the recovery the expansion of the quantity of money.

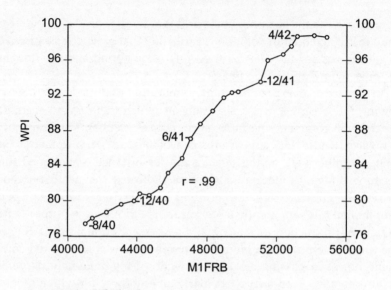

FIGURE 3.6.   Wholesale price and constructed *M1* money stock,
August 1940–June 1942.
(Data from *Federal Reserve Bulletin,* various issues.)

Concluding Observations

The interesting question then becomes whether any of those living in
the recovery identified the expansion of the money stock as key to the
ongoing recovery. Did economists use the quantity theory approach as
a vehicle to understand the recovery? If they did, what was their framework? These are some of the issues with which the next chapter is concerned.

CHAPTER 4

Decline of the Quantity Theory Paradigm

Postwar research singles out monetary expansion as a principal force promoting recovery. An interesting question is whether and to what extent economists living during the Depression recognized the important role of the expanding stock of money. Though many may have had reservations about the quantity theory as a vehicle for interpreting the economy, there nonetheless were few alternative macroeconomic frameworks. The Keynesian one was simply not a viable recourse, for several reasons. First of all, though the *General Theory* was published in February 1936, it was not digested until later. In addition, it was not well received in the United States, thereby further delaying its acceptance—witness Alvin Hansen's two negative evaluations, a review in the October 1936 *Journal of Political Economy* and an article four months earlier that concluded that "it is reasonably safe to predict that Keynes's new book will, so far as his theoretical apparatus is concerned, fare little better than did the 'Treatise'" (1936, 829). In fact, Keynesian economics did not become an important ingredient in American economic policy until into World War II (Colander and Landreth 1996).

Recognition Lag

Before turning to the evidence on economists' familiarity with the money-driven recovery, the question of the recognition lag must be addressed. Specifically, how long after the March 1933 trough was it before economists recognized recovery?

In a session devoted to "the history of recovery" at the December 1933 meeting of the American Economic Association, Willard Thorp, abstracting from a forthcoming "report on economic conditions throughout the world," indicated that "in eleven cases [an] upward movement began in 1933," cautioning however that "the upward swings are still young" (1934, 3). Curiously, the following year's meeting of the Association had no sessions or papers addressing the recovery.

Among the most useful sources for gauging sentiment about the economy were W[illiam]. L[eonard]. Crum's regular summaries of business conditions in the *Review of Economic Statistics*. In the first quarter of 1933, he noted "a change of great suddenness and intensity, occurred in public sentiment" (1933a, 69), this following the bank holiday. By November of that year, he was not yet confident that recovery was under way, noting "quite vigorous prosecution of *federal reserve policy* failed to bring about any large and sustained expansion in member bank credit [due to a] general impairment of confidence" (1933b, 190, emphasis added). This ambivalence carried through 1934. The following year was different: "The first quarter of 1935 brought an important expansion in the volume of business" (1935a, 34), with "the most striking features of the recent record for the member banks [being] the continued vigorous expansion in net demand deposits" (1935a, 38–39). The expansion had to be watched carefully, inasmuch as "the third quarter brought a mild contraction . . . a definite interruption" (1935b, 143). In retrospect, "economic improvement in the United States [in 1935] was more fully sustained, if not clearly more vigorous, than during any other year since the long cyclical advance of the 1920's culminated in 1929" (1936, 42). It thus was almost three years before Crum felt confident enough to recognize that indeed the recovery was under way.

Irving Fisher took a year less, though he previously had recovery occurring in the late summer of 1932 "as this book [*Booms and Depressions*] goes to press (September, 1932)" (1932, 157). In a May 1935 speech promoting the debt-deflation hypothesis of *Booms and Depressions*, he acknowledged that "the growing conviction the depression is nearing its end is justified" (*New York Times* 1935, 38).[1] This caution in recognizing recovery was quite pervasive, with the fear of retreating into contraction a continuing theme. In December 1935, for instance, Garfield V. Cox opined that the economy would drift into a recession because "this is the thirty-third month since business . . . began its rise from the extreme lows of the depression" (1936, 1). To put this in perspective, he noted that the National Bureau of Economic Research had documented only two longer peacetime expansions and that "the current recovery [was] taking an exceptional amount of time" due to "characteristics unusual if not unique in American experience" (1936, 2).[2]

In his December 1937 presidential address to the American Economic Association, which was midway through the 1937–38 depression, O[liver]. M[itchell]. W[entworth]. Sprague was still dubious about the recovery, because of damped investment—"the industries producing capital goods have shown little sign of complete recovery" (1938, 2).[3] His microeconomic focus, on capital goods, was central to Michael Bernstein's investigation (1987), whose detailed examination of various industries led him to view the entire decade as the Great Depression—"part of a long-term structural phenomenon" (1987, 185)—one in which there effectively was no recovery phase.[4]

Whether Sprague's damped business investment demand was due to a lack of demand for the products of firms or to credit tightening by banks or to some general notion of stagnation was not discussed. The theme of stagnation did however have many adherents, particularly as the decade wore on and the return to the prosperity of the previous decade seemed far distant. Prime among them was Alvin Hansen in his American Economic Association presidential address a year later. In it, he advanced the thesis that due principally to a declining population, which he believed imminent, the demand for capital would be lower, hence inducing a fall in investment. This would lead to investment levels insufficient to "give us full employment of our resources" (1939, 12). This concern over the economic implications of lower birth rates went beyond the United States. Sweden similarly was singled out (King 1937, 228). The prospect of stagnation was also a theme of Oskar Lange, who argued that "the view is widely held that the American economy has lost its momentum of expansion and reached a stage of more or less permanent stagnation" (1939, 503). This drift to stagnation was attributed to a "lack of sufficient inducements to invest" (1939, 513) under private capitalism.

That the recovery was not recognized until at least two years after it was under way seems a safe conclusion, particularly since it did not begin in earnest until September 1934, a year and a half after the trough.

Monetary Views of the Recovery

In the literature of the recovery, three themes stand out.[5] The first is that there was no satisfactory acknowledgment that the recovery was related to increases in the quantity of money, that it could be understood in terms of the quantity theory. There was, in fact, little discussion of the actual behavior of measures of the components of the money stock, much less attempts to link such movements to the evolution of prices and industrial production. The second theme deals with the growing volume of excess reserves and the inference that they implied an inability on the part of the central bank to stimulate recovery. The final theme relates to gold, first the devaluation and then the large inflows.

Prime among those who would have used a quantity theory framework were James Angell, Lauchlin Currie, and Irving Fisher, each familiar with a monetary aggregate. Angell and Currie assembled their own money stock series. Martin Krost and Milton Friedman as he experienced the decade are also considered. Fisher did not subscribe to the notion of an aggregate stock of money. He separated currency and demand deposits, terming the latter deposit currency. Fisher, the quintessential quantity theorist, is treated at length in the next chapter.

Before turning to the analyses of Angell, Currie, Krost, and Friedman, it is necessary to deal with economists' familiarity with and concern about the money stock. The professional literature has little to say about the actual measurement of it. Instead, there is more concern with what should be included. There also is a considerable literature on deposit multipliers, though the preferred orientation is bank credit, this due to C. A. Phillips's extraordinarily influential book of the same title (1920).

With regard to deposit- and earning asset-multipliers, or to use the term popular then, bank credit-multipliers, two of the most prominent monetary economists of the time wrote articles deriving formal expressions underlying the multiple expansion and contraction process. Each appeared in 1933, the first a two-part article by James W. Angell and Karel F. Ficek (1933a, 1933b), the other by James H. Rogers (1933a).

Angell and Ficek were concerned with getting things right regarding the activity of a single bank and that of the entire system. This reflected an elaboration on Phillips's seminal work. It also reflected a strong pedagogical statement intended to correct the position that "certain writers still hold to the view that a single bank . . . can expand its loans on the basis of surplus reserves by the reciprocal of its reserve ratio" (1933a, 9 n. 8). The likely source of such a view was the balance sheet of an individual bank holding fractional reserves. To that end, they arrived at "a fact long familiar [that the potential] expansion of loans and deposits is far greater when all or most of the banks expand together than when any one bank . . . attempts to expand alone" (1933a, 32). As to policy implications, "in the present depression, the converse proposition is especially relevant. Any one bank . . . can do very little by itself alone to expand" (1933a, 32).

Of more consequence, the authors calibrated multipliers—coefficients of maximum expansion (1933a, 17; 1933b, 157)—under various reserve requirement and currency-deposit ratio assumptions. The intent was to come up with the most satisfactory characterization of the U.S. situation. Though the bulk of their comments dealt with expansion, their basic assessment of the likelihood of combating the Depression through central bank policies was: "Whether a central bank can also deliberately control severe and protracted overcontraction, on the other hand, is a far more debatable question. The history of the last few years suggests, that . . . the question must probably be answered in the negative" (1933b, 193). Angell would return to this likely conclusion, which was articulated in the abstract rather than in a formal analysis, basing his answer on a quite detailed empirical study of the relation between movements of the economy and the quantity of money.

In much the same vein, James H. Rogers published in the inaugural issue of *Econometrica* an article reflecting the pessimism of the time. He similarly cited the pioneering work of Phillips (Rogers 1933a, 63). He derived earning asset and deposit multipliers for an individual bank and for the banking system, finding multipliers for the system larger than for an individual bank.[6] His main interest however was the policy implication implied by the ratcheting-down of deposits and loans in the Contraction, hence the puzzling title, "The Absorption of Bank Credit" rather than what seems more natural, "The Expansion of Bank Credit," the title used by Angell and Ficek. Rogers concluded:

In periods of general credit contraction, almost exactly the reverse situation holds. Once started, this process feeds upon itself. . . . In such a situation, lowering the rediscount rate is of little effectiveness in arresting the often accelerated liquation. At a time when the search for liquidity becomes little less than a mad scramble, the possibility of increasing debt at a Federal reserve bank *slightly more cheaply* provides no individual incentive to end the movement.

Should a large gold inflow appear, . . . a powerful, corrective, expansionary force would be felt. . . . In the absence of such beneficent inflows, . . . a remedy completely at the disposal of our central banking authorities . . . is apparently indicated. By Federal reserve "open-market purchases of bills and government securities," new funds . . . can be turned over to our hard-pressed banks.

Under present distressing conditions *easy money* is of little importance. *Plentiful money* would probably bring effective relief. (1933a, 70)

One sees here quite clearly Rogers's view that monetary expansion was the appropriate recovery policy and that the Federal Reserve should initiate and maintain an expanding monetary base through open-market purchases.[7] He argued consistently that monetary policy should be "plentiful money" and not "easy money," as gauged by interest rates (Steindl 1995, 106–9).

A second piece of evidence about economists' familiarity with the role of money is the running debate on the definition of money and the appropriate components of the money stock. One example of the former is the go-around between Raymond Lounsbury (1937) and Howard Ellis (1938) on whether it is the medium of exchange or the abstract unit of account, the *numéraire*, function that is money. Lounsbury's position is that money is the unit of account and currency is simply a medium of exchange. Ellis argues that both are relevant to defining money.

Of more consequence are discussions whether the concept of money should be expanded beyond the medium of exchange notion. As noted, the empirical work of Lin Lin (1937) argues for time deposits as part of the money stock. In contrast, Lawrence Towle (1935) maintains that generally falling prices between 1922 and 1928 in the face of rising bank reserves and earning assets were due to the public "impounding" its corresponding liquid assets in time deposits rather than in checkable ones. Had demand deposits grown commensurate with the rise in the earning assets of banks, the price level would have increased.[8]

Another foray was initiated by Charles Dice and Philip Shaffner (1939). They used data from individual banks to argue that the deposit balance on banks' books understated the relevant stock of money. The reason had to do with the check clearing process; in particular "the process of simultaneously offsetting debit and credit entries within a bank account at the time of bank posting releases a certain portion of the checks outstanding at any given moment from any dependence on deposit balances" (1939, 514). This assertion was quickly challenged, to which there were replies, further comments, and further replies. And then the issue died, not so much because of the logic of the argument but because of the difficulties, perhaps impossibilities, of obtaining satisfactory data. Of further note, it appears that Dice and Shaffner's argument had more to do with determining velocity than with measuring the money stock.[9]

There were also strident, vociferous debates concerning the several 100 percent reserve plans, in particular those of the Chicago Plan, issued under the name of Frank H. Knight (1933) but ascribed to Henry Simons (1934). Lauchlin Currie (1934b, 195–226) and Irving Fisher (1936a) also propounded 100 percent money proposals. Though much of the subsequent commentary spawned by the proposals dealt with questions of procedures and political viability, the central point remains: the ability of 100 percent reserves to foster economic stability through control of the money stock. The intensity of the debate is captured in Ronnie Phillips's careful discussion of the spate of commentary emanating from these, as well as from the later Maurice Allais and Milton Friedman proposals (Phillips 1995, 164–66). For present purposes, the important point is that the thrust of the proposals was to give greater control of the money stock to the Federal Reserve, in the belief that it would then execute policy to further the recovery, and that its actions would not be frustrated by banks or the public.

Finally, indirect evidence about the role of money comes from comments on the behavior of velocity, which in the absence of a (frequently implicit) monetary framework would have no meaning. For instance, Sumner Slichter in his comments on the state of and prospects for the American economy deals with the effect of wage cuts on "reducing the velocity of circulation" (1936, 204).

In the literature following the Great Contraction, very little was written about the behavior of the money stock. What there was came from James Angell, Lauchlin Currie, and Martin Krost.

James W. Angell

James W[aterhouse]. Angell, a professor for forty years at Columbia University, was one of the most prominent monetary economists of the decade, a theoretician who also did first-rate empirical work.[10] One of the substantive issues of investigation in the 1930s was that of circular velocity—a "concept itself [that] is fundamental to an understanding of the monetary and exchange processes of society as a whole" (Angell 1936, 130)—and in this Angell was prominent, as was Arthur W. Marget of Minnesota. The notion of circular velocity is that of the (average) number of times per period that money makes the "consumer-producer-consumer circle" (1936, 131).[11] It was in the quest for empirical estimates of circular velocity that Angell found it necessary to estimate a money series.

The first indication of his money stock data came in an article devoted to articulating the case for circular velocity (Angell 1933). No monetary data were reported; the values of "circular velocity" for 1909–28 were presented in a footnote (1933, 74–75 n. 4). They fell steadily. In an article immediately following, Currie presented his initial money stock estimates; he also included a table on income velocity, the values of which were generally twice as high as Angell's circular velocity.

The money stock data Angell used appeared with the publication of his well-regarded book (1936, 175–83). Here, he compiled annual June Call Date (1890–1934) essentially *M1* (circulating money) and *M2* (total money) series. His interest was in the narrower monetary aggregate, circulating money. He obtained estimates of *monthly* circulating money based on interpolations between the June Call Dates. These were for 1919 through 1934. There was a 25 percent fall in circulating money during the Contraction, which accords well with the Friedman and Schwartz estimate.

As to the recovery, he documented twenty-one months of data. On an annual basis there was evidence for 1934, the first year of recovery. In that year, circulating money increased 14.8 percent and total money 10.6 percent. Monthly data on circulating money exhibited a 25.5 percent annual rate of increase from April 1933 through December 1934.[12]

Much of Angell's formal analysis ends with the evidence through 1932, so it is not surprising that nothing of consequence was said about developments in 1934, even though the money increases were quite large and the first since 1929. There are two places where evidence for 1934 is presented. One is a graph of circulating deposits superimposed on industrial production (1936, 49) and the other a graph of the ratio of circulating to total bank deposits (1936, 169). Deposits exhibit a distinct increase in each. Yet, he chooses not to comment.

One reason may be that the sharp increases and decreases in industrial production in the immediate post-Contraction months did not warrant a firm conclusion that recovery was under way. The evidence for such a short time may have been deemed too tenuous to warrant even a provisional conclusion. Whatever the reason, the fact is that he did not call attention to the robust turnaround in the stock of money following the March 1933 nadir.

Of more consequence, even if he had explicitly acknowledged the sharp 1934 money stock turnaround, it is doubtful that he would have identified it as a prospective cause of the recovery. For it was only a year earlier that he cautioned, "due . . . to open market operations . . . by the Reserve Banks, the member banks alone already hold surplus reserves of close to 2 billion dollars" (1935, 171). A year later, those reserves were a billion dollars more. Moreover, for Angell, they were clearly regarded as surplus rather than desired reserves. Banks would not increase lending, hence pushing up the money stock, until economic activity took place: "Any general expansion [in economic activity would] transform this surplus into an increase in deposits perhaps six to ten times as large" (1935, 171).

On the basis of his several studies on the relationship between various measures of economic activity and his money stock data, he concluded that changes in the quantity of money were *not* an independent cause of movements in national income. The principal finding was:

> There is little in the data we have examined to support the belief that deliberately enforced increases in the quantity of money will produce a sound and lasting economic recovery. [T]he largest part of the money supply moves with or after business activity, not before it. A "moderate" enforced expansion of the money supply therefore seems likely to have little effect on current business activity, and may be absorbed chiefly in the "idle balances" discussed [earlier]. A large and continued expansion, on the other hand, will undoubtedly raise prices, but also seems extremely likely to bring on such a contraction of the real volume of economic activity, ending in virtual collapse. (1936, 160)[13]

For Angell, the appropriate recovery policy would have been to prevent the excesses that led to the Depression, the familiar refrain that the only sure cure is prior prevention: "that enforcing stability in the quantity of deposits would yield desirable results" (1936, 162).

In a subsequent, largely theoretical tract linking the cycle to changes in investment deriving from changes in anticipations, Angell (1941) extended his annual data through 1939. The framework had expectations, which he called anticipations, determining investment with a lag, which through the multiplier was the major variable dictating income movements in the business cycle. Changes in expectations were determined by past changes in income.[14] The money stock entered because he was interested in estimating the value of the multiplier, and to do that

> it is really necessary to know only two things. The first is the *average* length of time which elapses between the receipt of a given block of income . . . and the reappearance of the sums thus spent in the incomes of this or other individuals at a later date [the inverse of circular (i.e., income) velocity]. . . . The second necessary datum is the average size of the current additions to effective hoards which are being made out of current income receipts. (1941, 131)

The notion of money hoards was thus central to his intent to measure the multiplier and so the monetary dimension in his framework stressed changes in money demand, specifically changes in the distribution of money holdings between active balances and hoards.

To that end, he reported a circulating money (*M1*-type) series (1941, 337–38). Adjacent to the money column was national income. In an aside, quite remarkable for the times, Angell used his money stock data and estimates of national income to run a regression for three periods: 1899–1929, 1929–33, and 1933–39. The results were presented graphically. The correlation coefficients were at least 0.96, and the coefficient on the money stock was positive, and in excess of unity. His purpose, however, was not to relate the movement of income to that of the money stock. Rather, he was interested in measuring the circular velocity of money. The post-1933 recovery was not of interest. He simply did not comment on the then six-year recovery clearly evident in the data, nor did he say anything about the sharp late-1930s depression, for which his national income data showed an 8 percent decline in 1938, with the figure for 1939 still 2 percent lower than for 1937.

The money stock data were used to compute "active money" and "hoards" series (1941, 337–40), akin to early modeling of the Keynesian system in which money demand was broken into "active" and "passive" balances. The stock of money was still passive here: "Moreover, except when technical conditions limit the expansion of the money supply, the bankers are usually more followers than leaders" (1941, 38). From that point of view, Angell's search for a framework to understand the macro-economy would not have looked to movements of the money stock as a prime consideration. For him, it was the behavior of investment as it changed due to changes in anticipations, themselves endogenous.[15]

Even though his data clearly showed a recovery, he did not attribute it to the substantial growth in the stock of money. Even his model in which national income was regressed on the money stock for the 1933–39 period was not of sufficient consequence for him to acknowledge the recovery as being driven by increases in the stock of money.

Another who might be expected to have seen the monetary element in the recovery was Lauchlin Currie, whom David Laidler considers the first to identify the monetary contraction as basic to the Great Contraction and more specifically the first to argue that aggressive open-market purchases would have stemmed the slide (1999, 236).

Lauchlin Currie

One of the most interesting, and curious, cases is Lauchlin Currie.[16] In his well-received book (1934b) containing annual June 30 estimates of an $M1$-type money series, he documented a 24.5 percent decline in the stock of money during 1929–33. Further, he assigned primary responsibility for that to the Federal Reserve (Laidler 1999, 233–36). In particular, it was the System's real-bills orientation, "The Commercial Loan Theory of Banking," which was responsible. He firmly rejected that theory with its endogenous money stock, arguing that "variations in the money supply cannot be found in the variations in the demand for loans" (1934b, 125).

In his second edition, he added data for 1934. This showed a 15 percent *increase* (Currie 1935, 31–33). Yet this was not cause for comment, perhaps because the second edition was essentially unchanged.[17] The principal change was in the money stock data, revised "on the basis of additional information" (1935, xi). The main adjustment was an approximately $280 million reduction in the second edition's figures because the earlier edition had included gold coins before 1934 and then excluded them in subsequent revisions of its currency series.[18]

Given the sharp monetary turnaround in 1934, Currie might be expected to at least have acknowledged a sharp increase in the money stock after several years of decline. Yet, no comment was forthcoming, either in the book or in subsequent published and unpublished material. As with Angell, perhaps the one-year increase was regarded as insufficient evidence to warrant a conclusion about recovery. But even as the recovery continued, he never returned to the framework linking the behavior of the stock of money to the economy.

Instead, Currie turned his attention and considerable talents to other matters, among which were memorandums providing "a coherent justification for unbalanced budgets financed through borrowing" (Sandilands 1990, 69) in his capacity as an assistant to Marriner Eccles of the Federal Reserve Board, with whom he "shared a common enthusiasm for bold, unorthodox fiscal and monetary programs" (1990, 61).

In that position, his memorandums dealt with the state of the recovery, evaluations of current monetary policy (absent any reference to the money stock), and suggestions for policy actions. In contrast to his earlier exhortations, the behavior of the quantity of money was never indicated. In fact, Currie shifted his focus away from any monetary aggregates as he became increasingly concerned with the growing volume of excess reserves in banks, which he regarded as redundant, surplus reserves awaiting a resurgence of loan demand.[19] He was not alone in viewing with alarm those growing reserves.

The point, however, is that Currie now no longer interpreted the economy's behavior in quantity theory terms, as he had done in his seminal, early work. In fact, he abandoned that approach. He therefore did not see the recovery as the product of an increasing stock of money. For him, the quantity of money was now an endogenous variable, subject to the needs of business as it sought to borrow, thereby affecting deposits, money, and excess reserves. One arena to which he looked was fiscal policy, and in that he began developing a quantitative series on "Federal Income-Increasing Expenditures" (Sandilands 1990, 68–74). In this, Martin Krost assisted him.

Martin Krost

Martin Krost was "a brilliant young student . . . whom [Currie] had brought with him from Harvard" (Sandilands 1990, 62). Before finishing his dissertation, Krost took a position at the Federal Reserve Board,

renamed the Board of Governors by the Banking Act of 1935. His repu-
tation today derives from his work with Currie on the Federal Income-
Increasing Expenditures series, which culminated in his 1938 memorandum "The Measurement of the Net Contribution of the Federal
Government to National Buying Power." An earlier version had been
"vetoed by the Reserve Board's director of research" for publication
(Sandilands 1990, 72).[20] It did however circulate widely among Washington economists and indeed was cited in the professional literature
on deficit financing. His professional life ended with his "premature
death" (Sandilands 1990, 77; Stein 1969, 166).

In a roundtable chaired by James Angell, at the 1939 meeting of the
American Economic Association, Krost presented a paper entitled "The
Significance of American Deposit Movements since 1929" (1940). Half
of his comments dealt with the 1929–33 period in which he noted a 25
percent decline in an $M2$ money stock measure. But, "by 1939, the total
was 7 billion dollars above the 1928 peak" (1940, 80). Yet this more than
20 percent increase was not of consequence in explaining the post-1933
rebound. The reason is that examination of the "distribution of deposits
by classes of holders casts light on the question of how far the deposit
expansion since 1933 has placed deposits in the hands of those who
have *not* been induced to increase their expenditures [e.g., foreigners
and financial institutions]" (1940, 80). He then offered the unsubstanti-
ated observation that the "unwillingness of private firms and individuals to borrow also undoubtedly reduced the effect of federal spending
on the national income" (1940, 81). Here he most likely was drawing on
his work relating to Federal Income-Increasing Expenditures. His summary conclusion was a diplomatic denial of the quantity theory, viz.,
the monetary changes "helped to loosen the connection between
changes in total deposits and the flow of expenditures" (81), this exemplifying Angell's opening remark about the "shift of emphasis in monetary theory from the relation between money and prices to that
between spending and income" (80).

Milton Friedman's 1940 Business
Cycle Course

In the 1940 fall semester, Milton Friedman taught a course on Business
Cycles at the University of Wisconsin. His handwritten lecture notes
(Friedman 1940) consist largely of one-line entries on a topic, some-

times supplemented by a few comments. The basic structure of the course relied on the National Bureau of Economic Research approach. The key text was Wesley C. Mitchell 1927, with particular emphasis on its 127-page second chapter, "Economic Organization and Business Cycles," a book with which Friedman was quite familiar from his taking Mitchell's course on cycles in 1933–34 (Hammond 1996, 48). About a third of the course revolved around the discussions and statistical material of the "salient characteristics of the business cycle" (Friedman 1940). It was here that he distributed to the class hand-drawn charts. Among the graphs were manufacturing employment, industrial production, business failures, and stock prices, monthly from 1923 into early 1940, a period that included the Great Contraction and the 1937–38 depression. In all of this, there were no data on any monetary or credit variables: nothing on currency or deposits, nothing on interest rates, nothing on banks loans or debits. Likewise, there was no evidence of any discussion of the behavior of such in his lectures. Rather, discussions relating to monetary considerations came from the lectures out of Mitchell. These followed the organizing apparatus of the Fisherian equation of exchange. There was a general discussion, per Mitchell, on the Quantity Theory of Business Cycles in which "payments ($MV + M'V'$) made *today*" (a quote Friedman took from Mitchell 1927, 131) are related to PT. Mitchell's analysis of the relation between money and output had a real-bills orientation: "Thus, most of the time, P and T are the 'active' factors; . . . they bring about changes in M', V and V'; to a less extent they affect even M" (1927, 137). Friedman offered no commentary disagreeing with this.

In a discussion of plans for dealing with cyclical fluctuations, "the 100 percent bank reserve plan" is discussed, after which changing the monetary standard is considered, perhaps to stimulate discussion because the two standards mentioned are the (Fisher) "compensated dollar" and the "potato standard" (Friedman 1940). "Central bank control" is also mentioned along with fiscal actions such as public works and "direct subsidies not necessarily associated to need" in what appears to be a laundry list of possible recovery policies (1940). That "Central bank control" might be or in fact was destabilizing was not indicated.

His lectures also relied on Alvin Hansen's then recently published *Full Recovery or Stagnation?* (1938). The notes were cryptic, amounting to single-line entries of the titles of that book's chapters, so it is impossible to know the thrust of Friedman's lectures. One of the chapters dealt with the 1937 Recession, another with Pump Priming, and still another with the Fear of Inflation. In Hansen's book, there was no role for the behavior of the money stock; it is not even mentioned. Friedman's lecture notes also had no suggestion, no intimation, that the money stock's movements were pivotal to the post-1933 recovery and to the 1937 slide. Hansen saw the depression in terms of a fall in investment, to which the rise in reserve requirements may have contributed a bit because they induced an increase in long-term interest rates. Friedman's lectures apparently provided no antidote to that view in that there was nothing in his notes that indicated the importance of the stock of money.[21]

From this investigation of economists who could be expected to be familiar with the post-1933 increases in the stock of money, it is clear that none linked the recovery to those increases, neither Angell nor Currie, each of whom assembled money stock data, nor Krost, who used Board of Governors data, nor Friedman, who would become the pioneering proponent of the importance of the behavior of the stock of money.

Of the financial data that were readily available and widely discussed, the growing volume of excess reserves was a major concern and cause for apprehension. Krost's position about the "unwillingness of private firms and individuals to borrow" (1940, 81) was indicative of the general anxiety that the recovery was quite likely retarded because of the failure to borrow and spend.

The Problem of Excess Reserves

The second theme recurring in the discussion of the recovery relates to the growing volume of excess reserves. In the calendar quarter following the bank holiday, they averaged $354 million, down somewhat from their level in February.[22] Thereafter, they climbed steadily, rising to about $3 billion in the first two months of 1936, after which they drifted lower through August. The effect of the three-stage doubling of reserve requirements beginning on August 16 showed in the declining levels of excess reserves. They reached a low of $750 million in August 1937, three months after the final round of reserve requirement increases. Thereafter, they began increasing so that by the following March, they had doubled. The April 1938 reduction in requirements spurred further increases in those reserves, reaching $6.9 billion in October 1940.

These rising levels of excess reserves did not go unnoticed.[23] Many commented on them, in marked contrast to earlier times when they were virtually absent from any policy discussions. Without doubt this was because excess reserves then constituted a negligible fraction of total reserves, which was reflected in the assumption of an essentially constant reserve-deposit ratio in the calculation of bank credit and money multipliers (Phillips 1920, 79). In addition, the general view was that the amount of excess reserves in the system was near zero, because banks sought to be "loaned up." Economists now took the large and growing excess reserves as evidence of the ineffectiveness of monetary actions in promoting recovery, because of their interpretation that the reason for such excess reserves was that they were due to a lack of borrowers. Benjamin Beckhart, for example, argued that the large excess reserves implied no role for the System, that "the federal reserve banks no longer occupy the central position in the money market" (1936, 639). Another example was W. L. Crum, who regularly wrote "Reviews of the Economy." Several times he acknowledged the growing volume of excess reserves, at one point arguing that the "principal effect" of the "enormous increase in goldstock . . . was an expansion of member-bank reserves [that] merely enlarged already redundant reserves" (1936, 48).

Because it was widely held that the excess reserves were redundant, the doubling of reserve requirements was not regarded as a significant factor bringing about the late-1930s depression, because excess reserves were regarded as ample, even after the increases in reserve requirements (Hardy 1939, 170–71).[24] In what was to become a contentious postwar issue, the coexistence of large excess reserves with low interest rates was taken as evidence of a liquidity trap, one George Morrison investigated (1966).

Currie was one of the most influential economists holding that view, as he denied that those increases were either an initiating or a contributory factor to the subsequent depression.[25] His concern about the growing volume of excess reserves culminated in his memorandum of May 18, 1936, "Some Monetary Aspects of the Excess Reserve Problem." He argued for increases in reserve requirements to absorb the reserves he regarded as redundant: "Excess reserves constitute a problem because they lead to an excessive expansion of deposits. . . . The problem, however, is whether any further expansion would be advisable" (Steindl 1995, 71). This position was an unambiguous real-bills position, as it presumed that banks were not holding the assets they wished to hold, the presumption being that a "shortage" of borrowers restrained banks from making more loans, a position at complete variance with his earlier stance. Currie then moved to his recommendation: "Further expansion involves a risk [and therefore] it appears prudent, until we can see the way more clearly, to discourage further expansion by raising reserve requirements in the near future" (1995, 71).

This concern was widely shared, and so the increases in reserve requirements were broadly applauded. In a public lecture at the University of Minnesota, for instance, Arthur Marget, one of the most prominent and prolific monetary theorists of the 1930s, bemoaned the fact that the change "was limited to a 100 per cent increase" (1937, 25).

Against the chorus of approval for the increases, Melchior Palyi argued that the policy was ill conceived. He based his concern on "the underestimation of the banks' liquidity preference" (1938, 305), a theme he did not develop. A more satisfactory understanding of Palyi's concern appeared the following year, when he asked, "But would the banks be inclined to go along without excess reserves?" leaving little doubt that the answer would be in the negative (1939, 684). He then drew on the increased reserve requirement experiment, "a good case in point. It indicates that the excess reserves are no mere 'luxury.' . . . [B]anks are likely to continue their policy of maintaining them at substantial levels. . . . They need 'excess' reserves for current transactions as well as for emergencies" (685).

Another who demurred from the majority view of the redundancy of excess reserves was Paul Samuelson.

> It is more and more being realized that reserves do *not* perform the function of till money. Rather they are felt to be necessary for maximization of income over time in a world where uncertainty dictates diversification of portfolios. This the Reserve authorities overlooked when they raised reserve requirements in 1936–37. They were unprepared for the resulting pressure on the market for governments, since they regarded excess reserves as surpluses. Actually, the banks tried to reestablish old excess reserve ratios. (1942, 594)

To the extent that reserve requirement increases were held to have contributed to the 1937–38 depression, the argument was that banks, particularly central reserve city banks, liquidated their government securities, thereby increasing interest rates and raising the cost of capital.[26] At the same time, however, monetary policy was held to be "extremely easy," largely because of the considerable volume of excess reserves (Roose 1954, 117). Although Alvin Hansen saw other developments as more important to the downturn, he similarly held that by increasing interest rates, the reserve requirement increases might have been a factor. Thus, "more vigorous action should have been taken to sustain the government bond market" (1938, 271–72).[27]

In all of this, there was general ignorance of actual movements of the quantity of money. No one linked its behavior to the reserve requirement increases, and therefore no one tied the depression to changes in the money stock. Had this been done, $M1FRB$ would have shown slower increases in the four months following the initial (August 15, 1936) increase than in the four months prior to it. Subsequently, with the exception of a single month, $M1FRB$ declined each of the following sixteen months; reaching a low in April 1938 of 6 percent below the December 1936 peak. The quantity of money began to grow rapidly thereafter, abetted by the April 1938 reduction in reserve requirements, attaining in September its previous peak. The depression's revival began in late spring and continued until the economy's output was again back to its trend in mid-1942.

That there was general ignorance of the behavior of the quantity of money and that its movements were not used to try to understand the 1937–38 depression stands in marked contrast to analyses of the 1929–33 Depression (Steindl 1995).[28]

Gold

A third important theme in the literature related to gold, in particular the influence of large inflows on bank reserves. Most likely, the formal departure from the gold standard in 1934 was a prime factor in the bevy of articles on gold in the professional journals.[29] Not surprisingly, many dimensions were considered, including the question of whether gold should have been devalued (Paris 1938),[30] the maldistribution of the world's gold stock (Bowen 1936), historical analyses (Lester 1937), the regular reports on the economy by Crum and his colleagues, and the relation between growth of the gold stock and the price level in an expanding economy (Allen G. B. Fisher 1935).

The monetary base rose initially because of devaluation and then continued increasing because of gold imports. The effect of those imports was discussed in detail in the professional literature and in the Federal Reserve Board's 1938 *Annual Report*. In it, gold flows were linked to increases in member bank reserves and especially to excess reserves (Board of Governors 1938, 19–21). Elsewhere, Fritz Lehmann stressed that "the huge excess reserves . . . have been created in the Federal Reserve system by the influx of gold" (1939, 125), adding that "the American economy would probably have suffered if gold had been refused entry" (1939, 150). C. O. Hardy, though he recognized the role of the gold imports on excess reserves, denied that they had any noticeable economic effect because "the public is carrying much larger amounts of currency and bank deposits idle than it did a few years ago" (1941, 25). He did not present any data on such money holdings. Instead of interpreting the gold inflows as responsible for increases in the stock of money, he dealt with the demand for money. Evidently, what he had in mind was that the increased demand for money was of such magnitude as to move in step with the growing stock of it so that there was no excess supply of money and thus no economic responses.

With the exception of the increase in reserve requirements, the System was essentially passive through much of the recovery. The effect of the gold inflows, as well as the administration's gold policy, was to shift monetary policy to the Treasury as it paid for gold by drawing on its account at the Federal Reserve, thereby increasing the monetary base, and then replenishing its account by depositing at the Federal Reserve the gold certificates it printed.[31] This shift was not lost on the profession. Shortly after the formal devaluation of the dollar, Angell, for instance, wrote: "The central bank of the United States is no longer the Federal Reserve. . . . The central bank is the Treasury Department" (1934, 502). To underscore the central banking actions of the Treasury, Edward Simmons (1940), after arguing that the Federal Reserve's traditional policy instruments were unsuited to the task, maintained that the Treasury effectively could control bank reserve positions more satisfactorily by influencing the size of excess reserves through alterations in its deposit account at the Federal Reserve. Nor was the shift lost on the Federal Reserve Board: "Under existing conditions the Treasury's powers to influence member bank reserves outweigh those possessed by the Federal Reserve System" (Board of Governors, *Annual Report* 1938, 5).[32]

Concluding Observations

The dramatic economic recovery from the 1933 abyss seems best understood as largely a monetary phenomenon, one in which the processes of the quantity theory of money occupy a central place. This finding has been a robust result of postwar research.

Prior to the bottom of the Contraction, the quantity theory was an important macroeconomic model, the prevailing macroeconomic paradigm. Yet, for all the soul-searching, for all the attempts at understanding the developing recovery, no one in the literature surveyed here appears to have used it as a framework for understanding either the unfolding rates of recovery or the sharp depression occurring midway through it.

It is true that no official $M1$ or $M2$ money series existed. But neither had there been any official money stock data in the 1929–33 Contraction. That, however, did not serve as a barrier to using the quantity theory framework to analyze it, as was done for instance by Currie, Willford King, and Carl Snyder (Laidler 1999, 233–36; Steindl 1995, 61–69, 135–44, 148–52).

Monthly stock of money series could readily be constructed from the *Federal Reserve Bulletin*, the *M1FRB* and *M2FRB* series used here. If those constructed series were then related to monthly industrial production data, the monetary impulse driving the recovery would have been seen. In other words, if use had been made of the quantity theory framework, the economic recovery from the early 1933 trough would have been understandable and would certainly have given more reason for optimism.

Of course, that was not done. Instead, the quantity theory as a vehicle for understanding unfolding developments dropped from sight. Why that happened is now a matter of conjecture. Surely, however, the widely held impression that monetary ease had failed to stem the Contraction carried over to the recovery. This was especially the case with excess reserves, which themselves were regarded as evidence of the impotence of monetary actions.

One of the early episodes responsible for the self-doubt about monetary actions was the aggressively expansive policy in mid-1932, one that Rogers (1932, 247–49) and Henry Villard (1937) addressed in detail. In the second quarter of that year, the system engaged in an $888 million open-market purchase, up markedly from the first quarter's $32 million. The principal effect, however, was an increase in excess reserves as they almost quintupled from the first quarter's average $46 million. The subsequent continued increases in excess reserves were taken as a sign that banks were not lending, principally because of low loan demand. This implied that the money stock accordingly was not increasing (Crum 1936; Hardy 1939). As for interest rates, it increasingly came to be held that low rates, and these were always discussed as nominal rates, would not stimulate capital expenditures (Hubbard 1940). In other words, the failure of economists to use the quantity theory to understand the recovery may well have been due to their increasing disillusionment with it during the Contraction.

In a widely cited testimony to the quantity theory, Friedman (1956, 3–4) maintained that with the exception of the "oral tradition" at Chicago, a tradition that was not concerned with empirical considerations, the theory fell into disrepute in the 1930s and languished until at least the mid-1950s. One facet of that tradition held monetization of budget deficits as one method of increasing the money stock (Steindl 1995, 84–95; Tavlas 1997; Laidler 1999). In the 1930s literature examined here, there is, however, no evidence that any of the Chicagoans interpreted the recovery in monetary terms. In fact, Friedman himself appeared agnostic as to the causes of the Contraction, assigning no particular significance to the behavior of the Federal Reserve.

One other economist who needs to be considered is Irving Fisher. He commented frequently on ongoing economic events, many times in connection with one of his many crusades. The Great Contraction and the subsequent recovery were too important for him not to say anything, and it is to his analysis that the next chapter turns.

CHAPTER 5

◄o►

The Puzzling Case of Irving Fisher

The present concern is with Irving Fisher, the quintessential quantity theorist. If anyone would have been familiar with a monetary aggregate or would have used it to understand the recovery, it would have been him. Central to his framework of aggregative analysis, indeed synonymous with him, is the equation of exchange. Though it is not the quantity theory, a point he often made, it in fact is the core-organizing ingredient for his subsequent quantity-theoretic analyses. It has been argued that the quantity theory was central to Fisher's work, that "his fundamental premise and basis for all other analysis and policy prescription was this: money matters and matters most, [that he indeed was] the first of the modern 'monetarists'" (Allen 1977, 563).

Preliminaries

During Fisher's time, the Wholesale Price Index served as the metric for price movements. Since there were no official money stock series,[1] this raises the general question of the extent to which he had measures of its magnitude and movements and used those to understand the evolution of the economy. Of particular interest is the degree to which he recognized the behavior of the money stock during the 1930s, both during the 1929–33 Contraction and the subsequent recovery, because it was that era that was the theory's trial by fire, its time in the desert.

In developing the equation of exchange, Fisher had to consider the perennial question, What is money? To that end, currency was money, hence M, and V was its velocity.[2] "Bank deposits transferable by check," though a form of "circulating media" (Fisher 1911, 10–11), were not money; they were "deposit currency," denoted as M' for which the relevant velocity was V'. Together with the price level P and the volume of transactions T, this gave the equation of exchange

$$MV + M'V' = PT$$

In subsequent work, M and M' were never combined into a single money aggregate. They were always considered separately as money and deposit currency, with the latter the most frequently used monetary measure, largely because of the relative ease of obtaining data, particularly after the formation of the Federal Reserve System. He further assumed that the currency-deposit ratio, M/M', was constant (1911, 50). This assumption allowed him to sidestep questions of money stock mechanisms, ones in which he appears never to have been interested (Laidler 1991, 65). Under the gold standard, the existing monetary regime when he developed his framework, the "exogenous" M generates reserves that via a deposit multiplier gave M'. Under a managed money standard, the monetary authorities determined the reserve base that via the deposit multiplier then gave M'. Given the fixed currency-deposit ratio, M/M', the quantity of Fisherian money M was then determined.

He then set about testing the framework, both in the book and in an annual series of articles from 1911 to 1918 that appeared as "Equation of Exchange for 19xx" in the *American Economic Review*.[3] In this, he had to obtain monetary data. He was scrupulously careful in developing data that best corresponded to the theoretical basis of his money and deposit currency variables. He was thus quite knowledgeable about the detail and ingredients of the respective series. After the founding of the Federal Reserve, he tended to rely principally on the net demand deposit series, especially after 1929.

For the better part of two decades, from 1911 to the onslaught of the Great Contraction, he was pretty much concerned with things other than the continued empirical reaffirmation of the equation of exchange, which though not the quantity theory was indeed a most satisfactory framework for understanding its workings. And it was the quantity theory that formed the basis for his extended and extensive inquiries into price movements during the 1920s. But those investigations did not rely on documentation of movements in his measures of money. The price movements on which he concentrated were simply assumed to be the result of like movements in the quantity of money. An early sign of this disinclination to document changes in money and deposit data appeared in a 1914 tract to educate the public, *Why the Dollar Is*

Shrinking?, the analysis in it deriving largely from the quantity theory orientation of *The Purchasing Power of Money*.[4]

The concern about the shrinking dollar was later generalized to a crusade that would occupy Fisher for much of the rest of his days, namely, the issue reflected in his title *Stabilizing the Dollar* (1920). This time he proposed the compensated dollar as an antidote to the gold standard. The dominant concern in the prelude to his proposal dealt with documenting the behavior of price levels in various countries. There was little consideration of the actual behavior of any monetary measure. This, no doubt, was due to his strongly held belief that "throughout all history this [relation between money and prices] has been so. For this general broad fact the evidence is sufficient even where we lack the index numbers by which to make accurate measurements" (1920, 29).

The Purchasing Power of Money was devoted to comparative statics. A single short chapter explored the cycle, or as he preferred to term it, "Transition Periods" (1911, 55–73). That chapter apparently justified his later assertion that "the vast field of 'business cycles' is one on which I had scarcely entered before, and I had never attempted to analyze it as a whole" (1932, vii). It was in that chapter that the interplay of real and nominal interest rates drove movements in T.

Early in the 1920s, he reported preliminary results of an empirical attempt to understand the cycle in terms of the rate of change of the price level, one of "the two components of the real rate of interest" (1923, 1024). The model was an eight-month linear distributed lag of the rate of change of prices in relation to an index of the physical volume of trade. They were "correlated [at] 79 per cent" (1923, 1027). The behavior of the price level was implicitly assumed to be the result of proportionate movements of the quantity of money. No monetary data were explicitly considered.

The project's final report, published two years later, covered August 1915 through March 1923. He reported that a correlation coefficient of "94.1 per cent . . . is reached. Seldom before has a correlation so high been found in the efforts to explain 'the business cycle'" (1925, 179). Again, there was neither reference to the actual behavior of the money stock nor to any of its components in explaining the rates of price change. The quantity theory was implicitly employed. There was little doubt that he firmly believed the business cycle was largely a monetary phenomenon and that monetary stabilization, perhaps through monetary reform, was the key to mitigating its more pronounced movements: "Probably much of the remaining fluctuation of T, not explained by the factors here studied, is due to non-cyclical factors also. There can be little left in the fluctuations of T which can be said to be truly cyclical in character" (1925, 201).

In an extension of that paper, on which "during the last three years . . . I have had at least one computer in my office almost constantly at work" (1926, 786), he applied his distributed lag framework to deal with employment—the "I Discovered the Phillips Curve" inquiry. The correlation between the distributed lag of rates of price change and employment was "90 percent" (1926, 791).[5] Here again, there was no explicit reliance on monetary data. Rather, there was an implicit quantity theory strand from which the independent, that is, "exogenous," rates of price change explained movements in the index of employment, leading to the conclusion that "the 'dance of the dollar' [was] the key . . . to the major fluctuations in employment. [Thus] we have in our power, as a means of substantially preventing unemployment, the stabilisation of the purchasing power of the dollar, pound, . . . and any other monetary units" (1926, 792).

By the latter half of the decade, the validity of the quantity theory was so established in his mind that he began referring to inflation and deflation not as price level movements but as changes in the stock of money, that is, net demand deposits (Allen 1993, 200), as most clearly seen in his 1928 tract for the general public, *The Money Illusion*.

One of the interesting interpretations that came out of his empirical forays was that the quantity theory was not just a theory of prices. Rather, it was also a theory of output and employment. For him, price stability was a monetary phenomenon, and from it came output and employment stability.

Throughout the 1920s, indeed throughout his lifetime, Fisher wrote and lectured about money in his efforts to educate the public and mobilize popular opinion to the cause of monetary reform and stabilization (Allen 1993, 129). In these efforts, he did not make specific reference to the actual behavior of his money measures. The usual approach was to mention broad movements in money. It was here that he referred to increases and decreases in money as inflation and deflation, with the obvious implication of like price movements, a clear indication of his quantity theory outlook.

One last piece of evidence that Fisher tended not to examine monetary data in detail relates to his forecasting service, a description of which is given in Dominguez, Fair, and Shapiro 1988, 598, 607 n. 17. Two series were used: his "Ideal" index of commodity prices and an index of stock prices. On the basis of the respective behavior of these, pronouncements on the future course of economic activity were issued. Noteworthy was the absence of a monetary series.[6]

Two decades prior to the Great Contraction, Fisher showed in *The Purchasing Power of Money* that he was not only aware of the behavior of his monetary aggregates but that he was extremely familiar with difficulties in their construction. Having established via the equation of exchange the legitimacy of the quantity theory, he thereafter demurred from linking empirically the behavior of prices and employment to movements in money. This was to change with the onslaught of the Great Contraction when these notions were put to the test.

Debt-Deflation Driven Depression

Though initially slow to realize the extent and severity of the Contraction, Fisher turned his attention to the role of debt-deflation, a theme "first stated in my lectures at Yale in 1931" (1933a, 350). Its critical importance was highlighted the following year in *Booms and Depressions* (1932), "a brilliant solution of this puzzle [of] a deep and lasting depression" (Dimand 1994, 93). The debt-deflation theory was truly a radical departure from his earlier work in which he saw the business cycle as due to variations in the rate of change of prices, "one of the two components of the real rate of interest" (1923, 1024).

This latest exercise was indeed a strange book. Its audience appeared to be professional economists, as it hypothesized a business cycle model heavily tilted to explaining the Contraction phase of the cycle. Much of it read, however, like a popular tract intended to educate the public.[7] Thus, it was not surprising that it received poor reviews in the professional journals (Allen 1993, 241–42).

The subtitle, "Some First Principles," is instructive because it suggests Fisher would return to basics, namely, to an examination of the behavior of a monetary variable in an attempt to explain the ongoing deflation, and that is what he did, although not in the way one would have thought. The theory's theme is that deflation increases the real value of debt, thereby causing more bankruptcies, which in turn reduces aggregate demand and, thus, plunges the economy further into depression.

The central feature causing depression was overindebtedness. Though it was not the sole explanation, it "seems to me highly probable" that it and "deflation were strong and indeed the dominating factors" (1932, 85). He was primarily concerned with its consequences, not with its causes. He did however single out margin accounts for stock, "Investing in Equities on Borrowed Money" (1932, 72–73), the strategy largely responsible for wrecking his family finances (Allen 1993, 179–81, 185).[8]

The attempt to reduce overindebtedness resulted in a *"contraction of deposit currency*, as bank loans are paid off, and to a slowing down of velocity of circulation [thereby causing] *a fall in the level of prices"* (1933a, 342)—the joint interaction being a decline in the efficiency of money, by which he meant that the stock of money and its velocity fell. A further round of attempts to repay brought further declines in prices.

The formal debt-deflation framework had nine factors in the sequence, with debt liquidation as the first in the logical order (1932, 8–38; Dimand 1994, 97). Three points must be emphasized. First, and least important for present purposes, the interplay between real and nominal interest rates, which was central to his "Transition Periods" cyclical mechanism in *The Purchasing Power of Money,* was no longer of prime consequence, appearing at the end of the sequence, as changes in the earlier eight factors caused *"complicated disturbances in the rates of interest"* (1933a, 342), with nominal rates falling and real rates increasing.

Of more consequence was his altered view of the money mechanism. In previous writings, he held to the view that the money stock, both currency and deposit currency, were essentially determined by the central bank.[9] As such, the quantity of money was independent of the demand for loans.[10] With *Booms and Depressions,* this changed. Now the attempt at debt liquidation, the first step in the debt-deflation sequence, led to a fall in the level of deposits as loans were repaid. But his framework did not have banks responding to the consequent increase in their (excess) reserve positions by acquiring other assets; they now were passive agents whose asset acquisition activities were dictated by the demand for loans.[11] That is, in a "stampede of liquidation" arising from "a general state of *over*-indebtedness," the "new borrowings will by no means suffice to restore the balance, and there must follow a net shrinkage of deposits" (1932, 15). He did not argue that banks themselves were the ones who determined the composition of their assets, that they could have acquired government securities. Rather, he had them passive when it came to their earning asset portfolio, the size of which was to be dictated by the borrowing requirements of their customers.

He evidently accepted the passivity hypothesis because he never looked at Federal Reserve data to see if the fall in deposit currency could be understood from the supply side. Had he done so, he would have seen that bank reserves fell 21 percent while Federal Reserve credit increased only 12 percent between the fourth quarter of 1929 and the first quarter of 1932, the last one for which data were available to be included in the book. Ironically, his list of proposed remedies featured open-market purchases as a recovery vehicle (1932, 128–31, 213); yet System actions as summed up in Federal Reserve credit were evidently not something worth addressing as a potential cause of the slide.

Robert Dimand has argued that Fisher's analysis essentially predicted the actual U.S. experience insofar as there was a contraction of deposits even though the monetary base did not decline (1994, 98).[12] Fisher never made such a prediction. In fact, questions of the money mechanism simply were not of interest to him. That his framework could later be read to anticipate actual events was serendipitous, and certainly not by design.

The final point about *Booms and Depressions* is that it was here that Fisher returned to monetary data in order to document that the sharp decline in economic activity was in fact associated with the behavior of the monetary aggregates, especially net demand deposits. The inquiry took the form of a narrative suggesting likely economic responses to the events following the 1929 stock market crash.

The data were presented in an appendix (1932, 178–81) and depicted on a semilogarithmic graph showing the behavior of net demand deposits—his M' deposit currency—along with time deposits, which were *not* money for him (1932, 93–95). The former fell 16 percent from the end of June 1929 to the end of 1931. Time deposits were essentially unchanged for the first two years from June 1929, having increased slightly during the first year for reasons that were "little short of hoarding" (1932, 93). During the final six months covered by his data, they fell 18 percent.

His preferred method was not, however, calculating rates of monetary change. He, instead, coupled the money change with its respective estimated velocity movement; hence he looked at $M'V'$ rather than M'. These were his "efficiency of money" notions. From October 1929 to February 1932 "deposit currency of the member banks . . . fell 21 per cent . . . and the velocity in the same period fell 61 per cent, so that the efficiency of deposit money [was] only 31 per cent of what it had been in 1929" (1932, 96), that is, deposit currency's efficiency was $(1 - .21)(1 - .61) = .31$.

It was these declines in the efficiency of deposit currency, and not the behavior of deposits alone, that impressed Fisher as the by-product of the desire to reduce indebtedness. Ironically, the move to liquidation, the desire to reduce indebtedness, "left unpaid balances *more* burdensome . . . than the whole debt burden had been in 1929. . . . In a word, despite all liquidations, the 234¼ billions of 1929 became over 302 billions in 1932, if measured in 1929 dollars" (1932, 107–8).

Fisher's invention of the efficiency of money is an ingenious technique by which to gauge an excess demand for money. In the quantity theory, an excess demand results in falling prices, and those declines are taken as prima facie evidence of an excess demand, the method used at Chicago, particularly by Simons (Steindl 1995, 79–83). That approach is tautological. Fisher's efficiency of money method combines into a single number the joint effect of money stock and money demand movements; in other words, it captures the notion of an excess demand for money! Decreases in the stock of and increases in the demand for money, as captured by falling velocity, define excess demand, and Fisher's efficiency of money does just that.

A quantity theory explanation of the decline in prices would therefore take the falling efficiency of money as evidence of an excess demand for money. In order to combat that, the appropriate policy would be to increase the money stock, to the point where the measured efficiency would register neither an increase nor a decrease.

This was not Fisher's approach. He now had the decline in velocity implying a "liquidity trap" with its associated asymmetry in the effectiveness of monetary policy.

> In the case of a rising price level, the remedy [is] is taking the surplus M out of the overflooded circulation; for people cannot spend what they do not have. . . . On the other hand, people *can* hoard what they *do* have; so that in the case of a depression and a

falling price level, a mere new supply of money, to replace what has been liquidated or hoarded, might fail to raise the price level by failing to get into circulation. . . . For a prompt boost of the price level, therefore, a mere increase in M might prove insufficient, unless supplemented by some influence exercised directly on the moods of people to accelerate V—that is, to convert the public from hoarding. (Fisher 1932, 140)

In other words, he now held that no matter how much the stock of money is increased, the additional balances are not spent—the funds fail "to get into circulation." Individuals simply hoard additions to their money holdings. This surely is the notion of a liquidity trap, a view that came later to be associated with Keynes and his suggestion concerning expectations about the course of interest rates and their effect on the demand for money (Laidler 1999, 263–65, 281–87).

This was not an intractable impasse. He was not at a loss to suggest a velocity-enhancing policy, or as he phrased it, a "velocity control" measure (1932, 140), one in keeping with his fondness for radical, innovative policies. He became increasingly enamored with an antihoarding plan inspired by Silvio Gesell's *Schwundgeld:* the stamp scrip (stamped dollar) plan, which taxed hoarding of money (1932, 142). Although "this plan did not come to my attention until after this book had been finished" (1932, 140), he felt strongly enough to add four pages about it in an appendix (1932, 226–30). He also took time to write a short book exhorting its merits, *Stamp Scrip* (1933c).[13] The prospect of a liquidity trap remained a concern. His 100 percent reserve plan made provision for "velocity control," and this vehicle again was to be stamp scrip (1936a, 91 n. 3).

The chapter in which the liquidity trap analysis was presented is entitled "Remedies." One of the ironies is that Fisher advocated Federal Reserve actions—specifically "regulation through the rediscount rate [and] open market operations" (1932, 126–29). The setup for the discussion is an equation of exchange lead-in to the quantity theory as a vehicle to raise the price level, his overriding concern being reflation of prices to the 1926 level as the means to reduce indebtedness (1932, 122–24). The discussion of rediscount rate and open market operations is conventional, as would be expected of a book addressed to the general public. His summary assessment of Federal Reserve actions is that the "Reserve Banks can powerfully regulate the volume of the country's deposit currency—for good or ill" (1932, 130).

With this lead-in to the importance of bank reserves, it would seem a natural step to examine Federal Reserve data to see what actually had been happening. This he did not do. Had he, he would have seen a 21 percent reduction in member bank reserves through the first quarter of 1932, the last one available before the book went to press. Even if reserves had increased—as they did in the subsequent nine months of the year (to a level 2.5 percent less than three years earlier)—there was the issue of the growing volume of excess reserves. Would he have fallen in line with those who took those excess reserves as indicative of a "shortage of borrowers," or would he have interpreted them as desired by banks for precautionary liquidity purposes? He never addressed the excess reserves issue during the Contraction proper.[14]

The point, however, is that his strongly argued advocacy of the potency of monetary policy actions was not followed by an examination of actual Federal Reserve policies as they affected commercial bank reserves. True, he faulted the System in general terms, specifically for its failure to "exercise [its power] without due reference to the price level" (1932, 151), but he did not systematically investigate actual policy actions. If he believed that monetary expansion induced by the Federal Reserve was the appropriate course, why did he then advance the falling velocity hypothesis, coupling with it his stamp scrip solution? That avenue of escape, it should be emphasized, was not simply one on a shopping list of prospective alternatives. It was a desideratum, one about which he felt sufficiently strongly that in the midst of the exigencies of the depressed environment he took time to devote a book to it. If the issue was simply one of an excess demand for money, then why not advocate sufficiently aggressive monetary expansion? That would have been all that was required. Instead, he imposed the additional condition of a reasonably unbounded increase in the demand for money in which money stock increases would not be sufficient.

Fisher's analysis of the Great Contraction parted company from the quantity theory approach with which he was so intimately linked. One of the principal points of departure was his money stock mechanism. Formerly, currency and deposits were treated as essentially exogenous. Hence an excess demand for money, such as in the almost 50 percent price decline in the 1920–21 deflation, could be dealt with by monetary expansion. With the Contraction, he now modeled currency as exogenously determined by the Federal Reserve. Accordingly, the increase in Money in Circulation during 1930–31 was dismissed as "misleading" because the "increased quantity of Federal Reserve notes" "could, so far as is revealed by the figures for this so-called 'circulation' be in stockings or in other hoarding places and not circulating at all" (1932, 96). He reiterated the same point the following year, using virtually identical phrasing (1933b, 57 n. 8). That the Federal Reserve was accommodating an increase in the public's demand for currency, attendant on the wave of bank failures, was not something he acknowledged. Rather he consistently viewed the outstanding stock of currency as being determined by the monetary authorities (1932, 132; 1936a, 58).

Of more consequence, deposits and the composition of their earning assets were now taken to be outside the control of banks; they were perceived to adhere to a real-bills doctrine position; thus the fall in deposits was due to borrowers liquidating their debts. Banks could not now acquire other assets as replacements for those their customers extinguished. In addition, Federal Reserve actions could not be counted on to eliminate an excess demand for money, this because of liquidity trap considerations.

With the Contraction, Fisher demonstrated again his empirical monetary bent; he considered the actual behavior of his monetary measures. In these efforts, he wandered from the accepted notion of the quantity theory that changes in the independently determined quantity of money gave rise to changes in the price level, and in the short run to changes in real activity. For him, money was now endogenously determined, with the slide in prices and output resulting from attempts to reduce an exogenously given state of general overindebtedness. This represented a sharp break from his long-held views.

Fisher's writings during the Great Contraction stand out as a sharp break from the thread of his earlier studies. The issue is whether he returned to it in assessing the recovery.

The Role of Money in the Recovery

With the coming of the Roosevelt administration, Fisher essentially called a halt to his professional, scientific activity and moved to being a self-appointed activist-campaigner for policies he deemed essential to recovery. Among them was his crusade to raise the price level to its 1926 level (1933b, esp. 67 n. 3). This was part and parcel of his campaign for reflation.[15] There was to be no base drift; the price level was not to be stabilized at its low Contraction level. For over a decade he also investigated and campaigned enthusiastically for restructuring monetary arrangements to achieve 100 percent reserves (1936a). Robert Allen, for instance, has him writing to President Truman in 1947, "urging adoption of his 100 percent monetary reform" (1993, 293), a few weeks before he died at the end of April.

Shortly after the Contraction's bottom, he published his famous paper on debt-deflation (1933a, 356), which was largely a summary of *Booms and Depressions*. That same year, he also published a popular book, *After Reflation, What?* (1933b), a plea for and paean to price-level stabilization, or as he preferred to call it, stable money. In each, he included a graph portraying the September 1932 through August 1933 movements of net demand deposits and Money in Circulation, the latter inverted because "the more of it when hoarded, the worse. Hence to indicate improvement, the curve of it is here inverted" (1932, 57 n. 8).[16]

The graph vividly shows sharp declines to March 1933 in the currency and deposit series and a clear rebound thereafter. Among the other variables graphed are commodity prices and industrial production. The sharp declines in each through March and the strong rebounds thereafter stand out. Yet, there is only the cryptic remark "that immediate reversal of deflation is easily achieved by the use . . . of appropriate instrumentalities"—no other discussion, interpretation, or even comment on these movements (1933a, 346).

Although inverting the money-in-circulation series can be interpreted as a clever way of underscoring the decline and subsequent increase in the stock of money, such an interpretation suffers because Fisher never aggregated currency and deposit components. More likely, his purpose for inverting money-in-circulation was to underscore that the Federal Reserve's "exogenous" increase in currency was being thwarted by hoarding, hence the decline in the (inverted) money-in-circulation series. With his orientation that the System determined Money-in-Circulation, it is unlikely that he would have seen hoarding by the public as the reason for the rise in the currency, with the Federal Reserve simply accommodating the increase in currency demand. Because he regarded his currency variable M as exogenous, a liquidity trap interpretation of the public's demand was a straightforward conclusion.

In his generally available writings, there is (with one exception) no evidence that Fisher commented explicitly on the link between the growth of a monetary aggregate and the ongoing recovery, or on the deep 1937 depression. As Robert Dimand (2000) recently unearthed, Fisher continued his research on monetary considerations relating to the 1930s, with the results appearing in several obscure places. The focus of most of that was on velocity, specifically with demonstrating its approximate constancy.

The first of his velocity investigations was reported to a summer conference of the Cowles Commission (Fisher 1940). Here he set the tone for his future inquiries.

> The question of whether the velocity of circulation of money is a constant or a variable is of great importance.
>
> [I]f velocity is substantially constant, the so-called quantity theory of money has very definite validity. . . . [If it] is simply a cushion for changes of quantity, any attempt to control the price level or volume of trade by controlling money would be futile. (1940, 55–56)

He then summarized earlier work, including his own, on velocity estimates as a prelude to the leitmotif that would dominate his subsequent work. This was that the differences between pre- and post-1929 estimates of velocity were due principally to "the differences in the methods of collecting statistics" (1940, 57). An important factor was the pre-Contraction "misclassification" of demand deposits as time deposits due to banks seeking the benefit of the lower reserve requirement against the latter. Afterward, "banks were mending their ways on this subject" (1940, 58).

Nothing further was said on velocity until his Econometric Society report six years later (1946). He lamented that "the whole subject of the equation of exchange including the quantity theory of money . . . has been more or less shelved during recent years, because people have found . . . that velocity is tremendously variable," to which he would "show that the opposite is probably true: that the velocity of money varies little" (1946, 179). The key to his demonstration of the approximate constancy of velocity was the misclassification of demand deposits; banks were able "to palm off demand deposits as time deposits" (1947, 176). His report at the following year's meeting of the

Econometric Society, published the same month he died at age eighty, continued in much the same vein.

In none of those velocity studies was the recovery addressed. Almost by definition, nonetheless, if Fisher was engrossed in studies of velocity, he had to be aware of the aggregate behavior of his monetary variables. He however did not comment directly on their behavior and by extension on their relation to the ongoing recovery, much less on the depression two years prior to his velocity retrospective (1940).

His linking of the recovery to the growth of deposits occurs in two places. The first is in summary remarks in the preface to the second edition of *100% Money*, published just nine months after the first edition.[17] Of more consequence are his remarks at the Colorado Springs conference of the Cowles Commission (Fisher 1936b).

By way of setting the stage for his 100 percent reserves proposal, he asserts that "it is this very growth [of checkbook money] which has been leading us out of the depression" (1936a, vii). This growth is a cause for concern, because "if [it] is not controlled, it may lead us beyond recovery into an unwholesome boom" because of the "existence of huge excess reserves [which can be reduced by] raising the reserve ratios, as permitted under the new [Banking Act of 1935] law" (1936a, vii). Because the law's permissible doubling of requirements evidently would not reduce excess reserves sufficiently, it was of the essence to advance the 100 percent reserves proposal. "If the reserves could be raised to the full 100% there would be *no* excess" (1936a, vii).

This intimation that the recovery was due to an expanding stock of money, proxied by his preferred monetary aggregate, net demand deposits, was followed shortly by his July lecture to the Cowles Commission meeting. After a perfunctory admission that the cause of the Contraction was a complex matter—"many contributory causes"—he asserted that "one cause towers above all others, the collapse of our deposit currency. The depression was a money famine—a famine, not of pocket-book money but of check-book money, the money, or so-called money, recorded on the stubs of our check-books, our deposits subject to check" (1936b, 104; Dimand 2000, 332). He pointed to a 35 percent decline in net demand deposits between 1929 and 1933—"That is, our chief circulating medium had shrunk by $8 billion dollars" to $15 billion (1936b, 104).

He however did not assign responsibility for the decline to any particular set of circumstances, nor did he suggest any exogenous force reducing deposits. More likely, the decline can best be understood in terms of his debt-deflation hypothesis and its affiliated real-bills focus, given that he neither assigned any role to the Federal Reserve nor did he amend his earlier real-bills oriented analysis. It followed directly from his "over-indebtedness causing debt-deflation" thesis. It was the flight from overindebtedness that led to the downward spiraling of deposits due to banks' passivity in acquiring other assets. The contraction of deposits was not laid at the feet of the monetary authorities. Hand in hand with his debt-deflation view was the real-bills deposit mechanism he adopted in which attempts to reduce debts lead to a fall in deposits. The liquidity trap is still prominent. How else does one interpret the fact that he still maintained that virtually the entire "15 billions" stock of 1933 "check book money [was] still largely left idle" (104–5). Why the hoarding?

He then moved to discuss the rebound in deposits from their Contraction low. After observing that the "right remedy was to increase the money supply," he pointedly observed that the increase was "not [brought about] in the usual way by business men borrowing of banks [*sic*] but by the Government selling its bonds to the banks" (1936b, 105).[18] Indeed, from the beginning of the recovery through May 1936, the most likely recent month for which he would have had data for his presentation, bank reserves rose 137 percent and bank holdings of U.S. government securities increased 112 percent. The rise in bank reserves was not due to Federal Reserve policy. Federal Reserve credit actually declined, being at that point 1 percent *lower*. The rise in reserves was attributable principally to a 157 percent increase in the gold stock.

Had he employed a correlation analysis that he used in the mid-1920s to relate the business cycle to movements in the rate of change of prices (Fisher 1925), he would have observed the relation between industrial production and net demand deposits as shown in figure 5.1 for a sample period through May 1936. The presence of the high degree of variability in the early months of the recovery serves to generate a correlation of 0.60, one that by conventional standards is not particularly strong. But the positive trend of the regression line is graphic evidence of a clear rebound, one that becomes much clearer as recovery progressed. Had he continued to relate the two series, he would have witnessed something akin to figure 5.2, for which the correlation coefficient is 0.916. This is a value only slightly smaller than the one he characterized in a related context as "seldom before has a correlation so

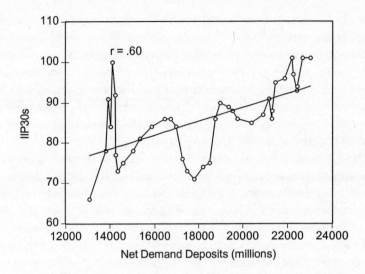

FIGURE 5.1.   Recovery of industrial production, April 1933–May 1936.
(Data from *Federal Reserve Bulletin,* various issues.)

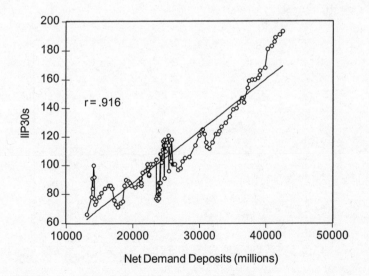

FIGURE 5.2.   The full Fisherian recovery, April 1933–June 1942.
(Data from *Federal Reserve Bulletin,* various issues.)

high [94.1 percent] been found in the efforts to explain the business cycle" (1925, 179).

The relationship between wholesale prices and net demand deposits is shown in figure 5.3. From this, it is reasonably clear that the rebound in prices for which he so much campaigned was well under way, and that the rising stock of deposits was the fundamental reason. This certainly is impressive evidence that the then three-year-old recovery was in large part the result of monetary expansion.

These three figures, for which the requisite data were readily available, would have been convincing evidence as to the role of the growth of money in the recovery. Yet, Fisher did not pursue such an investigation. He chose instead to follow another course, that of casting doubt on the robustness of the money stock mechanism. It was the seemingly anomalous situation in which deposits increased because of bank purchases of governments rather than "the usual way," borrowing by businesses, that was further ammunition in his campaign for 100 percent reserves: "it is the smallness of our reserve requirements which makes possible the contraction and expansion of the deposit currency" (1936b, 106). Coupled with the growing excess reserves, this led him to take a positive view of the soon-to-be-implemented doubling of reserve requirements, expressing at the same time skepticism that it "may not be enough" (1936b, 106).

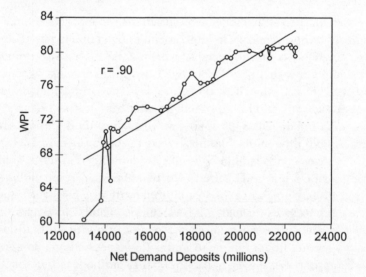

FIGURE 5.3.   Recovery in wholesale prices, April 1933–May 1936. (Data from *Federal Reserve Bulletin*, various issues.)

Though he appeared agnostic as to the reasons for the excess reserves, whether it was "borrowers fail[ing] to come forward" or banks "afraid to lend,"[19] the logic of the matter is that he believed fundamentally that the excess reserves were due to a failure of borrowers "to come forward." Had he thought they were due to bank caution, he would not have crusaded for higher reserve requirements.

Suppose banks were "afraid to lend." The implication would be that they raised their credit standards and perhaps increased their desire for liquidity. The two options open would then have been to employ those reserves either to acquire more U.S. government securities, adding to their already doubled holdings, or simply to maintain those reserves for precautionary, liquidity purposes. Banks would in the latter case have had a demand for them; the reserves would not have been surplus, redundant assets. The banks did not employ their reserves to buy all the more governments; had they done so, there would have been no excess reserves issue. Banks must therefore have held those reserves as a desired asset. Given the logic of the excess reserves question, if Fisher had in fact subscribed to this position, he could not as a matter of consistency have campaigned for higher reserve requirements, a battle that took on the characteristics of a single-minded crusade for total elimination of partial reserve requirements.

There was however not a modicum of concern that the increases in reserve requirements might have a deflationary effect, as banks in their attempts to rebuild their reserve positions would have let their loans, hence deposits, run off. Ironically, the consequences of such adjustment by banks would have been identical with the actions of borrowers in his debt-deflation theory. That he did not recoil from such a likely upshot adds further weight to the argument that he in fact believed that the large volume of excess reserves was attributable to a deficiency of borrowers.

The 100 percent reserves proposal was a typical Fisherian pose, characteristic of his many crusades. Perhaps he was caught up in the righteousness of his crusade so that he did not think through the money stock consequences. Perhaps this reflected his lifelong disinterest in money mechanisms. More likely, his attribution of a shortage of borrowers as the underlying cause of the banking system's large excess reserves was another variation on the real-bills orientation in *Booms and Depressions*. This time it was based on banks being unable to decide the composition of their assets because "the usual way" of lending was not operational due to "borrowers fail[ing] to come forward."

Thereafter, he did not return to any formal analysis of the relationship between (deposit) money and the economy (Dimand 2000, 336–44). The bulk of his remaining monetary work had him and his coterie concentrating their energies on establishing the approximate constancy of velocity, even to the point of arguing that "the drop [in velocity] between 1929 and 1933 . . . was probably more apparent than real," a position that contrasted with his 1936 Cowles Commission lecture.

Summary and Conclusions

There is little to indicate that in the recovery Irving Fisher had abandoned the views he adopted during the Contraction. Through it and the subsequent recovery, he continued to adhere to the quantity theory position that changes in the stock of money affected the economy. He now viewed the changes in deposits and money as due to the vagaries of individuals and businesses, and not to Federal Reserve actions or gold stock movements. The principal influences on the stock of money came from individuals and businesses as they became overindebted or unwilling to borrow (further). In the former case, their attempts to reduce their debts led to a spiraling down of the money stock, which then lowered prices and output—the Great Contraction. In the latter, the reluctance to borrow, perhaps a normal, understandable response to earlier overindebtedness, led to a buildup of excess reserves. These in turn portended a substantial, potential rise in the stock of money, hence in inflation, as the reluctance to borrow abated.

The logic of his support for reserve requirement increases implies his continued adherence to the debt-deflation thesis and real-bills doctrine integral to *Booms and Depressions*. Though he continued to view changes in deposits and money as basic to the course of prices and output, he no longer saw Federal Reserve actions as fundamental to their movements; perhaps he is best viewed as not being a practicing quantity theorist, in that he did not use the theory to analyze the behavior of the economy. Fisher's later work, particularly that presented in his Cowles Commission lecture (1936b) with its real-bills orientation, liquidity trap exposition, and embracing of substantial reserve requirement increases, indicates that he used other factors to understand the economy.

In the previous chapter, no one saw the recovery as due to the rising stock of money, that is, no one employed the quantity theory. In the current chapter, at least Fisher was aware of the link between the expanding money stock and the recovery, but he chose not to lay emphasis on it for reasons articulated at length previously. In a fundamental sense, his allegiance to it waned, at least as he practiced its dictates.

The decline (and fall) of the quantity theory paradigm is puzzling in at least two respects. First, why was it that professional economists did not employ available theory in their attempts to fathom what was happening, and in the course of so doing attempt to implement it empirically? Was intuition, supplemented perhaps by seat-of-the-pants empirical judgments, of greater consequence than formal theory? If so, why?

Second, the late Thomas Kuhn argued that progress in science normally occurs as a new paradigm appears in response to anomalies in an existing one. Such a crisis presumably was attendant on the quantity theory. Yet, on the basis of the evidence in this and the preceding chapter, such was not the case. The theory was abandoned, and without any empirical justification, before any alternative macroeconomic paradigm surfaced. Here then is a case fundamentally at variance with Kuhn's hypothesis: the quantity theory paradigm was abandoned well before a new macroeconomic paradigm was advanced and adopted. The irony in this is that the recovery seemingly could have been understood from the viewpoint of that theory.

One of the extraordinary events of the decade was the sharp, deep depression midway through. An inquiry into that depression is the subject of the following chapter.

CHAPTER 6
―◦―

The Depression of 1937–38

The sharpness of the economy's deterioration beginning late spring 1937 was more dramatic than in any previous depression. Along with this, the existence of more data resulted in greater resort to empirical forays to understand it. Though there was some debate over when the economy began to decline—late spring or late summer—and how long the depression lasted—a year or nine months—the assessment was still much the same, namely, that the depression was no recession, no rolling readjustment; it was indeed sharp and deep. Kenneth Roose's masterful examination of that depression began, "Every writer, when evaluating the success of government action in promoting . . . recovery in the thirties, faces the necessity for examining the recession and revival of 1937–38" (1954, 1). As to its causes, most explanations stressed a multiplicity of factors. Roose listed forty-one, arranging them in five general categories (16–17). The factors to which the revival was due were fewer, with Roose noting eight (19).

The chapter begins by considering several of the more important factors that caused the downturn. It then moves on to deal with elements deemed crucial to the revival. In this, there is heavy reliance on Roose. The third section considers the role of the money stock in the slide and recovery. Of particular note is the May 1938 nadir, which gave all indications of further despair. The liquidity trap prospect is also examined, since the interest rate on short-term government securities was virtually zero (cf. the zero-bound problem of contemporary monetary policy). Also of consequence, the uncharacteristic behavior of simultaneous deflation, monetary growth, and rapid economic recovery is considered, a matter that warrants consideration in a later chapter.

Industrial production, having increased from the low point of the Contraction, stalled in March 1937. It was constant through May, followed by three months of almost uninterrupted modest decline. Beginning in September, it fell rapidly the rest of the year, declining at a 60 percent annual rate. The rate of decline abated to 16.2 percent through the trough in May 1938. On the basis of this history, it was understandable that some would choose September 1937 as the month in which the depression began (Roose 1954, 3). However, this essay takes May as the start of the depression.

Causes of the Depression

As can be seen in Roose, the roster of possible causes bordered on a shopping list. One he did not consider was that it "was perhaps due in part to nothing more than the familiar rhythms of the business cycle, which dictated some inevitable measure of contraction after four years of expansion" (Kennedy 1999, 351). That explanation would have gotten short shrift, in part because of the propensity to search for identifiable factors, and not to fall back on "nature." In addition, in the activist atmosphere of the time, the demand to "do something" required identification of the cause(s) for which actions were to be taken. Of the causes, the three most widely considered were fiscal policies, price-cost maladjustments, and monetary actions.

Fiscal Actions

One of the most widely cited factors was the altered fiscal stance of the federal government, the decline in the net government contribution to the income flow, to use the phrase popular at the time, largely due to the series that Lauchlin Currie and Martin Krost (1938) originated.[1] This was a monthly series. The decline in the net government contribution during 1937 was principally because of the joint effect of the cessation of the June 1936 Veterans' Bonus[2] and the increased payroll taxes in 1937 resulting from the Social Security Act of 1935, which moved the budget toward surplus.[3] Arthur Gayer's results showed the monthly net contribution series falling almost continually during 1937 and into the following year until it reached zero in November 1938, a month before his presentation to the American Economic Association (1938, 107). Henry Villard similarly had the net contribution of government declining in 1937, becoming negative in September of that year and February of the following one.[4]

The notion that fiscal policy was in part responsible for the depression continues to the present. In his history of the Federal Reserve, Allan Meltzer argues, "There were two large, contractive changes in fiscal policy in 1937. One was the reduction of soldiers' bonus payments and passage of the undistributed profits tax; the other was the beginning of Social Security tax payments"[5] (2003, 521).

Not all agreed that the decline in the net government contribution was of foremost importance. Gayer (1939, 102), C. O. Hardy (1939, 173), Joseph Schumpeter (1939, 1032), Sumner Slichter (1938, 102), and others were skeptical about acknowledging its primacy as a cause of the depression. Among the reasons were lags and timing, what now are known as impact lags, and the strength of consumer spending. The bonus was "pump priming," and so its termination returned expenditures to their pre-bonus levels. Roose's assessment was that, on balance, "the evidence would seem to support those who tend to minimize the direct responsibility of the decline in net government contribution for the recession" (1954, 76).

Price-Cost Maladjustments

Another set of explanations for the depression related to "price-cost relationships"—the "maladjustment" issue out of which came serious economic dislocation, to use a popular phrase of the time.[6] The prototype was a narrowing of price-cost margins dampening profit expectations, thereby reducing investment expenditures. Among the cited instances were rising raw material prices and increasing labor costs in the building industry, the electric power industry, and the steel industry (Roose 1954, 126–41). Sumner Slichter (1938) articulated a lucid statement of difficulties owing to such relationships. After an impressive examination of likely reasons for the downturn, in which he dismisses "underconsumption and shortage of capital theories," he leans to "remarkably" low profits and the nonrealization of business expectations (1938, 107–9).

At the end of the twentieth century, it is difficult to have much sympathy for analyses that look for cyclical turning points in altering price-cost relationships, particularly those in individual industries. During the 1930s, however, a leading paradigm among economists attributed the problems to structural concerns—"the defects" of capitalism (Hawley 1966, 11)—and this view was not restricted to economists. After all, the Roosevelt administration's preferred vehicle for recovery was the NIRA, which showed their structuralist agenda that emphasized coordination between firms to abate "destructive competition," as well as coordination between industry and labor to allay "maladjustments."

Monetary Actions

A third cause of the depression related to monetary policy. In this, both the Federal Reserve and the Treasury were indicted: the former, understandably, for raising reserve requirements and the latter because of its institution of a gold sterilization program in December 1936. Based on the belief that excess reserves were redundant, idle funds posing an inflationary threat, the Board in mid-August 1936, using its recently enacted power to alter reserve requirements, launched a "preemptive strike," raising requirements to the legally mandated ceilings prescribed in the Banking Act of 1935.

The gold sterilization program was initiated by the Treasury at the behest of the Federal Reserve as a means of preventing "the gold then flowing to the United States in growing quantities from Europeans worried about the possibility of war" from adding to already "excessive" reserves (Blum 1970, 188). The sterilization was announced on December 22, 1936, and went into operation two days later (Johnson 1939, 133–34). It was formally abandoned in April 1938, though it effectively ended two months earlier.[7]

With the exception of a few economists, such as Hardy (1939, 170–71), Schumpeter (1939, 1029), Slichter (1938, 103–4), and Currie (1980),[8] the general tenor of commentary scored the Federal Reserve's doubling of reserve requirements.[9] The decision to raise requirements, widely applauded by economists and "responsible bankers,"[10] was based on the view that the large volume of excess reserves represented a potential inflationary threat and that an increase in requirements would "mop up" some of those redundant reserves, leaving monetary conditions still quite "easy."

Lauchlin Currie in his capacity as an Assistant Director of Research (and de facto adviser to Marriner Eccles) was a prime advocate of increases in reserve requirements. He denied that the increase had anything to do with the subsequent depression (1980, 325–29). In a memorandum written in April 1938, but not published until 1980, he laid the blame instead on a combination of factors. One of the principal ones was the sharp decline in net federal income-increasing expenditures: "It is in the net federal contribution to community expenditures that the greatest decrease took place in the factors tending to increase business activity" (323).

The tone of criticism regarding the reserve requirement increases by those living then differed markedly from postwar ones. The latter stressed the effects of the increases on the reduced rate of growth of the money stock resulting from banks attempting to rebuild their reserves relative to their deposits by letting their loans run off. In contrast, the condemnation of the increases when they were instituted dealt at one level with the effects on interest rates and stock prices, and their influence on the capital market. Another level of analysis dealt with the effects of differential adjustment by banks in different geographical reserve categories. The two strains, however, were not disjoint.

Had economists at the time explored the money stock effects of the reserve requirement increases, they would have used measures akin to *M1FRB* and *M2FRB*. Figure 6.1, which also includes the December 1936 institution of the gold sterilization regime, is such an examination. Following the August 1936 increase of 50 percent, the money stock, whether *M1FRB* or *M2FRB*, began growing less rapidly and then fell,

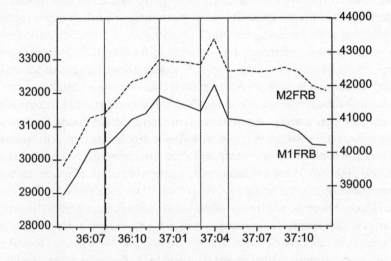

FIGURE 6.1.   Money stock responses to reserve requirements and gold sterilization, May 1936–December 1937.
(Data from *Federal Reserve Bulletin*, various issues.)

with the start of the gold sterilization policy. The March 1937 increase saw an unexplainable April blip and then a decline in each money measure to a level less than when the second reserve requirement increase was instituted. The response to the May increase was a continued fall in each of the stocks until their low points in April of the following year, when reserve requirements were lowered. The money stock increased the following month, the bottom of the depression. But at that time such an examination was not to be. Economists did not examine money stock data, and so it was not surprising that none linked its behavior, and the economy's, to the increase in reserve requirements.

At that time, member banks fell into one of three reserve requirement classes, for which higher requirements prevailed for demand than for time deposits. The class with the highest requirements was Central Reserve City banks—the largest banks in New York City and Chicago. Next were the requirements for Reserve City banks, which comprised banks in large cities, including some in New York and Chicago. The remaining bulk of the banks were classified as Country banks, and their requirements were the lowest.

Banks in the central reserve cities liquidated some of their security investments to meet the higher requirements because they did not have sufficient excess reserves. Although the aggregate volume of reserves was more than adequate for the banking system to meet the higher requirements, individual banks were not able to do so, the central reserve city banks in particular.[11] The problem the central reserve city banks experienced was of the same kind as in the National Banking System—withdrawals by non–central reserve city banks. As the requirements were raised, those banks withdrew their balances from the central reserve city banks, choosing to restructure their assets by converting those balances into legal reserves. This pulled reserves out of the central reserve city banks, thereby compounding the difficulty of their meeting the new higher requirements.[12]

Other banks, even though they could meet the higher requirements through running down their excess reserves, similarly chose to use additional portfolio adjustments to meet the higher requirements. The effect was "weakness in the bond market" as interest rates rose when banks sold some of the security investments. According to the *Economist* (Oct. 16, 1937, 118): "The Government bond market had to absorb over $2,000 millions of bonds in six months when the large banks, the biggest buyers in the last four years, turned sellers" (Roose 1954, 105).

Alvin Hansen was representative of this sentiment. Seeing the higher interest rates as a direct consequence of the reserve requirement increases, he believed that, accordingly, "more vigorous action should have been taken to sustain the government bond market" (1938, 271–72)—presumably open market purchases, which would have negated the interest rate increases. Such action would however have been in direct conflict with the intent of the policy of increasing requirements. In sum, Hansen with the benefit of hindsight thought the policy of increasing requirements was wrong.

With the increase in interest rates, some borrowers were deterred. Others found it more difficult to borrow, as banks raised their credit standards. Investment spending accordingly was reduced. In summarizing the effects of the reserve requirement increases, Roose found, "Even though monetary conditions were extremely easy, compared with any previous period, Federal Reserve policy cannot be cleared of important responsibility in the recession" (1954, 117).

Currie disagreed. He presented his case in a "memorandum [Currie 1980] that was destined to assume the status of a kind of New Dealers' Nicene Creed" (Kennedy 1999, 355). The basic thrust was that the recession was due to a decline in federal income-increasing expenditures. He denied that the rise in interest rates was occasioned by banks selling governments. Rather the rise was attributable to profit taking owing to rising commodity prices the previous six months and to increased bond sales by federal and municipal governments (1980, 327–28). Eccles went a step further as he denied "that the increase in reserve requirements . . . parched the flow of credit into the economy and thereby precipitated the recession of 1937–8" (1951, 293). His argument followed Currie's in assigning the rate rise to nonmonetary causes. It went further through an implicit investment-interest nexus because "the levels reached were not high. Neither were the degrees of change large compared with previous periods, nor was the rise in rate [sic] long sustained" (293).

Based on timing patterns, Philip Bell argued that the second of the reserve requirement increases did not cause a spike in interest rates. He argued further that to have held the Federal Reserve responsible for the recession, investment had to be sensitive to interest rate changes, which he denied, using an interest inelasticity argument (1951, 349–50).

As for investment spending, an additional factor adduced as contributing to its decline was the rise in labor costs following strikes to organize major industries. Combined with higher interest rates and the growing belief that the Roosevelt administration was becoming more hostile to business—in practice, as shown by the undistributed profits tax of 1936, and in perception, as the "anti-business" rhetoric—this raised current and prospective tax rates and costs of capital (Roose 1954, 238–39).

Postwar studies tended to emphasize the effect of the increase in reserve requirements on the stock of money. For Friedman and Schwartz the rise in reserve requirements was an important factor responsible for the severity of the depression (1963, 517–32, esp. 526–27). The effect of those increases was to reduce the growth of the stock of money, almost entirely by increasing banks' desired ratio of reserves to deposits, as they "sought to restore their excess reserve position" (526). The "impact of the rise in reserve requirements . . . first sharply reduced the rate of increase in the money stock and then converted it into a decline" (544–45). They concluded that "consideration of the effects of monetary policy [the rise in reserve requirements in particular] certainly strengthens the case for attributing an important role to monetary changes as a factor that significantly intensified the severity of the decline, and also probably caused it to occur earlier than otherwise" (544).

Allan Meltzer's (2003) more recent study of the depression is an exhaustive examination of Federal Reserve policy-making. In the present circumstance, he deals at length with the internal debate within the System concerning the decisions to increase requirements. The discussion is nuanced by the interplay of political considerations relating to the November 1936 election and the interchange between Marriner Eccles and Henry Morgenthau, the secretary of the Treasury, particularly as it related to the December 1936 decision to sterilize gold. Because the sterilization policy effectively made the Treasury another monetary policy authority, it understandably led to contentious disputes between the two (Blum 1970).

Meltzer singled out for extended analysis reserve requirement increases and the gold sterilization policy.

Changes in reserve requirements were part of monetary policy, and monetary policy was part of government policy. The data on interest rates, risk premiums, changes in the monetary base and money suggest that the Federal Reserve did not offset the effects of the change [in requirements]. Monetary policy became more restrictive. The proximate causes of the monetary policy change were (1) the increase in reserve requirement ratios, not offset by open market purchases, and (2) the shift in December 1936 to gold sterilization. (2003, 521)

In short, the policy "not only contributed to the recession but also failed to reduce the Federal Reserve's concern that it could not prevent future inflation" (2003, 520).

His examination relies heavily on internal Federal Reserve documents. After reviewing accounts in which policy was believed to be easy, namely, reliance on a variant of the Riefler-Burgess framework in which excess reserves now substituted for borrowings at the Federal Reserve as a criterion for ease, he arrives at his overall assessment.

Once again, the monetary base and the money stock tell a different story. . . . Growth of the monetary base turned negative following gold sterilization. . . . The base fell throughout 1937. . . . The money stock lagged behind. . . . [Its] growth remained negative until the early months of the recovery. With inflation . . . rising . . . real money balances fell. (2003, 525–26)

He thus agrees that among the prime causes of the depression were actions that caused the rate of growth of the quantity of money to decline.

Though he had interests beyond developments in the 1930s, George R. Morrison (1966) spent a goodly amount of effort on the liquidity trap concern that was basic to the decision to increase reserve requirements.[13] Had banks been in such a trap, they would not have reacted to the increases. He found that banks in fact reduced their investments and deposits. The problem he faced was to develop a framework in which to understand this. There were two possible rationales, each of which implied a shift in the banking system's liquidity preference function. One was a shock effect and the other an inertia effect hypothesis. The former had the increase in reserve requirements inducing banks to increase their demand for reserves, quickly and abruptly. The inertia effect hypothesis had the rise in reserve requirements inducing banks to become "more cautious in estimating their permanent deposit creating potential, i.e., the maximum volume of reserves . . . which can be safely used to support deposits without risking a costly scramble for liquidity" (1966, 115).

Though the hypotheses are not mutually exclusive, each represents a tractable way of gauging the response of banks. His evidence supports the inertia effect hypothesis, that banks did respond to the increase in reserve requirements by gradually, rather than abruptly, increasing their demand for additional liquidity, that is, for more excess reserves. The essential point is that banks are viewed as having a demand for excess reserves and that the increase in reserve requirements induces them to rebuild their excess reserves, which leads to a reduction in the stock of money. The clear implication is that the decision to raise reserve requirements was a mistake. "The proper policy [in 1936 and 1937] would have been to allow reserves to continue to climb through gold inflows, and to reinforce this by vigorous open-market purchases" (1966, 117).

Another study emphasizing a demand for excess reserves is by Peter Frost (1971). The distinguishing feature is an adjustment cost hypothesis that derives from profit-maximizing considerations. At low interest rates, banks do not wish to incur the costs associated with constantly adjusting their reserve positions because those costs are in excess of any "interest earned on short-term securities" (1971, 821). It "implies that substantial amounts of excess reserves are held only at relatively low interest rates" (819). As a result, it gives rise to a kink in the demand function at very low interest rates, which he estimates to be rates between 30 and 50 basis points. At that point, the demand function becomes quite flat. The demand for excess reserves then depends essentially solely on the interest rate. At rate levels that may be considered normal, bank holdings of excess reserves would be virtually zero.

After estimating a stable demand for excess reserves, Frost turns his attention to the liquidity trap issue. The question of concern is whether a shock to the banking system, such as the increase in reserve requirements, could best be understood in terms of his adjustment cost framework in which banks would alter their excess reserve holdings in response to an interest rate change. The competing view, as framed by Morrison, would be the shock- and inertia-effect frameworks, each of which has the demand for excess reserves increasing in response to the reserve requirement increases. In neither of these can "the large accumulation of excess reserves . . . be solely attributed to the low level of the short-term interest rate" (1971, 818). Frost finds, not surprisingly, that his adjustment cost hypothesis better explains the excess reserve experience of the 1930s.

Of greater concern here is that his framework is another piece of evidence indicating that the Federal Reserve's decision to increase reserve requirements was an important factor causing the depression. In Frost's framework, the reserve requirement increases would have induced banks to pursue actions to adjust their excess reserves back to their original levels, absent any marked increase in short-term interest rates. Though he did not formally address the increase in reserve requirements, the implication from his adjustment cost model of the demand for excess reserves is that it would have resulted in a decrease in the stock of money. That is to say, banks were not caught in a liquidity trap.

Not all of the postwar literature found that the reserve requirement increases were a factor in the 1937–38 depression. Charles W. Calomiris and David C. Wheelock maintain "that the reserve requirement increases of 1936 and 1937 did not precipitate the recession of 1937 and 1938" (1998, 38), citing Frost (1971), Currie (1980), and an unpublished 1996 manuscript of theirs, "The Neutrality of Reserve Requirement Changes in the 1930s." (That paper was not available at the time of preparation of this book; in answer to an e-mail query, David Wheelock said, "Frank—Charlie and I never went back to that work," and in response to the same question, Charles Calomiris wrote, "The paper with Wheelock is still dormant, although we are about to return to it" [March 20, 2001].)

Currie certainly denied that the increases had anything to do with causing the depression. Calomiris and Wheelock's lumping of Frost in with those who abjured linking the depression with the reserve requirement increases is suspect. It is difficult to see how Frost's model could be interpreted to imply a framework in which the reserve requirement increases were not integral to the reduction in the stock of money.

Sources of Revival

There is a far more voluminous literature on the causes of the depression than on revival. One reason may be that the recognition lag was so long for the revival. By the time it was realized, the trough had passed

and the pressing economic issues had changed to war and the requirements of a wartime economy. With the advent of the war, there was
increasing attention to the "effect of war developments on American
Markets."[14]

A factor that may have been responsible for a lengthy recognition
lag was the continued decline of prices. Though industrial production
reversed course after May 1938, wholesale prices declined until August
1940, and falling prices tended to be regarded as symptomatic of
depressed economic activity.[15]

Roose's examination led him to conclude that the lack of attention to
the rebound was "due to a broad consensus that renewed government
spending in the spring and summer of 1938 initiated the revival" (1954,
15). Indeed, there was considerable commentary about the altered fiscal stance. To the extent that it was censorious, it called attention to the
delay, indeed failure, to increase federal government expenditures
(e.g., Hansen 1941).[16] With the resumption in net income-increasing
expenditure in 1938, the general tone was that it was responsible for the
revival (Villard 1941).[17] Whether the turnaround from depression to
revival could be due to the increases in such expenditure was more
controversial, principally because it implied an impact lag so short as to
strain credulity (Angell 1941, 232).

Other factors may be regarded as exogenous developments, such as
a rebound in investment expenditures, induced by "improvements in
the relations between businessmen and government" (Roose 1954,
18).[18] James Angell sounded an early version of a mean-reversion force
in a business cycle. He regarded the depression as "first . . . a fairly 'normal' self-generating cyclical affair in its origin, and one which would
have come about even in the absence of government intervention; but
that, second, it was intensified by the government's own actions" (1941,
230–31). So also with the revival: "The start of this new recovery phase
hence also appears to have been, in the main, a relatively 'normal' and
self-generating cyclical phenomenon" (232).

In what perhaps is a testimony to the times, monetary considerations
were virtually absent in discussions of the revival. One instance in
which it was mentioned was Martin Krost (1940) who simply noted the
level of deposits in 1939. Two monetary actions that were mentioned as
contributing to the turnaround were the desterilization of gold inflows
in February 1938 and the reduction in reserve requirements in April
1938.[19] What tended to be emphasized was the effect of each on excess

reserves. There was no reference to the money stock in the context of its growth as a factor in the revival. The *Federal Reserve Bulletin,* in its monthly commentary on the economy, did mention the movement of deposits once in a while, but it did not go beyond simply presenting the facts.[20] Its emphasis tended to be on the behavior of bank credit. In his summary of the evidence of the contribution of these monetary actions to the recovery, Roose acknowledged that they "undoubtedly facilitated the recovery. . . . The best guess seems to be that such actions would have done little to promote recovery if unaccompanied by other favorable factors" (1954, 117–18). What those were and the basis on which he arrived at that conjecture can only be surmised.

Friedman and Schwartz also commented on the revival, singling out the resumption of increases in the money stock and the gold inflow to which it was due: "Recovery came after the money stock had started to rise. . . . Munich [September 1938] and the outbreak of war in Europe were the main factors determining the U.S. money stock in those years, as Hitler and the gold miners had been in 1934 to 1936" (1963, 545).

Another investigation is that of John Burbidge and Alan Harrison (1985), who conducted a sophisticated examination using modern time-series analysis. The technique consists of estimating a four-variable vector autoregression (VAR) model. The data are monthly observations of a short-term interest rate, wholesale prices (*WPI*), industrial production (*IP*), and an *M1* money stock series they constructed.[21] The variant on which they cast their analysis is historical decomposition. The concern is the determination of the role of the money stock on output and prices during the entire Depression decade.[22] It is the results bearing on the late 1930s that are of interest.

Their investigation assesses the procedure as well as the role of money, so it is not surprising that the estimates do not track the actual behavior of the economy very well. For instance, the fall in prices at the start of the depression is overstated—"the projection is some way below the [actual] series" (1985, 50). They do, however, anticipate the dramatic September 1939 price increase. Thereafter, the "projection captures (albeit slightly prematurely) the rise in *WPI* up to the end of the data period in December 1941" (1985, 50–51). The results for movements in industrial production are more satisfactory: movements in money "play an important role in the behavior of *IP*, with the . . . projection if anything accounting for more of the deviation of the actual series from the base projection than in the case of *WPI*" (1985, 51).

Of most interest were the revival results. They found "much firmer evidence" of the impact of the increases in the stock of money "between 1938 and 1941" (1985, 52). There is an interesting contrast between analyses in the 1930s and after the war. The earlier ones concentrate on interest rates and excess reserves; here there is the nascent germ of the soon-to-be-articulated notion of a liquidity trap. Monetary policy is held to be easy because of abundant excess reserves and near-zero short-term interest rates. The later studies ignore these and deal with the impact of the stock of money.

Money in the Revival

Another way in which to understand the role of the money stock in the depression and especially in the revival is to consider the following situation. As in spring of 1938, suppose interest rates are near zero, prices are falling, Federal Reserve credit is declining, loans by banks similarly are falling, and excess reserves are extraordinarily high and mounting. What would be the prognosis for the economy over the next year? This is the situation in which the U.S. economy found itself.

The economic data for this extraordinary period appear in table 6.1. The dates on the columns correspond to the beginning of the depression (May 1937), the trough (May 1938), the last month of the twenty-

TABLE 6.1.   Deflation and Economic Performance

	May 1937	May 1938	Aug 1939	Aug 1940	June 1941
Industrial production	100	67.4	90.3	106.3	134.3
Wholesale prices	100	89.4	85.8	88.6	99.7
Federal Reserve credit	100	100.7	95.7	97.2	88.5
T-bill rate	0.41%	.05	.05	.04	.12
Real rate (U.S. government bonds)	2.76%	13.15	6.18	−.01	−10.48
Commercial loans	100	88.5	85.9	90.9	107.7
Excess reserves	100	272.4	497.0	710.0	577.2
M1	100	95.0	112.2	129.7	148.2
M1FRB	100	96.6	117.4	131.4	150.8
M2	100	97.3	109.5	121.7	135.7
M2FRB	100	98.2	113.9	122.2	140.2
Monetary base	100	105.8	135.8	162.1	170.2
Gold	100	108.3	137.7	174.1	189.9

seven-month fall in prices (August 1939), and the end of the deflation (August 1940). The June 1941 column represents the month in which prices returned to where they were at the depression's start.[23] Except for the rates on short-term treasuries and real interest, all data are indexed at 100 in May 1937.[24]

In the depression, industrial output fell 33 percent.[25] Unemployment increased from the previous year's 14.3 percent to 19 percent in 1938. Wholesale prices declined 11 percent during the depression and fell another 3 percent over the next fifteen months, until August 1939, thereby falling 14 percent from the start of the depression two and a quarter years earlier.[26] If the September–October price surge associated with the start of the war in Europe could be regarded as an aberration, as surely it was, the duration of deflation was forty months, since prices fell another 2.5 percent into the following August.

After increasing a paltry 0.7 percent during the depression, Federal Reserve credit contracted 5 percent during the first fifteen months of the revival. The interest rate on three-month treasuries fell from 41 to 5 basis points in the depression. Thereafter, it averaged 4 basis points in the subsequent fifteen months. These extremely low levels were instrumental in causing the economy to be perceived as caught in a liquidity trap.

The real interest rate rose sharply during the depression, almost quintupling, which would not be unexpected in the face of deflation. Thereafter the real rate fell by August 1939 to less than half its depression trough level, then fell further to essentially zero percent by the following August. This two and a quarter year slide was surprising, given that prices were still declining. After August 1940, it continued declining even as prices increased, a consequence that is not unexpected.

Loans at banks also declined through August 1939, falling 14 percent, of which 3 percent occurred after the May 1938 trough. They then increased the following year but still were 9 percent lower than at the May 1937 cyclical peak. Business loans marched in lockstep with total loans as they similarly fell 3 percent after the trough.[27] Excess reserves at the end of the depression were $2.5 billion, 172 percent higher than a year earlier, largely because banks sought to rebuild their reserve positions as a result of doubling of reserve requirements. They continued rising, so that by August 1940 they were over 700 percent of their May 1937 level.

Anyone but the most extreme optimist viewing the economy in late spring 1938 would have foreseen a continuation of the sharp slide that began the previous year. To all appearances the outlook was among the darkest. But the economy did not emulate the Contraction of 1929 into 1933—it instead rebounded sharply. Over the next twenty-seven months, prices continued falling while industrial production increased 58 percent, an annual rate of 22 percent. Real GNP rose 19 percent, an annual rate of 8 percent. Unemployment fell from 19 percent in 1938 to 17.2 to 14.6 percent over the following two years. What happened? How could an economy with essentially zero short-term interest rates, deflation, decreased bank lending, restrictive Federal Reserve policy, and increasing excess reserves rebound so dramatically? How could an economy that by all appearances seemed to be in a liquidity trap spring back so impressively?

The answer to a large extent seemed to be monetary expansion. The M_1 and M_2 quantities of money increased 37 and 38 percent respectively, after declines of 3 and 5 percent in the depression.[28] Those increases were not due to Federal Reserve policy. Though reserve requirements were reduced in April 1938, Federal Reserve credit, unchanged during the depression, actually declined. Though it increased slightly in the last year of the deflation, it was still less than at the bottom of the decline.

The principal driving force in the monetary expansion was the rise in the monetary base, and this was due to the massive inflows of gold. The base expanded 53 percent during the revival phase, up markedly from its 6 percent increase in the depression. The gold stock rose 61 percent, up from its 4 percent increase in the depression, thus contributing almost entirely to the expansion of the base.[29] The evidence from the recovery from the depression, which had the mien of a liquidity trap, seemingly demonstrated vividly that expansionary monetary actions were not to be emasculated by near-zero interest rates.

The economy continued to expand as the base and money stock continued to grow. In the fall of 1939, the economy was back to where it had been a decade earlier, when the Great Depression was in its early stages. Prices reversed their downward course in mid-summer 1940, getting back to their 1926 = 100 base level in October 1942. The recovery from the deep depression of the late 1930s was remarkable. It seemed clear that a principal factor in the revival was the behavior of the money stock, whose increase was due virtually entirely to the inflow of gold. To the extent that the gold sterilization policy was rescinded, the base continued growing. The reductions in reserve requirements allowed for a somewhat larger money multiplier, and that allowed for the increasing stock of money to have a greater influence on the recovery.

The Price Puzzle

One of the most puzzling developments is the decline of prices in the twenty-seven-month period from the depression's trough, culminating in August 1940. This episode appears not to have caught much attention among observers, either at that time or later. Friedman and Schwartz would seem prime candidates for addressing the issue, but they did not even comment on it. Another would be Christina Romer (1999), who is concerned with understanding price movements in the 1930s.

Friedman and Schwartz's concern was with the markedly greater rise in wholesale prices relative to the growth of the stock of money in 1933 into 1937. This contrasted with previous recoveries from deep depressions, "despite a probably higher fraction of the labor force unemployed and of physical capacity unutilized" due to "autonomous forces raising wages and prices" (1963, 498). The nature of those forces was clear: "*increasingly* strong unions and *increasingly* strong monopoly groups in the process of raising their wages and prices to levels consistent with their newly acquired monopoly power" (1963, 498–99 n. 4). They did not go beyond 1937 and so did not investigate the revival with its falling prices and increasing money stock.

The theme of "autonomous forces" is a not-so-veiled allusion to the NIRA of the "hundred days" and to the 1935 National Labor Relations Act (Wagner Act). In line with the dominant economic thought of the times, the role of the NIRA was to rein in "destructive, predatory" competition by implementing codes of industrial self-government intended to promote "fair" competition. Antitrust was to take a back seat.[30] Included in the NIRA were the establishment of minimum wages and the right to organize into unions. In its brief life span, over 550 codes covering virtually the entire nonagricultural private sector were promulgated. The Supreme Court's unanimous decision in the Schecter case struck down the NIRA in May 1935, three weeks short of its second birthday.

The impact of the NIRA on prices and wages was the subject of a careful study by Michael M. Weinstein (1980). He found that despite the downward pressure on wages because of high unemployment, "the industrial codes had a more than offsetting inflationary impact on wages," and the codes "increased prices . . . by two mechanisms. First [through increased wages and] secondly, the codes conferred increased monopoly power to industries" (1980, 29). His estimate was that the codes increased wages "as much as a 26 percent annual increase" and prices by "a 14 percent annual increase" (1980, 29),[31] results that support Friedman and Schwartz's conjectures as far as the first few years of the recovery are concerned.

A more extensive investigation of prices was conducted by Christina Romer (1999). The task was to track the course of the implicit GNP price deflator. As in her earlier work (1992), she took 1942 as the year the economy returned to trend. Her data were annual, as she addressed the conundrum of rising prices in the face of an economy well below trend, viz., "almost any conventional model of price adjustment would suggest that such huge deviations of output from trend should have led to continued deflation through much of the recovery period, not moderate inflation" (1999, 168).

To that end, the initial setup had her estimating a modified Phillips curve model, the results of which confirmed the "well below trend implying deflation" hypothesis. In contrast to the prominence she earlier assigned the growth of the money stock in promoting recovery, the gold-driven increases were not of consequence in understanding the recovery's inflation. The increases in the stock of money would only have served to lessen the deflation, but "inflation certainly should not have occurred" (1999, 168).[32] Accordingly, the money stock did not enter any of her subsequent probes.

The irony is that the growth of the quantity of money was fundamental to her earlier explanation of the recovery (1992), yet it played no role in explaining the decade's rising prices. This is an inversion of the quantity theory, for that theory holds that the behavior of the money stock affects prices, both in the short and long run, and has no long-run effect on output. Her orientation, empirical that it is, has no role for the quantity of money in affecting prices, but a powerful one for influencing output.

In a bit of hyperbole, she held that scholars had ignored the phenomenon of inflation in the 1930s. The assertion that prices should not have risen because of the severely depressed state of the economy relative to its trend was an exaggeration. The normal course of a recovery, whether from a mild or deep depression, has prices rising.[33]

To understand the rising prices, a growth-rate effect to account for increases in aggregate demand was added to the modified Phillips curve formulation, capturing the idea that prices depended "also on the growth rate of output. As a result, the rapid growth of output as the United States recovered from the Great Depression was a force mitigating the deflationary effect of the low level of output" (1999, 176). The data were annual observations on real GNP and the implicit GNP price deflator during 1880 through 1932. The inflation rate estimates for the 1930s were then derived from a dynamic simulation.

The results indicated that the growth-rate effect dominated the deviation-from-trend effect. As a result, that "specification . . . explains much of the mysterious behavior of prices during the recovery" (1999, 179).[34] The growth-rate effect more than offset the dampening influence of high levels of unutilized resources in operating below trend.

The estimate had the GNP deflator falling 1.3 percent in 1937 as contrasted with its actual increase of 4.7 percent. Each declined the following two years, with an estimate of a 1.9 percent decline against the actual 1.6 percent fall in 1939. That is, she found prices continued falling after the revival began.

To obtain a more satisfactory understanding, the influence of the NIRA was then considered. The root mean-squared error was reduced by over 75 percent from the growth-rate effect model, and over 91 percent from the initial modified Phillips curve estimates. Here again, the estimates showed falling prices in 1937, as contrasted with an actual increase, and then declining prices in the next two years, with the estimate of a 1 percent deflation in 1939, which was smaller than the actual 1.6 percent decline. Given her concern with modeling price movements during the entire recovery, no attention was paid to the atypical deflation in 1939.

The conclusion was that "most of the mysterious behavior of prices during the recovery from the Great Depression has now been accounted for" (1999, 192). It was the combination of the growth-rate effect and the NIRA that raised prices in much of the recovery. Because the NIRA nullified the deflationary pressure on prices, Romer suggested that it might well have been a force "holding back recovery" (1999, 197).

The puzzle nonetheless remains: How can we explain the deflation during the first two and a quarter years of revival? Romer's framework does not appear helpful. In 1939, both nominal and real output grew dramatically, GNP by 6.9 percent and real output by 8.1 percent. The consequent growth-rate and return-to-trend effects should then have resulted in prices rising. Furthermore, the NIRA-unionization effect could not have decreased wages, hence prices; in fact, it would have exerted upward pressure.[35]

Other Revival Possibilities

A widely held view was that the revival was principally attributable to fiscal policy, a demand shock. In particular, as William Barber has shown in "the struggle for the soul of FDR" (1996, 114), there was a U-turn in the president's thinking about the relationship of budgets to the economy.[36] In April 1938, over "the objections of the Secretary of the Treasury [Henry Morgenthau Jr.]" he consciously advocated fiscal stimulation in his proposal for "more than $3 billion worth of spending or lending . . . for relief, public works [and] housing" (1996, 114). The succession of increasing deficits could then be easily linked to the recovery from the depression. So to many, the recovery was a fiscal policy success; in taxonomic terms, a demand shock.[37]

Another example of such a shock was the "exogenous" increase in investment beginning in spring 1938. With the war clouds in Europe, the prospect of a wartime economy may have induced anticipatory attempts to add to capacity, the long-term consequence of which would be an increase in aggregate supply. But to accomplish that, it was necessary to increase investment. An indication that there may have been attempts to increase capacity was the 60 percent rise in real investment in producers' durable equipment through the second quarter of 1940, after which prices began increasing. At the same time, real business inventories increased at more than double the rate at which they fell during the depression.[38]

A demand shock view is, however, an unsatisfactory explanation of the evolution of the economy. Such a shock would have both output and prices increasing. In fact, the conundrum under investigation has the two moving along opposite trajectories.

Was there instead a supply shock, an increase in aggregate supply? The logic of the situation suggests this may not be an implausible explanation. If there were a supply shock, output would have increased and prices decreased, which was what was observed. The shortcoming of a supply shock approach is that such a shock would have a short-term influence, a one-time effect, as output and prices moved to their new levels. It would not result in output continuing to rise and prices continuing to decline, unless there was a succession of such shocks. But then, what developments, what events, what circumstances occurred that were the driving ones for a succession of such shocks?

Another difficulty with the supply shock view is that in assessing the evolving economic situation it is not easy to attribute such a shock to any particular, identifiable event. If anything, the looming international difficulties suggest that aggregate demand shocks would be more likely due to anticipatory attempts to increase expenditures on durables as well as heightened investment to enlarge capacity.

Neither the demand nor supply shock approaches appears to be a satisfactory framework. An alternative view, one for which there is historical precedent, emphasizes the demand for money in a quantity theory framework. The point of departure is an increase in the demand for money relative to the expanding stock of it—a decrease in velocity, the consequence of which is a fall in prices. Given that the quantity of money and output increased (substantially) while prices fell, velocity must have fallen. There are good reasons why that was the case.

One reason the demand for money would have increased relates to the sharpness of the depression, coming as it did when the economy was far from recovered from the shock of the Contraction. As Meltzer acknowledges, "it is no wonder that many feared the 1929–33 disaster had returned" (2003, 522). This would have increased uncertainties about the future and the durability of a recovery. Another consideration relates to the understandable tendency in the 1930s to identify declining prices as synonymous with bad times, a direct consequence of the Contraction's fall in prices. Symmetrically, there would be the propensity to link improving economic circumstances to rising prices. The falling prices in the depression could seem an omen of future difficulties, which would increase the demand for money. Still another factor that would have increased money demand is that the depression's fall in prices would have increased expectations of further deflation, in which case money is an attractive asset.

The hypothesized fall in velocity can be seen in the data, as shown in figure 6.2. The data are quarterly; real GNP data come from Balke and Gordon (1986) and the $M1$ from Friedman and Schwartz (1963). The clear downward movement is apparent. The velocity of M1 fell at a 6 percent annual rate from the cyclical peak in the second quarter of 1937 across the next three years through the second quarter of 1940, after which prices began increasing. From the cyclical trough in the second quarter of 1938, the fall in velocity was at the somewhat reduced annual rate of 4.8 percent (for the importance of this velocity behavior, see chap. 9).

Just as there were reasons for the fall in velocity, there should be recognizable circumstances that led to desires to hold smaller real money balances relative to real incomes. One important consideration was the growing recognition that the war in Europe would impact the United States. Perhaps the effect would be direct; certainly the vigorous debate leading to the September 1940 resumption of conscription with its unmistakable message that the United States might well be involved in a war would have been a factor. Perhaps the influence would be indirect, as when the president initiated what was to become the lend-lease program with the fall of France in June 1940. Whatever it was, it signaled "an end to isolation" (Leuchtenburg 1963, 299).[39] The shift from fear of continued depressed conditions to concern about war and the "prosperity" it brings would have moderated the increased demands for money, again relative to the growing stock.

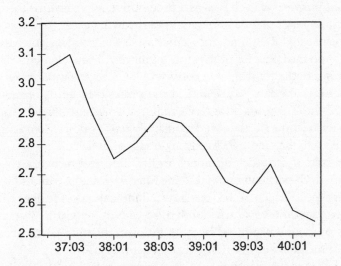

FIGURE 6.2.   *M1* velocity with falling prices, 1937.2–1940.2. (Data from Friedman and Schwartz 1963; Balke and Gordon 1986.)

The behavior of output can be understood as a tendency to return to trend, the tendency to revert in an "exogenous-like" manner to its normal growth path. In the parlance of contemporary theory, the behavior of output is characterized by a mean-reversion thrust. The notion is that the economy contains within itself mechanisms that propagate endogenously the movement of output toward its trend.

The notion of mean-reversion is largely a product of postwar studies of the time-series properties of economic variables, though there were hints of this in the 1930s, in the work on business cycles (Angell 1941).[40] The notion of trend implies the tendency to operate neither systematically above nor below but on average at the trend value; it assumes that the economy has self-correcting tendencies.[41] The importance of this is basic to understanding the recovery (chap. 9).

Concluding Comments

The chapter examined at length the 1937–38 depression. It began by considering factors identified as important in causing the depression. Prime among them was monetary restriction brought on by actions in 1936, the Federal Reserve's doubling of reserve requirements beginning in August, and the Treasury sterilizing gold in December. The avowed purpose of each was as a preemptive move against the incipient inflationary potential inherent in the growing excess reserves. Monetary criticisms then tended to emphasize the effect on interest rates and not on the behavior of the stock of money. Then, elements deemed important to the revival were considered. On this, comparatively little was said, in the late 1930s, and in the present. In terms of monetary actions, the lowering of reserve requirements and abandonment of gold sterilization were viewed as useful steps at best. More emphasis was given to the emergence of growing fiscal deficits.

The role of the stock of money in the slide and recovery was then examined. Of particular note was the May 1938 nadir, with its liquidity trap prospect, which at the time gave all indications of further despair. The economy, however, rebounded, seemingly by virtue of increased stocks of money produced by gold inflows, this due to the abandonment of the gold sterilization policy in February 1938.

Of major consequence was the anomalous behavior of simultaneous deflation, rapid monetary growth, and vigorous economic recovery.

Any analysis that relied on increased aggregate demand would be faulty because it could not account for falling prices. A supply shock rationalization was also rejected, partly because a one-time shock cannot result in continuing deflation; in addition, no express sequence of such shocks that would have had prices declining could be identified. The explanation instead revolved around a fall in velocity serving to reduce prices. The increase in output was understood as due to endogenous propagation forces of mean-reversion, the response of the impulses in an economy below trend inducing movements back toward it.

CHAPTER 7

The Influence of the Budget

Discussion of the use of the federal budget to influence the course of the economy, that is, fiscal policy, swelled in the last half of the 1930s, due perhaps to the influence of Keynes and his *General Theory*. Herbert Stein argued, however, that "it is possible to describe the evolution of fiscal policy in America up to 1940 without reference to [Keynes]. . . . [B]y the outbreak of the war a large part of the fiscal revolution had already occurred. It was accepted policy that we would run deficits in depressions, that we would not raise taxes in depressions in an attempt to balance the budget" (1969, 131).

This chapter considers some of the fiscal policy discussions in the 1930s along with early postwar views. The emphasis is on assessments of such policy for the entire recovery and not for selected fiscal incidents. As an example, there is much commentary on the impact of the budget swing toward surplus as a factor responsible for the late-1930s depression. Similarly, the frequently mentioned role of growing fiscal deficits as war loomed at decade's end is not of relevance here. The chapter then assesses the empirical evidence on the role of fiscal policy in the recovery. There can be little doubt that the depressed state of the economy in conjunction with the apparent political change of budget regime was a prime consideration in the substantial interest in the effects of the budget.

Early Budget Analyses

One of the earliest statements dealing with the budget and recovery issued out of a roundtable at the University of Chicago a few months before the Contraction's trough (Bane et al. 1933).[1] It dealt with President Hoover's early 1933 proposed budget for the fiscal year beginning on July 1 of that year. One of the principal suggestions was that the budget be balanced "over a period of years, taking account of the swings of the business cycle, rather than attempt to balance each annual budget without reference to the effects of such policy on business and social welfare" (1933, 26). Deficits owing to emergency expenditures, including those for public works, were to be financed by borrowing. Because the roundtable's format considered the budget in the conventional sense, notably absent from the proposals was a discussion of financing the prospective fiscal 1934 deficit through monetization. This would be a feature that became prominent in Chicagoans' later budget deficit proposals (Steindl 1995, 79–96).

In the literature prior to 1936–37, two themes that stand out can be seen in works of J. Ronnie Davis (1971) and Herbert Stein (1969). The thesis Davis develops is that even before the *General Theory* there was a goodly amount of opinion along a wide spectrum of economists that deficits were an appropriate counterdepression policy. Not only that, but budget policy was to follow a compensatory ambit, one in which depressions meant conscious deficits and booms surpluses.[2]

Though there were many who advocated what came to be called fiscal policy as a means of promoting recovery, it nonetheless is true that the dominant view was that a balanced budget, euphemistically called "fiscal stability," was the appropriate budget policy. The Brookings Institution, for instance, in its late 1936 inquiry argued strongly for budget balance. It regarded deficits as "*a problem of major difficulty.* . . . [A]n early balancing of the federal budget is economically possible. . . . If fiscal stability is not achieved, the resulting financial and monetary disorganization and price inflation would in due course completely disrupt the process of constructive economic expansion now under way" (1936, 538). By 1940, this view of deficits had changed significantly: "Under New Deal policies liberal spending and lending have been put forward as desirable methods of diverting a greater portion of the national income into consumption channels. A balanced budget is viewed as an outworn fetich" (Crawford 1940, 236).

Herbert Stein concentrates more on the political and business reactions to Roosevelt's budget proposals. As is well known, Roosevelt scored the Hoover deficits in his 1932 presidential campaign. Through his first term, the default position was a balanced budget; deficits were regarded as departures, necessary but nonetheless aberrations, from the desired state. One of the clearest examples was in 1936 when an undistributed profits tax was proposed and enacted. In contrast to the redistributive, social grounds for his 1935 tax increases,[3] "the decision to raise taxes was predicated on the need for revenue" (Stein 1969, 86).[4] There also was the political consideration that with the November elections, a show of fiscal rectitude would not hurt.

With the 1937–38 depression that perspective changed. There followed "an intense ideological struggle" (Kennedy 1999, 356). Various camps in the administration advanced their preferred policies. Should it be balanced budgets in the hope of stimulating private investment? Should it rather be repeal of the undistributed profits tax, as a sign that the New Deal was not "anti-business"? Another possibility was reverting to some form of planning, a constitutional NIRA. And there were advocates of other policies. Lastly, should the depression be dealt with by a conscious, planned increase in spending, in short fiscal policy, as was argued at a meeting in the White House in November 1937 (Kennedy 1999, 356)? The answer came in the president's message of April 14, 1938. Recovery was to be engineered by fiscal policy; the budget was to be a fiscal policy vehicle in that it was to be formulated with an eye to promote revival.

Formal economic analyses specifically dealing with fiscal policy similarly were spawned by that depression. Prior to it, federal budget discussions tended not have a fiscal policy thrust. In a Brookings Institution study of the recovery (1936), fiscal policy was virtually absent. The budget chapter was a conventional presentation of data on receipts, expenditures, and the public debt (1936, 277–318). The notion of a fiscal policy was absent, appearing neither in the chapter text nor the index. It appeared in a negative light in a brief commentary on the likely effect of increased government spending: "An earlier and more rapid expansion might have occurred had [business] confidence not been impaired by fiscal policy" (459). It was not surprising then that one of the fundamental policy requirements was a balanced budget (541).

Of the studies prior to the war (chap. 6), the ones by Arthur Gayer (1938) and Henry Villard (1941) were among the first to bring to bear data examining fiscal policy. By later standards, the analyses were not sophisticated. They tended to be tabular presentations of deficits along with aggregative measures of the economy, hence lending a "correlation implying causation" tone.

Postwar Analyses

The professional literature on fiscal policy exploded following Keynes's *General Theory*. From about fifty articles in the 1936–40 period, the number of articles tripled in 1941–45, then increased to over two hundred by 1946–50.[5] Many of the articles were conditioned by the experiences of the 1930s. To a large extent, they could be read as sympathetic to the role of fiscal policy, particularly to the view that it was the main recovery vehicle, especially the growing deficits immediately preceding World War II. This tended to be true even of those that were formal theoretical exercises, including work on multipliers, balanced-budget multipliers, the proper mix of monetary and fiscal policy, and deflationary gaps.

An extreme example was the wide-ranging essay by Arthur Smithies (1946) for the American Economic Association. The task was an assessment of the economic role of the federal government in the 1930s. In line with the generally prevailing gloom characteristic of the times, he saw the private sector as "tending to depress the level of national income" (1946, 23). For example, declining population growth and "the high rate of construction of business plant and equipment . . . during the twenties . . . increased the stock of capital . . . and thus made for abnormally low investment in the thirties" (1946, 23). The presumption was clear: in the absence of federal fiscal policy, the economy would not have moved back to trend. That it instead rebounded was due to fiscal policy: "The single factor operating in the opposite direction was the expansionary fiscal policy of the federal government, which afforded a strong positive stimulus to national income" (1946, 24).

A tour through the years before budget policy became fiscal policy, when budget balance would have been achieved except for emergency expenditures, yielded Smithies's judgment: "Nevertheless, the rate of expansion between 1933 and 1936 was remarkable. . . . After 1938 the fiscal actions of the federal government again made its full contribution to an unspectacular recovery through 1940" (1946, 25–26). "My main conclusion . . . is that fiscal policy did prove to be an effective and indeed the *only* effective means to recovery" (25, emphasis added).

In the mid-1950s, a seminal paper appeared that markedly altered views of fiscal policy. It was prompted by the "question of how effectively fiscal policy promoted recovery in the 'thirties . . . [an issue that] has agitated a good fraction of the profession at one time or another" (Brown 1956, 857). To that end, it systematically explored through use of national income and product account data "the direct annual static effects of fiscal policy on demand in the 'thirties" (857). In Brown's analysis, fiscal policy meant the actions not only of the federal government but of all governmental levels.

That paper was a landmark. It was the first systematic study that used national income accounts data for total government to examine the effects of fiscal policy at a full employment level. The frame of reference was the effect of such policy on the shift in the private sector's demand for final goods and services at a full employment level of output.[6] The base of comparison was 1929; if fiscal policy—that is, total government expenditures minus taxes less transfers—contributed more to an increase in private aggregate demand at a high employment level of output in any particular year in relation to what it did in 1929, then fiscal policy was judged to have promoted recovery that year. The use of the full employment budget, Brown being the first to develop it, was to examine the influence of the budget on a benchmark level of activity.

One of the principal conclusions related to total governmental fiscal policy. Only in 1931 and 1936 were fiscal actions "clearly relatively stronger in the 'thirties than in 1929" (863); in each of those years, the reason was the same, namely, the payment of the Veterans' Bonus, "programs passed by Congress over the vigorous opposition of both the Hoover and Roosevelt administrations" (863). In two years, 1933 and 1937, fiscal actions were "markedly less expansionary than in 1929" (863). For the other years, they were either about the same or slightly more expansive. Accordingly, his widely quoted judgment about fiscal policy was:

> For recovery to have been achieved in this period, private demand would have had to be higher out of a given private disposable income than it was in 1929. Fiscal policy, then, seems to have been an unsuccessful recovery device in the 'thirties—not because it did not work, but because it was not tried. (863–66)

A second conclusion related to the separate, disparate effects of federal relative to state and local fiscal policies. Here the federal government's policies were clearly more expansionary than in 1929, though less so at the end of the decade—"not of sufficient size to approach that of 1934–36" (867). The fiscal actions of state and local governments became more restrictive after 1930, such that federal actions essentially offset those of state and local governments. This was captured in his summary: "It took the massive expenditures [of] the second world war to realize the full potentialities of fiscal policy. Until then, the record fails to show its effective use as a recovery measure" (869).[7]

Subsequently, Larry Peppers (1973) reexamined Brown's procedure for calculating the federal government's high employment budget. Peppers dealt only with the federal budget. He argued that Brown's implicit assumption that taxes were unitarily elastic with respect to GNP was inappropriate, that taxes were in fact income elastic. The effect was to introduce an expansionary bias.[8] He disputed Brown's finding that federal fiscal policy more than offset contractionary state and local policies. He concluded that his improved estimates "contradict [for over half the 1933–39 years] Brown's finding that federal fiscal policy was more expansionary throughout the thirties than it was in 1929" (1973, 201). Accordingly, aggregate fiscal policy seemed all the more "to have been an unsuccessful recovery device in the 'thirties" (Brown 1956, 863).

The change in economists' views of fiscal policy in the recovery was such that Alvin Hansen (1963) felt compelled to offer a partial rehabilitation of it.[9] His argument was impressionistic. Further, it had the character of linking recovery with the growth of federal deficits in a *post hoc, ergo propter hoc* manner. The argument had two dimensions. The first, and most important, was that the collapse during the Contraction left much "'debris', so-to-speak, [to be] cleared away," and these "salvaging operations performed a useful purpose" (1963, 321). Fiscal policy thus was a necessary step. The second point was that the 1933–37 recovery was "amazingly strong . . . choked off in 1938 . . . by a desperate effort by the administration to balance the budget. . . . Had the recovery been allowed to proceed at the same rate as that achieved from 1933 to 1937, we should have reached a GNP by 1940 very close to full employment" (321–22). This was a carryover of his earlier analysis, where he argued that though fiscal policy made "a fairly good showing . . . up to 1937, . . . [f]or the most part, the federal government engaged in a salvaging program and not in a program of positive expansion" (1941, 84).

The advent of structural macroeconometric models in the 1960s was not lost on scholars of the Great Depression. John Kirkwood (1972) used an *ISLM* framework and found neither monetary nor fiscal policy to be of much consequence in the recovery. His assessment of the fiscal thrust mirrored Brown's, that only in 1931 and 1936, the years in which the Veterans' Bonus expenditures occurred, were fiscal actions stimulative. He concluded that "government policy during the Depression must not be faulted for having contributed somewhat to the decline in income, but for not having contributed enough to its recovery" (1972, 834).

For Kirkwood, the driving force in the Depression was investment: "The sharp decline and incomplete recovery of investment must be held responsible for the Great Depression" (1972, 834). Monetary actions were not effective. One reason was the low interest-elasticity of investment when interest rates already were so low. The other was that at such low rates his constant elasticity money demand function required inordinately large increases in the money stock to reduce rates further. Though reluctant to commit formally to a liquidity trap view of the impotency of monetary policy, he in effect acceded to it: "Whether that situation should be called a liquidity trap or not, monetary policy was not much different than trading cash for cash" (1972, 829).

Thomas Beard and Douglas McMillin explored the effects of federal expenditures and deficits, using monthly Firestone (1960) data. Theirs was a five-variable vector autoregression (VAR). The sample period ended in June 1938, a bit after the trough of the late-1930s depression. Based on variance decomposition, they found only weak, transitory effects of the deficit. Specifically, "the results for deficits are broadly consistent with the predictions of the Ricardian equivalence hypothesis [in that we] find small or insignificant effects of deficits" (1991, 263).

A second study in conjunction with Prosper Raynold dealt specifically with the effects of federal expenditures (Raynold, McMillin, and Beard 1991). As in the previous study, the federal budget data were from Firestone. The model and VAR approach were much the same as in Beard and McMillin 1991. The principal finding had increased expenditures having "only a modest impact on production and a trivial impact on prices," a conclusion "not at odds with earlier studies by Brown and Peppers which found an inconsistent role for fiscal policy" (1991, 26).

J. R. Vernon (1994) used a large-scale structural macroeconometric model in his study. His empirical estimates were based on multipliers drawn from the Federal Reserve's MPS—MIT-Penn-SSRC model. The strategy was to detail fiscal actions, such as expenditures, personal and corporate taxes, and social insurance taxes, and apply the relevant MPS multipliers. Those multipliers captured the direct and induced effects of each fiscal action. His emphasis was on post-1940 fiscal policy. For recovery through 1940, he seconded Brown's finding for the 1930s. In contrast, fiscal actions were the principal driving force in 1941 and 1942, years in which real output increased dramatically. With recovery at best half complete by the end of 1940, fiscal actions left it "only 13.3 percent short of completion" by the fourth quarter of the next year (1994, 851), thereby leaving "very little to be explained by monetary policies and other factors" (1994, 863).

One of the more recent studies dealing with fiscal policy was that of Christina Romer (1992), discussed earlier in connection with her assessment of the role of monetary forces. Fiscal policy was measured by the annual change in the ratio of the real federal deficit, measured by the administrative budget, to real GNP. The strategy revolved around calculating the actual path of output with what it would have been under "normal" policy. Her simulation results showed that the fiscal influence was essentially absent inasmuch as the actual and normal paths were basically coincident. Fiscal policy accordingly "contributed almost nothing to the recovery from the Great [Contraction]. Only in 1942 is there a noticeable [influence] and even in this year [it] is small" (1992, 767).

There certainly was a substantial literature on fiscal policy that boomed in the last half of the 1930s and continued thereafter, focusing on fiscal policy and its contribution to the recovery. Of most consequence were the empirical studies. Every one failed to detect any meaningful role for it during the 1930s. None argued that it was perverse, except in selected years, but none found that overall it contributed meaningfully to the recovery. The positive thrust of fiscal actions was identified repeatedly as owing to the Veterans' Bonus. Other than that, the empirical research failed to unearth evidence of a marked role for fiscal policy in promoting recovery.

A second strand was a belief that if not fundamental, fiscal policy at least was important. This thread was largely impressionistic, relying on seeing the recovery moving in line with growing budget deficits and concluding that the latter were the driving force of the former. Hansen's position was basically sympathetic to this view, but he demurred from a full endorsement because he viewed the failure of fiscal policy to be effective as due to the smallness of the expenditure programs. In one sense, Brown was not all that different from Hansen. Though his empirical evidence failed to uncover a fiscal impetus, his basic orientation led him to conclude that the failure to stimulate was due to timidity of the policymakers.

Some Additional Empirical Evidence

The previous analyses generally use lower frequency, annual data. In this section, monthly data are utilized. The framework is a regression model assessing monetary and fiscal influences on industrial production. Before presenting the results, it is necessary to discuss the monthly Firestone (1960) series on federal receipts and expenditures.[10]

There are several accounting systems that measure government receipts and expenditures: the Daily Treasury Statement basis, the consolidated receipts and expenditures basis, the National Income and Product Accounts (NIPA) basis, and the administrative budget. Firestone uses the first of these to generate a series beginning in January 1879. From then until July 1942, the series is called "unrevised receipts and expenditures." They represent "the receipts and expenditures, on a cash basis, for carrying on the government's day-to-day business" (1960, 3). As such they do not include transactions of the trust accounts, such as Social Security and highways. It would be preferable to use the NIPA measures of receipts and expenditures, as Brown did. Unfortunately, these are not available on a monthly basis. The Firestone series is the only monthly federal budget series currently available.

Because the data are monthly, there is the likelihood of considerable seasonal variation. The separate expenditures and receipts series, accordingly, are adjusted by the "ratio-to-twelve-month-moving-average method," the then-standard National Bureau of Economic Research procedure for handling seasonal variation.

The model deals initially with monetary and fiscal policy via a quasi-reduced form procedure, in part because of the current skepticism of large-scale structural models. It has industrial production influenced by the money stock and the budget. After looking at the direct influence of monetary and fiscal impulses, the additional avenue of an interest rate effect is considered, because changes in the money stock and the budget affect the price level and nominal interest rates, hence the real interest rate. Monetary growth increases the price level, which through the Fisher Effect initially reduces real interest rates. Increases in the budget deficit increase the nominal interest rate. As a result, the real interest rate increases, though Ricardian Equivalence considerations may negate the influence of a greater stock of government securities.[11] The model thus is expanded to allow for the direct and indirect influences of monetary and fiscal policies.

For the econometric investigation, the variables are:

IIP = index of industrial production, 1977 = 100
M1FS = Friedman and Schwartz *M1* series
RFGR = real receipts of the federal government, millions of dollars
         in 1926 (WPI) prices
RFGE = real expenditures of the federal government, millions of
         dollars in 1926 (WPI) prices
RINT = real interest rate, Moody's Aaa bond rate minus WPI infla-
         tion rate

The formal specification of the model is

$$IIP_t = \alpha_0 + \alpha_1 M1FS_t + \alpha_2(RFGR_t - RFGE_t) + \alpha_3 RINT_t + \varepsilon_t \qquad (7.1)$$

In conformity with current custom, all variables, except the real interest rate, are written as natural logarithms. The variables thus become approximations to rates of growth. The notation for industrial production accordingly is *LNIIP*. A difficulty occurs when there is a deficit. Define *RBB* as the *ratio* of real receipts *RFGR* to real expenditures *RFGE*. Then, *RBB* is definitely positive. It is greater than unity when the budget is in surplus and less when there is a deficit. Denote the logarithm of the budget balance term as *LNRBB*. The data then are *LNIIP*, *LNM1FS*, *LNRBB*, and *RINT*.

The next step is to check for a unit root in any of the four series. The test statistic is the Augmented Dickey-Fuller Unit Root Test (ADF) where the MacKinnon critical values are used to test the null hypothesis of such a root. The ADF is computed for two and four lags of each variable. Table 7.1 presents the results, which are strikingly unambiguous. For a 1 percent criterion, the MacKinnon critical value is −3.49. Of the series in their levels form, only the real interest rate, *RINT*, does not contain a unit root. The hypothesis of a unit root cannot be rejected for each of the three variables written in terms of logarithms. When each variable is first differenced and evaluated at two and four lags, respectively, the null hypothesis of a unit root is always rejected at the 1 percent level.

The first model relates the movement in industrial production directly to changes in the stock of money and the budget deficit.

$$DLNIIP_t = \alpha_0 + \alpha_1 \, DLNM1FS_t + \alpha_2 \, DLNRBB_t + \varepsilon_t \qquad (7.1')$$

The appropriate number of lags is determined by examining the Akaike Information Criterion (AIC). This occurs with two lags. Though this is an empirical procedure, the reality of fiscal and monetary impulses is not that their effects show up within three months. More likely, the impact lags are at least a half-year.

Table 7.2 presents the OLS estimates. The sample covers the entire recovery. Due to using the change in the logarithm and including two lags, the sample begins in July 1933; in that way data from the beginning of the recovery are utilized, rather than from the end of the Contraction.

The signs of the coefficients accord with their theoretical expectation, that is, the money coefficients are positive and the fiscal ones negative. None of the latter is significantly different from zero.[12] The coefficients of the current and two-period-lagged growth of the money stock are significant. The summary statistics are satisfactory, though the R^2 value indicates that over 50 percent of the variation in industrial production is not accounted for by the money and budget variables. The evidence in the table thus captures the general thrust that the

TABLE 7.1.   Unit Root Statistics

Variable	Level 2 Lags	Change in Level 2 Lags	Change in Level 4 Lags
LNIIP	−1.94	−6.84*	−4.78*
LNM1FS	0.69	−5.39*	−4.32*
LNRBB	−1.84	−9.01*	−5.57*
RINT	−4.95*	−8.88*	−7.04*

*Significant to reject unit root hypothesis at 1% MacKinnon critical value of −3.49 as well as the 5% critical value of 2.89.

recovery can be understood as a response to the growth of the stock of money and that fiscal actions did not play a meaningful, quantifiably significant role in it. As such, the evidence in that regression model corroborates the mounting evidence heretofore advanced.

It could be argued that the deficits were crucial because they gave rise to increases in the stock of government securities, which banks purchased by restructuring their assets from excess reserves. Whether banks bought newly issued or extant governments is beside the point. The apparent driving force was the money stock increases. The evidence is that fiscal policy had no measurable influence on the recovery.

Since monetary growth coupled with increasing deficits can be expected to alter the real rate, it is included in the next regression. On the basis of the AIC, the number of lags is again two. The results of estimating the regression are shown in table 7.3. The signs of the coefficients of the monetary and fiscal variables accord with their theoretical

TABLE 7.2. Monetary and Fiscal Effects on Industrial Production

Variable	Coefficient (*t*-statistic)
C	−0.008
	(−2.104)
DLNIIP(−1)	0.472
	(6.185)
DLNM1F	0.628
	(3.151)
DLNM1F(−1)	0.069
	(0.337)
DLNM1F(−2)	0.476
	(2.425)
DLNRBB	−0.002
	(−0.150)
DLNRBB(−1)	−0.016
	(−1.017)
DLNRBB(−2)	−0.024
	(−1.824)
R^2	.477
Adjusted R^2	.440
Standard error of regression	.024
Sum squared residuals	.060
D.W.	1.915
AIC	−4.513

expectation, as does the negative sign of the contemporaneous real interest rate. All coefficients of the growth of the *M1* money stock coefficients are statistically significant, as they were in the previous model. None of the fiscal coefficients, current or lagged, is significantly different from zero.[13] Though it is extremely doubtful that either of these macroeconomic influences would have a quantitatively measurable impact in as few as two or so months, it turns out that the conclusions are the same when the lag structure is extended to a year, namely, that the money stock and real interest rate effects are significant and the fiscal ones are not.[14]

TABLE 7.3.   Monetary, Fiscal, and Interest Rate Effects on Industrial Production

Variable	Coefficient (*t*-statistic)
C	−09.007
	(−1.852)
DLNIIP(−1)	0.479
	(5.882)
DLNM1F	0.587
	(3.033)
DLNM1F(−1)	0.073
	(0.370)
DLNM1F(−2)	0.451
	(2.344)
DLNRBB	−0.008
	(−0.562)
DLNRBB(−1)	−0.008
	(−0.522)
DLNRBB(−2)	−0.013
	(−0.975)
RINT	−0.0004
	(−2.459)
LRINT(−1)	0.0002
	(1.270)
RINT(−2)	0.0003
	(1.774)
R^2	.525
Adjusted R^2	.476
Standard error of regression	0.024
Sum squared residuals	0.054
D.W.	2.009
AIC	−4.552

The most interesting finding was the significant negative coefficient for the real rate of interest. It was generally believed in the 1930s that interest rate declines were ineffective in stimulating investment. One of the frequently cited keys to recovery was held to be investment, but the traditional policy route by which to affect it, through interest rates, was believed to be nugatory, for two reasons. First, since rates were low, there was little room for reductions. Of more consequence, investment was widely held to be interest inelastic (Hubbard 1940).[15] The interest rates on which discussion concentrated were nominal rates, and in terms of those, there was a general consensus that interest rate considerations were so small a factor in investment decisions as to make them inconsequential, hence the interest inelasticity.

Though the model does not deal directly with the interest elasticity of investment, it does indicate that the movement of real interest rates had an empirically significant influence on the movement of the nation's output. To the extent that investment is the one of the principal magnitudes on which interest rates bear, it is one of the avenues through which the empirically identified interest rate effect would work. It is ironic that for all the attention given to fiscal policy in the literature, the movement of real interest rates appears to have more to do with recovery.

The R^2 value, though a bit larger than in the previous model, indicates nonetheless that almost 50 percent of the variation in industrial production is not accounted for by the included variables. The evidence mirrors that in the previous table; fiscal actions, in accord with postwar assessments, do not play a quantitatively significant role. The money stock and now the real interest rate appear to be the principal driving forces. Since the real rate is not influenced directly by policymakers, the apparent driving force is the growth of the money stock. As such, the evidence in the models corroborates the mounting support for the importance of the money stock's increase.

Concluding Observations

This tour through the literature on fiscal policy can be summarized succinctly: Though there was much early speculation that it was in large part responsible for the economy's return to trend, subsequent empirically based inquiries fail to detect any such influence.

It is ironic that the professional theoretical literature in the first several post-Depression decades so heavily emphasized the role and effects of fiscal policy when the empirical evaluations found so little. Paradoxically, the literature on monetary influences on the economy in those times was meager, but the actual force of those monetary impulses appears to be quite important.

Notwithstanding the importance of increases in the stock of money, there still remains about half of the adjustment to full capacity that must be explained. One possibility is the influence of the credit channel. Still another is the intrinsic dynamic of the economy, the endogenous propagation mechanism.

The next chapter addresses the credit channel. Though Fisher (1932) highlighted it as the major factor in the Contraction, it was Bernanke (1983) who brought it center stage as he stressed the importance of credit restriction in exacerbating the effects of the monetary restriction that was fundamental to the Contraction. The pertinent question is its role in the recovery. There was after all considerable interest in the banking system and its credit policies, as they may not have contributed to the recovery. In light of the extended time in which the economy operated below capacity, there was more concern that those policies may in fact have impeded recovery. In particular, we have to wonder whether "banking policies in regard to loans to business enterprise [were] a dominant reason for our inability to achieve a lasting economic recovery" (Kimmel 1939, v). Did they further strengthen the movement back to trend, or were they of little consequence?

CHAPTER 8
◄O►

Empirics of Credit Channel, Fiscal, and Monetary Effects

The credit channel and its prospective role in advancing the recovery are introduced in this chapter. Though not formally called that in the 1930s, its operation was acknowledged as banks and their lending practices were scrutinized for their likely contribution. The channel is typically regarded as ancillary to monetary actions. "The so-called credit channel . . . has been receiving a lot of research attention in recent years," Mishkin notes (1996, 1), due in large part to Ben Bernanke's (1983) finding that decreased lending by banks, because of their increased costs of credit intermediation, added to the deterioration of the economy in the Contraction—a 1930s version of a credit crunch. The intellectual inspiration was Irving Fisher and his debt-deflation hypothesis (1932, 1933a), so that it is not unusual to see it labeled Fisher-Bernanke (Calomiris and Wilson 1998, 26).[1] The Fisherian view had debtors attempting to reduce their bank borrowings, which led to a fall in deposits and therefore in the price level. This increased the real value of debts, leading to another round of attempts to reduce indebtedness, hence "The Debt-Deflation Theory of Great Depressions" (1933a).

The credit channel refers to the relationship between monetary policy as it affects bank lending and the effects of such on real economic activity. The literature identifies several avenues for credit channel mechanisms. One of the earliest theoretical bases stresses the idea that banks have a comparative advantage in certain types of credit intermediation, specifically in their "specialized evaluation and monitoring function" (Bernanke and Gertler 1987, 91). As a result, "banks provide the only available conduit between savers and certain types of investments" (1987, 90). Another emphasizes the effects on bank lending of changes in banks' capital (Calomiris and Wilson 1998). Bernanke and

Mark Gertler (1995, 40–44), Stephen Cecchetti (1995, 85–87), and Anil Kashyap and Jeremy Stein (1994, 222–52) present theoretical explications, as well as empirical evidence favorable to the hypothesis.

There are some who questioned the channel's importance, based on empirical grounds rather than theoretical frameworks. Among those advancing such evidence were Jeffrey Miron et al. (1994), Christina Romer and David Romer (1990, 1993), and Valerie Ramey (1993).

This chapter attempts to identify the extent to which the credit channel was operative in the recovery. This emphasis is based on two considerations. First, there is the evidence that the 1929–33 money stock reductions were unable to explain sufficiently the depth of the Contraction; the added role of banks in reducing the supply of credit gave a more satisfactory account. In a manner symmetric to that in the Contraction, the stimulative dimension of the bank lending channel should, therefore, be operative and discernibly important in further promoting the recovery (Romer 1992, 781 n. 54). Second, though much of the current discussion of the channel deals with the impact of monetary restriction (Cecchetti 1995, 95), the complementary case for monetary ease needs investigation. Bernanke and Mark Gertler (1989), for instance, have an economic recovery increasing the net worth of business firms, which serves to reduce the monitoring costs of banks, thereby leading to increased lending as the financing vehicle for firms' investment.

Background

A major concern in analyses of credit markets is whether the observed volume of bank loans is principally the result of loan supply or demand. The credit channel approach emphasizes the effects of banks altering the supply of loans (Peek and Rosengren 1995, 3–4). However, during the Contraction, many economists viewed the growing volume of excess reserves as evidence that the demand for loans had essentially evaporated, suggesting that there was a "shortage of borrowers."[2] If bank lending were principally determined by borrowers' decisions, the notion of a credit channel would be vacuous. There is considerable reason to be skeptical of a hypothesis in which the credit channel can be dismissed so casually. One implication would be that banks were holding neither the assets nor the composition of them they wanted—that they were passively impaled on the crucible of disequilibrium. If banks were not holding their desired array of assets, why not? Why did they not adjust? Why would they remain in a state of disequilibrium?

Another consideration relates to bank responses to the doubling of reserve requirements. Banks responded by rebuilding their excess reserves, increasing them to even higher levels. They held excess reserves rather than employing them as a basis for additional lending (Friedman and Schwartz 1963, 520–27). Hence, the sustained decline in bank loans through the first two and a half years of recovery and the sharp fall through almost two years of depression and revival in the late 1930s would be the obverse of the increased demands for excess reserves, the corollary of which is a decrease in loan supply.

A further piece of evidence is the study by C. O. Hardy and Jacob Viner on "the availability of bank credit in the Chicago Federal Reserve district in the period from the bank holiday to September 1, 1934" (Friedman and Schwartz 1963, 456–57). They conclude "that there exists a genuine unsatisfied demand . . . by solvent borrowers, [but banks' desires] to avoid a recurrence of the errors to which they attribute much of the responsibility for the . . . bank failures" led banks to raise their loan standards (1963, 457).

The National Industrial Conference Board undertook an inquiry into the availability of bank credit. The motivation was the allegation that "in the past few years it has been repeatedly stated or implied that the banks have adopted too cautious an attitude toward industrial and commercial loans. [The] restrictive banking policies retarded the upward trend in business that ended in 1937 and contributed to the sharp recession in 1937–38" (Kimmel 1939, 47). The format was a questionnaire. Of 9,000 firms, 19.5 percent responded. A fourth had no dealings with banks, most likely, Kimmel speculates, because of corporate policies—"One of the basic tenets of the financial policy of many corporations is the attainment of the highest possible degree of independence of banks and other financial institutions" (1939, 54), a questionable hypothesis. Another 12 percent reported refusals or restrictions. These were smaller firms, "concerns with capital of $500,000 or less" (1939, 141). Though no formal analysis of the refusals was undertaken, he found a substantial number of cases where the "record of earnings and current financial condition of the applicant fully justified the [negative] decision of the bank. There are other cases [that] seemed to be unjustifiable" (1939, 141). The criteria used were not indicated, so it is impossible to know if the refusals he seconded were due to the imposition of higher credit standards. Of the refusals that were "unjustifiable" in his eyes, they most likely occurred because of tighter lending standards by banks.

On balance, the survey found evidence of some credit restriction but did not uncover any substantial reduction in the availability of bank credit. Banks were essentially making the loans they thought were economically viable but with somewhat stricter standards. Bank balance sheets were in equilibrium at those levels of lending, and that equilibrium was achieved in part by making fewer loans because of self-imposed tighter lending standards.

Another piece of evidence further underscoring that loans were the result of bank lending decisions comes from the *Annual Reports* of the U.S. Office of the Comptroller of the Currency. One theme is that "strengthening the capital structure of banks" is a prime concern to bank examiners, hardly surprising given the earlier high rate of bank failure (1935, 3). Banks would be expected to be more discriminating in lending; to raise their credit standards. The concern with the condition of banks can be seen in the self-congratulatory tone of the 1937 *Annual Report*: "only eight primary charters were issued [in order to prevent] the recurrence of the over-banked condition which has been regarded as a contributing factor to the banking collapse of March 1933" (1937, 14).

Concern that the actions of bank examiners hindered the recovery led to the 1938 "Uniform Agreement on Bank Supervisory Procedures," an understanding in which the Comptroller of the Currency, Federal Reserve, and Federal Deposit Insurance Corporation agreed to subordinate traditional examination to valuation forbearance, that is, to alter examination procedures to gloss over asset and capital losses, in order "to dampen the procyclical tendencies of examiners to be critical of loan values in times of economic distress" (Simonson and Hempel 1993, 250). Bank examination thus was to be employed to bolster the effectiveness of monetary policy. To the extent that banks were viewed as responsible for the meager pace of bank loans, valuation forbearance was to be the incentive for greater lending activity. Economists at that time, Jacob Viner and George L. Bach for instance, generally supported the agreement (1993, 251). These concerns about banks not lending sufficiently aggressively add to the presumption that the behavior of loans was a supply phenomenon.

A recent contribution bearing on the credit channel is Charles Calomiris and Berry Wilson's (1998) study of member banks in New York City. The focus is on the role of a "bank capital-crunch" (1998, 7) in inducing a reduction in the supply of bank credit. The capital crunch arises because loan losses and anticipations thereof are an incentive for depositors to withdraw funds, especially the larger ones whose balances exceed the insurance coverage. This prospect induces banks to shore up their balance sheets. One avenue is the issuance of (higher-cost) capital. Another is to reduce the loan portfolio by not replacing maturing loans.

The finding was that banks pursued the latter tack: "Loans did not decline solely because of reduced opportunities for profitable lending. Banks scrambled to shed asset risk during this period, to restore their default risk to the low long-run desired level, and to avoid the high cost of issuing capital as an alternative means to reduce default-risk" (1998, 32). The relative decline in loans at banks was not due therefore to a decrease in the demand for loans. It owed to bank decisions about the structure of their assets, a key ingredient in the intermediation function central to the credit channel.

With the clear exception of the 1937–38 depression, the gathering strength of the recovery would have manifested itself in greater demands for borrowing. Yet loans fell as a percentage of earning assets (chap. 2, fig. 2.10). These considerations indicate that the observed behavior of bank loans is principally the result of bank lending actions.

Evidence

It is more likely that the excess reserves buildup reflected asset allocation decisions by banks associated with a tightening of their credit standards, the "move to quality" in banking jargon.[3] The supposition that the increased excess reserves resulted from bank decisions on the structure of their assets appears particularly plausible in the two and a quarter years following the mid-1938 trough. This was then that the rapid growth in industrial production, a 23 percent annual rate, would have sharply increased the demand for loans; excess reserves, nonetheless, increased at a 49 percent annual rate.

The credit channel focuses on business firms' borrowing to finance investment, inventory and fixed.[4] The loan category that most satisfactorily captures such lending is commercial and industrial loans. Such a series, however, does not exist for the entire recovery. What does exist is a series on aggregate loans, but that is unsatisfactory as a measure relevant to the credit channel because it includes among other things securities loans.[5]

However, it is possible to construct a commercial and industrial loans series back to September 1934, the month corresponding to the beginning of the recovery in earnest (see appendix for the details).[6] To put the loan series in real terms, the Wholesale Price Index is used. The loan series is denoted *RCI* (real commercial and industrial loans) and is used to capture the credit channel. Figure 8.1 depicts its behavior against the Index of Industrial Production (1977 = 100). *RCI* declines slightly (2 percent annual rate) through February 1936, as industrial production increases at annual rate of 21 percent. The correlation during that time is –0.57. Thereafter loans increase sharply, so that by May 1936 the correlation had risen to zero and then to 0.83 by the start of the depression a year later. Real loans continue rising well into the depression, and this is the next point to note.

While industrial production was falling 33 percent, *RCI* increased, rising 16 percent during the first half of the depression and then falling

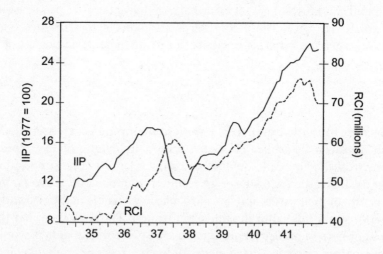

FIGURE 8.1.   Industrial production and RCI loans, September 1934–June 1942.
(Data from Board of Governors of the Federal Reserve System 1985; Board of Governors of the Federal Reserve System 1943.)

off for a net increase of 9 percent, which gives a correlation of −0.83 for the twelve months of depression. Finally, though industrial production increased by 25 percent during the first twelve months of revival, *RCI* continued falling. In June 1939, loans then climbed, reaching in July 1940 the peak attained in January 1938.

In his pathbreaking contribution, Bernanke (1983) addressed the credit channel in a variety of ways. Professional attention concentrated on a monthly model of various influences on the growth in industrial production relative to trend, denoted y_t. This was regressed on several forces, including its first two lags, several lags of the monetary innovation variable (the difference between the actual and predicted rates of growth of the $M1$ money stock), and two measures of the increased cost of credit intermediation.

Because no direct measure of bank lending relevant to the credit channel was available, proxies designed to capture the changing cost of credit intermediation effects on loan behavior were employed (specifically, the first difference in the real deposits of failed banks and the change in the real liabilities of failing businesses). These served to capture the nonmonetary financial impact of the Contraction. An increase in either would have the effect of reducing the rate of growth of industrial production.

The strategy begins by estimating a model without the two credit intermediation proxies. The model has two lagged values of y_t and the contemporaneous plus three lagged values of the monetary innovation. The results are "disappointing [because] they capture no more than half of the total [Great Contraction's] decline of output" (1983, 269). To the basic model, the two cost-of-credit-intermediation variables along with their first-order lags are added. Inclusion of the two proxies explains better the decline in industrial production, providing "at least a tentative confirmation that nonmonetary effects of the financial crisis augmented monetary effects in the short-run determination of output" (1983, 270).

The availability of the *RCI* series allows a direct test of the credit channel. To that end, the original Bernanke model is estimated. The results duplicate his, thereby providing assurance that any subsequent results could not be attributable to having employed a framework other than his.[7] To see if the credit channel is influential in boosting the rate of recovery, the basic Bernanke model is adapted by using the relevant commercial and industrial loan series rather than his two proxies.

The influence of the credit channel was investigated by including the change in the logarithm of *RCI*, denoted *DLNRCI*. The unit root in *RCI* dictated first differencing. The logarithmic change gives an approximation to the growth of lending as a factor contributing to the growth of industrial production, y_t. Since the commercial and industrial loan series was available from September 1934, first differencing gave rise to a month shorter estimation period. The percentage change in industrial production adjusted for the trend rate of growth is y_t. The monetary innovation, M_t, is estimated as the residual from a regression of the growth of $M1$ on four lagged values of itself, the growth of industrial production, and the percentage change in wholesale prices (1983, 268). The equation has low explanatory power, $R^2 = 0.176$.[8] The influence of the credit channel is captured by including *DLNRCI*. The estimates for two lags are shown in the second column of table 8.1. At six lags, the AIC is minimized. Accordingly, the results of this are shown in the third column. Bernanke's model employed three lags of the monetary innovation, M_t, and so the present one likewise uses three lags of it in column two.

The estimates mirror his; each money innovations variable has a positive coefficient, but only the contemporaneous one is statistically significant. He did not report a value for R^2 so it is not possible to compare the present one with his. With regard to the lending channel, none of the coefficients of *DLNRCI* is significantly different from zero. A Wald test of the hypothesis that the *DLNRCI* coefficients are jointly zero could not be rejected. As the six-lag regression shows, the contemporaneous monetary innovation variable is significant. Only the fourth lag of *DLNRCI* is significant, but negative, a clearly anomalous result in that there is no theory that has increased lending reducing output growth.[9] As to the overall influence of lending, the Wald test of the hypothesis that the seven *DLNRCI* coefficients are jointly zero could not be rejected. This suggests that the lending activity of banks was not sufficiently aggressive to promote recovery. An alternate interpretation is that the growth of the economy was essentially independent of the lending activity of banks.

For the Bernanke-type formulation, there does not appear to be a bank-lending channel promoting recovery. Its failure to be significant may be model-specific, or it may be that the channel, in fact, is not an economically relevant mechanism.

Still another approach to identifying the credit channel is to assess

TABLE 8.1. Estimates of Credit Channel

Variable	Coefficient (*t*-statistic)	Coefficient (*t*-statistic)
C	.003	.004
	(1.226)	(1.595)
y(t–1)	.646	.669
	(5.751)	(5.823)
y(t–2)	–0.156	–0.214
	(–1.495)	(–1.894)
M(t)	.468	.591
	(2.377)	(3.232)
M(t–1)	.206	.282
	(1.008)	(1.458)
M(t–2)	.337	.319
	(1.609)	(1.621)
M(t–3)	.008	.016
	(0.039)	(.084)
M(t–4)		.086
		(.463)
M(t–5)		.372
		(2.052)
M(t–6)		–0.156
		(–0.847)
DLNRCI(t)	–0.044	.108
	(–0.319)	(.820)
DLNRCI(t–1)	–0.170	–0.188
	(–1.115)	(–1.290)
DLNRCI(t–2)	–0.010	–0.164
	(–0.069)	(–1.082)
DLNRCI(t–3)		.174
		(1.181)
DLNRCI(t–4)		–0.459
		(–3.086)
DLNRCI(t–5)		.275
		(1.876)
DLNRCI(t–6)		–0.068
		(–0.529)
R^2	.515	.639
Adjusted R^2	.461	.557
Standard error of regression	.021	.018
Sum squared residuals	.036	.024
D.W.	1.796	2.004
AIC	–4.801	–4.498

the effects on industrial production of commercial and industrial lending, along with fiscal and monetary variables. The lag is six months. Table 8.2 reports estimates of the regression of *DLNIIP* on the current and the previous six months' *DLNRCI, DLNM1FS,* and *DLNRBB*.

The R^2 of 66 percent is significantly different from zero. A strongly significant, positive coefficient of money growth, as found in recurrent probes into the recovery, also appears here. None of the lagged coefficients is, however, significant. The commercial and industrial lending coefficients exhibit a pattern of positive and negative signs, of which none is significantly different from zero. Only the fourth lag is statistically significant but negative, the same anomalous result as in the previous table. Bank lending as assessed in this framework thus appears not to have stimulated the course of the recovery. The fiscal variable is

TABLE 8.2.   Money, Fiscal, and RCI Lending Effects on Output

Variable	Coefficient (*t*-statistic)	Variable	Coefficient (*t*-statistic)	Variable	Coefficient (*t*-statistic)
C	0.002 (0.350)				
DLNIIP(–1)	.530 (5.066)				
DLNM1F	0.734 (3.560)	DLNRCI	0.143 (0.992)	DLNRBB	0.009 (0.669)
DLNM1F(–1)	0.327 (1.438)	DLNRCI(–1)	–0.303 (–1.868)	DLNRBB(–1)	0.005 (0.376)
DLNM1F(–2)	0.240 (1.111)	DLNRCI(–2)	–0.141 (–0.857)	DLNRBB(–2)	–0.004 (–0.259)
DLNM1F(–3)	–0.168 (–0.816)	DLNRCI(–3)	0.217 (1.371)	DLNRBB(–3)	–0.005 (–0.317)
DLNM1F(–4)	–0.133 (–0.662)	DLNRCI(–4)	–0.455 (–2.873)	DLNRBB(–4)	0.014 (0.911)
DLNM1F(–5)	0.364 (1.856)	DLNRCI(–5)	0.231 (1.482)	DLNRBB(–5)	–0.012 (–0.838)
DLNM1F(–6)	–0.136 (–0.684)	DLNRCI(–6)	0.006 (0.045)	DLNRBB(–6)	0.006 (0.450)
R^2	.662				
Adjusted R^2	.546				
Standard error of regression	0.019				
Sum squared residuals	0.023				
D.W.	1.801				
AIC	–4.886				

again nugatory: none of the coefficients is remotely statistically significant.

These results provide additional evidence that the recovery seems best viewed as due to the monetary impulse rather than to the credit channel or fiscal policy. At the same time, however, the inability of the model to account more fully for the movement of industrial production indicates that there are other forces affecting output.

Another technique with which to estimate potential influences employs a polynomial distributed lag. The attraction of this approach is that the lag distribution need not be linear. Another advantage is that the net effect of the lags can be assessed, in that the sum of the lag effects and their statistical significance are calculable. The basic equation is a fourth-degree polynomial with no endpoint constraints. Again, six lags are employed.

Table 8.3 reports the results. The explanatory power is somewhat greater than 60 percent, in accord with the previous linear distributed lag approach. The monetary influence, shown in the first two columns, stands out, both in the significance of the contemporaneous and first lag effect, and importantly in the total effect. This is additional evidence of the seeming importance of monetary considerations. The striking result for lending, the third and fourth columns, is that none of the coefficients is significant. The overall effect is negative, though not statistically significant, indicating that recovery proceeded independently of lending. Fiscal policy's influence, shown in the final two columns, is nil. None of the coefficients is statistically significant, nor is the aggregate influence, as shown in the sum of the lags. This result corresponds to the evidence found earlier, namely, that there does not seem to be any evidence that federal fiscal actions promoted recovery.

This model then is further evidence that neither the credit channel nor fiscal actions can be viewed as forces useful for understanding the recovery. The growth of the money stock again shows up as being of consequence, this adding to the accumulating, indeed burgeoning, evidence of its seeming importance in the recovery.

A vector autoregression (VAR) framework is commonly used in systems of interrelated time series. It is an alternative to a structural model. It sidesteps such modeling by treating each endogenous variable in the system as a function of the lagged values of all the endogenous variables in the system. Instead of models in which the endogenous and exogenous variables are designated a priori, a VAR can be used to detect monetary, fiscal, credit channel, and other influences. A five-variable model with endogenous *DLNIIP, DLNRCI, DLNRBB, RINT,* and *DLNM1FS* is the basic framework. The typical procedure by which to detect the effect of an unanticipated change, that is, a shock, is the impulse response function (IRF). The graph of the IRF depicts the response of a variable to a shock, an innovation, in a second variable. The shock is taken as a one-standard-deviation increase. It further is customary to include a two-standard-error band around the IRF.

To capture the importance of commercial lending on industrial production, *DLNRCI* is placed first in the ordering, followed by *RINT, DLNRBB, DLNM1FS,* and lastly by *DLNIIP.* An IRF in the positive quadrant indicates a positive response to the shock. If the operation of the credit channel stimulated the recovery, the impulse response func-

TABLE 8.3.   Polynomial Distributed Lag Estimates of Money, Fiscal, and RCI Lending Effects on Output

Variable	Coefficient (*t*-statistic)	Variable	Coefficient (*t*-statistic)	Variable	Coefficient (*t*-statistic)
C	-0.002 (-0.473)				
DLNIIP(-1)	0.486 (4.617)				
DLNM1FS	0.673 (3.303)	*DLNRCI*	0.036 (0.262)	*DLNRBB*	0.005 (0.359)
DLNM1FS(-1)	0.455 (2.193)	DLNRCI(-1)	-0.171 (-1.517)	*DLNRBB(-1)*	0.013 (0.657)
DLNM1FS(-2)	0.067 (0.418)	*DLNRCI(-2)*	-0.122 (-1.583)	*DLNRBB(-2)*	0.008 (0.397)
DLNM1FS(-3)	-0.144 (-0.879)	*DLNRCI(-3)*	-0.047 (-0.512)	*DLNRBB(-3)*	-0.000 (-0.010)
DLNM1FS(-4)	-0.085 (-0.602)	*DLNRCI(-4)*	-0.041 (-0.559)	*DLNRBB(-4)*	-0.007 (-0.370)
DLNM1FS(-5)	0.078 (.448)	*DLNRCI(-5)*	-0.062 (-0.547)	*DLNRBB(-5)*	-0.011 (-0.663)
DLNM1FS(-6)	-0.077 (-0.401)	*DLNRCI(-6)*	0.066 (0.522)	*DLNRBB(-6)*	-0.019 (-1.420)
Sum of lags	0.967 (2.318)		-0.339 (-1.460)		-0.011 (-0.140)
R^2	.608				
Adjusted R^2	.518				
Standard error regression	0.019				
Sum squared residuals	0.026				
D.W.	1.840				
AIC	-4.875				

tion would lie there. This is the expected result if the credit channel is an avenue spurring recovery. Should the IRF coincide with the horizontal axis, the variable upon which the shock is acting would be unaffected by the innovation. This would be the case if the lending operations of banks did not stimulate the recovery. An IRF in the negative quadrant signals a deterioration in the rate of recovery, an anomalous result for which there is no theoretical basis. It may be regarded as akin to the more recent price puzzle wherein federal funds rate innovations lead to increases in inflation.

The resulting IRFs are shown in figure 8.2.[10] To highlight the most interesting results, the five IRFs dealing with the responses of *DLNIIP* are shown, rather than all twenty-five (five for each of the five variables). The variables' ordering is of no consequence, in that the conclusions are unaltered by alternative orderings, including reversing. The upper-left graph portrays the influence on output of a shock to *DLNRCI*. The most prominent feature is that none of the responses is significant; none is more than two standard errors away from the zero response line. The string of twenty-four nonsignificant responses is further evidence that the activities of banks contributed essentially nothing to the recovery. This may be interpreted as banks impeding recovery in that they acted as a drag on its pace, a result in agreement with the views of many, and the basis for the 1938 "Uniform Agreement on Bank Supervisory Procedures" among the regulatory agencies. The present finding extends Bernanke's conclusion about bank actions exacerbating the Contraction in that their actions carried over to the recovery.

The second graph in the first row shows the IRF for an innovation of the real interest rate. The output response is significantly negative through the first two periods, after which it is insignificant. That an increase in the real interest rate should dampen output growth is the expected result, but not one in which policy in the 1930s had much faith. There was widespread dismissal of interest rate effects. One reason for the skepticism is that analyses concentrated on movements of nominal rather than real rates of interest.[11] The VAR evidence stands in sharp contrast to the rhetoric of those times.

The behavior of industrial production exposed to a fiscal shock is shown on the last graph in the first row. The IRF hovers around the zero line and is never significant. Output is not at all significantly affected by a fiscal shock.

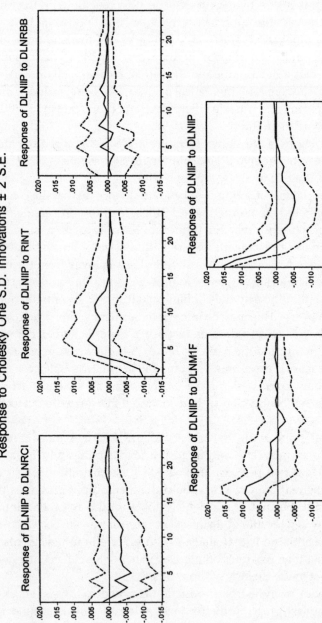

FIGURE 8.2. Impulse response functions for money supply, fiscal policy, RCI loans, and real interest on industrial production. October 1934–June 1942.

The importance of the monetary impulse is apparent in the first graph in the second row. The IRF lies with two exceptions in the positive quadrant and is significantly positive for the first three months, clear evidence that the growth of the money stock appears to have a marked positive effect on the course of industrial production. The final graph shows the usual, expected behavior of the adjustment of a variable to a shock to itself. From an initial large deviation, the movement back is damped.

Concluding Observations

The principal focus of the chapter was an inquiry into the role of the credit channel. Inasmuch as it had been identified as a factor exacerbating the Contraction, it was natural to inquire into its role in the recovery. Was there room for it as a transmission route, as a mechanism whereby banks due to their comparative advantage in assessing and monitoring loans extended credit to business firms who in turn used the proceeds to finance their real activities?

In the various frameworks investigated, no evidence was uncovered suggesting that increased accommodation of firms by banks stimulated the growth of output. The reduced pace of lending was due to banks striving to improve their balance sheets, perhaps on their own account but surely also in response to examination pressures by regulators. An understanding of the factors responsible for the recovery would not, therefore, include the credit channel as a positive influence. In not accommodating certain kinds of borrowers, banks more likely served to draw out rather than accelerate the recovery. As such, the credit channel operated in the recovery much in the manner that Bernanke first identified in the Contraction, where it intensified the economy's decline. In the recovery, it appeared to prolong the adjustment of an apparent monetary-driven move back to trend.

The return to trend similarly was not due to federal fiscal actions. In the several models in which it appeared, it failed to be a significant factor promoting recovery, a result fully concordant with the previous assessments of it.

Similarly, the evidence adduced here adds further support to the view that the recovery was apparently due to monetary influences, which were more pervasive than those of the growth of the stock of money alone (though that was of marked consequence). Of particular note is the significant response of output to declining real interest rates. This finding is at variance with widely held beliefs about the inefficacy of interest rate effects. Neither "specialness" of banks in providing credit to particular classes of borrowers nor fiscal action was a factor.

That the recovery was driven by the growth of the gold-flow induced money stock appears to be a robust conclusion. Yet, there are some reservations as to its seeming dominance. For example, no matter what the empirical model, there remains a substantial movement of industrial production for which there is no explanation. Of more consequence is the anomalous behavior of the price level in the twenty-seven months following the trough of the 1937–38 depression, in which prices fell while industrial production and the quantity of money grew rapidly. This suggests that other influences were operating to move the economy along the path to full recovery, and that is the subject of the next chapter.

Appendix

The data on commercial and industrial loans are constructed from *Banking and Monetary Statistics* (1943, 148–62), "Weekly Reporting Member Banks in 101 Leading Cities, Principal Assets and Liabilities," and *Banking and Monetary Statistics* (1976, 160–64), "Assets and Liabilities, Member Banks." The series begins in September 1934 "when the weekly [bank] reports were considerably expanded" (1943, 128). From then until December, 1937, the series is monthly averages of Wednesday figures for the category "Other loans to *customers*" (emphasis added), a series that "provided for the first time [data] composed largely of loans for commercial, industrial, and agricultural purposes" (1943, 128). These loans average 44 percent of total loans for the period. They do not include "loans to brokers and dealers in securities" (12.8 percent), "loans to others on securities" (24.2 percent), and "real estate" loans (13.3 percent).

This series is spliced to one resulting from the May 1937 revision of the bank reporting form. The new series is designated "Commercial, industrial, and agricultural" loans. To this is added "Open market paper," the reason being that data for "Commercial, industrial, and agricultural loans" for the overlap year 1941 from *Banking and Monetary Statistics* (1976) are identical to the 1941 data from the *Banking and Mon-*

etary Statistics (1943) volume when such "Open market paper" is added to the 1943 volume's series on "Commercial, industrial, and agricultural loans."

For 1942, the data are monthly averages of weekly figures of the series "Commercial, Industrial, and Agricultural" loans. The overlap year, 1941, establishes that the monthly averages of the weekly reports in the *Banking and Monetary Statistics* (1976) volume are the monthly data of member banks in *Banking and Monetary Statistics* (1943); that is, "open market paper" is included in "commercial, industrial, and agricultural loans."

CHAPTER 9

◄○►

Endogenous Propagation to Trend

The previous chapters emphasized aggregate demand mechanisms. They looked at the relative importance of monetary, fiscal, and credit channel impulses, as reflected increasingly in the postwar literature and as gleaned from extant theory and available evidence in the 1930s. The chapters treated the recovery in terms of conventional macroeconomic aggregate demand mechanisms, an understandable approach much in line with the predilections of current-day economists.[1] The evidence supported the burgeoning literature that holds as central the growth of the quantity of money.

The money stock growth was not due to Federal Reserve actions. It resulted initially from the 1933 devaluation and then to the continuing inflow of gold from Europe, due largely to the anxieties over the growing threat of the National Socialists.[2]

According to this interpretation, the recovery owes its existence to two exogenous developments, one domestic, the other foreign. The domestic one is "the establishment of a new policy regime" on the part of the Roosevelt administration, signaled by rising prices as key to the initiation of recovery (Temin and Wigmore 1990, 484). The difficulty with this is that it stands in marked contrast to the price experience of the revival from the late-1930s depression. How could rising prices in the 1933 turnaround be fundamental to the recovery but not in the more vigorous later recovery, when prices actually fell? The exogenous foreign development has the continuation of the recovery due to events in Europe. There is little intrinsic to the U.S. economy that contributed. Presumably, had there been no continuing inflow of gold raising the monetary base and money stock, the economy would have languished until the demands of World War II made their impact. Is it true therefore that there would have been little recovery for almost seven years except for the brewing, adventitious German vagaries that were to become World War II? In other words, to put it in brutally frank terms, would there have been no recovery had there been no Adolf Hitler?[3]

This chapter cautions against a near unequivocal, unabridged acceptance of the monetary understanding of the recovery. It instead considers the role of forces inherent in the economy that move it to its natural rate of expansion, toward its trend rate of output growth. In the parlance of the finance literature, this means that the economy displays mean-reversion, a tendency to adjust toward its trend rate of output. Thus, when the economy is below trend, in fact well below as the United States was in the Depression, the most likely direction is not a further deviation, but rather a movement toward the rising trend, that is, a regression toward the mean.

In contrast to mean-reversion in financial markets, where stock market valuations differing from fundamental values lead to price adjustments toward the levels based on fundamentals, mean-reversion in economics is asymmetric. As in the Depression, the economy could be below its capacity trend rate of growth; hence mean-reversion implies moving up to trend. The trend rate of growth however represents an upper bound to the economy's potential, one determined by its effective resources, technological state, and techniques of organization of those. As such it is not possible to be above the ceiling of maximum feasible output.[4] Accordingly, the notion of mean-reversion refers not to a symmetrical phenomenon of reverting back to trend, whether from above or below. It instead relates to moving up toward the trend rate of output.

The factors determining the trend rate of growth lie in the province of growth theory. Among the key factors identified in that literature are population growth, technological advance, physical and human capital accumulation—knowledge, especially learning-by-doing—and openness of markets. The manner in which these interact to promote (and increase) the trend rate of growth is the proper subject matter of that theory. That growth is associated with these factors is not really in question. It is the particulars of the interaction of these, and perhaps other factors, that remain to be understood; as of now, those are still the subject of intensive inquiry. What is clear is that no one of these is susceptible to being affected in any significant manner by short-run developments.[5]

Built-In Adjustment

The suggestion that the economy has a built-in tendency to adjust to trend would have been thoroughly discounted if not outright ridiculed in the 1930s. It would have been viewed at best as not meaningful but more likely as utterly wrong. The persistence of unemployment, buttressed by tales of "riding the rails," as well as the 1937–38 depression would have been regarded as prima facie evidence discrediting any natural rebound hypothesis. The literature after all was replete with theories of underemployment equilibrium, low-level equilibrium employment traps, and secular stagnation. The widespread despair about (ever) operating near full capacity was an important factor in the increased interest in planning as an alternative to the market system, whether in the ways envisioned by Rexford Tugwell (1932) or by adoption of an alternative economic system, what James Rogers called state capitalism (1938, 6–8). And this skepticism about the likely inability of a market economy adjusting toward trend continued into the postwar years, as evidenced by the economists' rapid and almost complete adoption of the Keynesian model with its highly elastic money demand and relatively inelastic expenditure functions, these emphasizing the likelihood of deficient aggregate demand. It was this that judicious use of fiscal policy was to fill. And it was the search for such uses that prompted economists' research, as reported in the substantial fiscal policy literature.

The notion of mean-reversion became prominent in the past fifteen or so years, largely the result of the pioneering work of Eugene Fama and Kenneth French (1988) and James Poterba and Lawrence Summers (1988). Those investigations concentrated on formal empirical testing employing modern time-series techniques, spurred by the fundamental work of Charles Nelson and Charles Plosser (1982). Whether stock prices display mean-reverting propensities is still an unsettled question. What is interesting is that those who find mean-reversion do so on the basis of empirical results.[6]

At much the same time that financial economists investigated mean-reversion, other economists devoted attention to its relation to the macroeconomy. Illustrative of this is work by John Cochrane (1988), J. Bradford DeLong and Lawrence Summers (1988), Ben Bernanke and Martin Parkinson (1989), and Milton Friedman (1993), each of whom identified a tendency for the economy to revert to its trend rate of growth.[7] Two studies that argued for mean-reversion in the recovery were DeLong and Summers (1988) and Bernanke and Parkinson (1989). The former concentrated on output while the latter's interest was employment. Cochrane and Friedman did not offer comments relating specifically to the recovery.

DeLong and Summers investigated whether postwar aggregate demand policies resulted in a difference between the experience of the pre-Depression (1889–1929) and postwar (1947–87) years. Their procedure was to examine the time-series behavior of output.[8] They drew implications for the economy on the basis of econometric time-series tests. There were no considerations of the influence of different policy initiatives in either of the periods; neither was there room for the likelihood of different shocks to the economy. They concluded that aggregate demand policies had stabilized output in the postwar period: "recent macroeconomic performance has been good. . . . [There has been] a sizable relative improvement in performance since World War II" (1988, 470).

This was contentious. Christina Romer argued, "They provide no evidence that stabilization policy is what actually accounts for any stabilization that we observe. Policy could have stabilized the economy. But it is also possible that shocks to the economy could have been different in the two periods" (1988, 486).[9]

They found that the pre-Depression period "shows strong signs that fluctuations . . . were as a rule transitory; it is possible to reject the null hypothesis that there was a sizable unit root in output" (1988, 452). In other words, the pre-Depression period exhibited a business cycle. The evidence for the postwar period was the converse: "there has been an improvement in macroeconomic performance—a reduction in the size of the transitory components in output—since World War II" (1988, 454).

The Depression fell between the two periods. Such a gap did not go unnoticed. The strategy used to understand it was to calculate the probability of the actual movement of output in the Depression if it followed a random walk. On the basis of probabilities of 1 percent or less, they opted for a mean-reversion explanation: "The low probabilities of such a recovery argue against the random walk hypothesis and so favor a model of mean reversion" (1988, 468). The recovery "is particularly striking given that so many of the mechanisms that economists rely on to produce hysteresis [the dependence of an equilibrium upon initial conditions] were at work during the Depression. Net capital formation [for instance] was nil" (1988, 469). Accordingly, the recovery was best viewed as a rebound due to the inherent dynamics of the economy: "The substantial degree of mean reversion . . . is evidence that shocks to output are transitory" (1988, 467).[10] The mechanisms involved in reverting to trend were not suggested.

Bernanke and Parkinson argue that the "self-correcting tendencies of the 1930s economy were probably much stronger than is generally acknowledged" (1989, 210). The basis for this is an error-correction employment model whose estimates indicate employment adjusts quite rapidly. The formal structure of the model has as the key link the change in employment related to the gap between normal full employment and actual employment; there are other variables in the framework, such as unanticipated inflation, but these are not of interest at present.[11] The critical consideration is the estimate of the coefficient of the employment gap. Given an unanticipated increase in unemployment, "the economy is estimated to make up over half of the difference between actual and full employment in the first three quarters after the shock" (1989, 211); this is a quite rapid rate of adjustment and is the basis for their assertion about the strength of the recovery's self-correcting tendencies. The particular avenues on which the much stronger than generally acknowledged "self-correcting tendencies of the 1930s economy" (1989, 210) traveled were not singled out, but their existence was not in doubt.

The previous studies deal directly with the 1930s. The following are concerned with ferreting out reversion tendencies by examining much longer periods. John Cochrane "reexamines the long-run properties of [the logarithm of real per capita] GNP" for 1869 through 1986 (1988, 893). He calculates the variance of growing differences between observations, where the differences range from one to thirty years, concluding "that GNP does, in fact, revert toward a 'trend' following a shock. However, that reversion occurs over a time horizon characteristic of business cycles—several years at least" (1988, 893). Thus, "annual growth rates of GNP contain a large temporary component. . . . [T]he pattern . . . is consistent with a deterministic trend, which has *no* permanent or random walk component, and whose fluctuations are entirely temporary" (1988, 898). The evidence accordingly has output moving slowly toward its trend value. To capture this visually, he presents a graph of the logarithm of real per capita GNP over 1869 through 1986. It "looks as if it has a [linear] trend in it. Fluctuations occur [the sharpest being in the Great Depression] but the level of the series always returns to the 'trend line'" (1988, 898–99).[12]

Milton Friedman (1993) also used long-run data to construct a "plucking model" framework suggested by empirical regularities.

> Output is viewed as bumping along the ceiling of maximum feasible output except that every now and then it is plucked down by a cyclical contraction. . . . When subsequent recovery sets in, it tends to return output to the ceiling; it cannot go beyond, so there is an upper limit to output and the amplitude of the expansion tends to be correlated with the amplitude of the contraction. (1993, 172)

His approach does not employ more recent time-series techniques. Rather, it uses traditional correlation and graphic analyses.

The physical analogy is that of a string secured to the underside of a board. When plucked, it is further below the underside than when at rest. Having been plucked, it rebounds, but clearly it cannot go above the board. The vigor of the rebound is related to the strength of the pluck. The economy is viewed likewise.

The basis for the "plucking model" conjecture was a study of the serial correlation of the amplitude of several series from 1879 to 1961: "the results were striking. . . . [T]he correlation was trivial between the amplitude of an expansion and the amplitude of the succeeding contraction. On the other hand . . . the correlation was high and statistically significant between the amplitude of a contraction and the amplitude of the succeeding expansion" (1993, 171). When data for 1961 to 1988 were examined "they did not contradict the asymmetrical correlation pattern," though none of the correlations was statistically significant (173). Visual examination of the rates of change provided "much stronger evidence connected with the 'plucking model'" (173).

The insight is that whatever causes a downturn, the economy rebounds with much the same vigor as in the decline. Thus, sharp, deep contractions are followed by vigorous recoveries and mild ones by less robust revivals. Asymmetry comes to play in that no such relationship holds for contractions following expansions.

The relevance of the "plucking model" for the recovery is that the movement back to trend appears to be a normal reaction. For Friedman, the principal "plucker" is a reduction in the rate of growth of the M_2 money stock, an aggregate demand orientation. Likewise, the likely prime mover in the rebound is the aggregate demand stimulus of the monetary impulse. But the late-1930s revival cannot be satisfactorily understood in terms of the behavior of aggregate demand. Though increases in the behavior of the money stock seem to be of importance, that does not imply that other forces are not at work.

It is a frightfully difficult undertaking to isolate the independent effects of a variable. There are the many short-term influences that buffet the actual course of output, including monetary and fiscal actions, white-noise supply and demand changes radiating from the international and domestic sectors, and lagged effects from earlier policy innovations. In addition, the normal evolution of output has interrelated movements of policy and private-sector variables that secondarily influence its short-term behavior, so that disentangling their collective, commingled influence from the forces responsible for output's independent, "exogenous" movements adds to the difficulty.

An attempt at disentangling the influences of the individual forces is thornier in normal times, when there is relatively little variation in the variables, as they tend to march in step. As an early exponent of this problem asserted, the "major defect of the data on which economists must rely . . . is the small range of variation they encompass. In consequence, it is difficult to disentangle systematic effects from random variation since both are of much the same order of magnitude" (Friedman 1952, 612). Accordingly, "data for wartime [and other extraordinary] periods are peculiarly valuable. At such times, violent changes in major economic magnitudes occur over relatively brief periods, thereby providing precisely the kind of evidence that we would like to get by 'critical' experiments if we could conduct them" (612).

One of the salient reasons for the fascination with the Depression is its extreme pathology—its "violent changes in major economic magnitudes." There is then understandable intellectual appeal to studying it. There also is a greater likelihood of observing events outside the normal range of experience. This makes examination of the decade unusually valuable. It is from the understanding of outlier events that economists can arrive at an enhanced, richer knowledge of the economy's workings.

Understanding Deflationary Revival

Recall that in the twenty-seven months following the spring 1938 trough, industrial production increased 58 percent and the $M1$ money stock 36 percent. Wholesale prices, however, fell 7 percent.[13] As through the entire recovery, the source of the rising money stock was gold, with Federal Reserve credit remaining essentially unchanged.[14] This is summarized in figure 9.1.[15] The graph is divided into two sections, representing the periods immediately before and after the beginning of the European war. The correlation coefficients refer to the relation between the money stock and industrial production for the entire period and between wholesale prices and the quantity of money in each of the periods surrounding the outbreak of the war. There is a close link between money and output, and a significant negative one between money and prices.

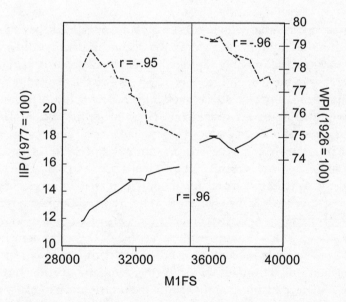

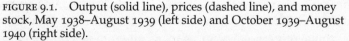

FIGURE 9.1.   Output (solid line), prices (dashed line), and money stock, May 1938–August 1939 (left side) and October 1939–August 1940 (right side).
(Data from Friedman and Schwartz 1963; Board of Governors of the Federal Reserve System 1985; *Federal Reserve Bulletin*, various issues.)

The revival from the depression with its uncommon, surprising, indeed counterintuitive, movements of prices, money, and output provides a particularly valuable opportunity for study. The conventional view is that increases in the stock of money raise prices and output, at least when it is below trend.

The suggestion was made that the immediate years of revival could not be understood as due either to supply or demand shocks. Instead, it was attributable to a combination of an increase in the demand for money relative to the expanding stock of it, which would have caused prices to decline, and to forces inherent in the economy pushing it toward its trend value, what here is called "endogenous propagation," in the sense that forces endogenous to the economy interact to generate movement toward its trend rate of output.

Why Prices Fell When Money and Output Increased

The present concern is with understanding the puzzling behavior in the top half of the figure, which shows the decline in prices as the money stock increased reasonably rapidly. The explanation revolves around an increase in the demand for money relative to the expanding quantity, that is, a fall in velocity, as shown in chapter 6, figure 6.2. Associated with that figure is a discussion of reasons for the decline. The following expands a bit on that.

The puzzlement comes because the normal expectation is that velocity would increase as a result of the revival's rising income. One reason it did not, why the demand for money increased in excess of what might be expected, is the sharpness of the 1937–38 depression. In the minds of many, its severity conjured up fears of the not-so-long-past Contraction, which would result in an increase in the demand for money (as had previously happened). The depression may also have "confirmed" in the minds of many the transiency of the recovery, thereby reinforcing uncertainties about the future, and especially about the durability of any recovery. It was not only the seeming transiency, but of more consequence, the increasingly likely view that the economy was permanently mired in a less-than-full-employment state, a situation captured in the popular and professional literature and reinforced by the just-experienced sharp depression (Hansen 1939; Lange 1939). After all, it was going on ten years since satisfactory economic conditions existed. Still another factor increasing the demand for money relates to the understandable tendency in the 1930s to identify declining prices as synonymous with bad times, a direct consequence of the 1929–33 fall in prices.[16] In a symmetrical fashion, there would be the propensity to associate improving economic circumstances with rising prices.[17] With prices falling during the yearlong depression, many individuals would translate that into an omen of future difficulties; hence they would have increased their demands for money. Finally, the deflation would have led to expectations of further price declines, an incentive to increase money demands.

Endogenous Propagation of Output

The behavior of output during this extraordinary postdepression period can best be understood in terms of the tendency for it to return to its trend path: its predisposition to revert in an "exogenous-like" manner to its normal growth path, that is, as behavior summarized by a mean-reversion thrust. The economy is viewed as containing within itself mechanisms that endogenously propagate output movements toward trend.

The forces making for the trend growth of output are the proper focus of the study of economic growth, where a key consideration deals with identifying forces relevant to determining that trend rate, the equilibrium path along which the economy travels. An important related question is whether and to what extent differing intensities of any of the factors affecting the growth rate may also increase it. Questions relating to likely mechanisms operating when the economy is, say, below its trend potential typically lie outside the exploration of economic growth. While this may be analytically convenient, it should not distort the fact that the economic system is not so bifurcated. There is no growth sector and no cycle sector. The economy's movements are the result of the interaction of the extant forces. The theory of growth concentrates on the ability of the society to produce more efficiently, a supply orientation. The data used to measure growth come from the market observations in which aggregate supply and demand forces interact, and not from aggregate supply alone, which in fact is unob-

servable. Growth observations thus imply that the increased productive potential must have had as a corollary increased income and
spending.

One of the remarkable developments for which more than a hundred years of data are available relates to the growth of the U.S. economy, which John Cochrane characterizes as "fluctuations occur but the
level of the series always returns to the 'trend line'" (1988, 898–99). Figure 9.2 updates Cochrane's real per capita output data to the present. It
depicts the logarithm of per capita real GNP (in chained 1996 prices),
along with its logarithmic linear trend.[18] The data are taken from Louis
Johnson and Samuel Williamson (2002). The actual series is well
approximated by the trend. The economy returns to trend following
any deviation from it, as noted by Cochrane.

Growth represents continual increases in productive capacity, an
aggregate supply phenomenon. For the 133 years recorded in the figure, growth occurs at a rate of almost 2 percent per annum. The upward
progress of real per capita income is the result of the successful implementation of prospective improvements in the ability to produce, these
deriving in large part from growth in human capital. How those poten-

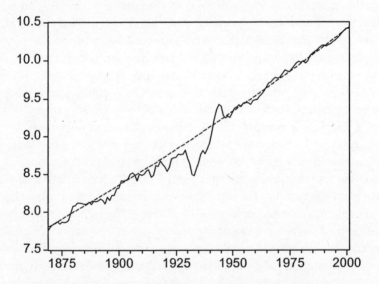

FIGURE 9.2.   Log of real per capita GNP and linear logarithmic
trend, 1869–2001.
(Data from Johnson and Williamson 2002.)

tial developments get realized is part of the mystery of growth.[19] Education, for example, is one of the influences most highly regarded as critical to growth. How does it in fact operate to enhance productivity and growth? What is the behavioral pattern that leads from increased education to innovations in production and product development, other than through the sobriquet "learning to think"? To uncover those avenues and processes is to find the Holy Grail of growth. The response of agents to the incentives and opportunities inherent in those prospective improvements is also what drives endogenous propagation.

The data in figure 9.2 are based on market observations in which both aggregate supply and demand are involved. Aggregate demand thus must have been increasing at least at the same rate as aggregate supply. What is it about aggregate demand that keeps it increasing with the growth in productive capacity, the effect of which has the economy tending to operate at the growth trend? The argument is that it is the forces of endogenous propagation that generate income sufficient to absorb the increasing output, and it is in this sense that the tendency of the economy to operate at trend is evidence of it. The documentation of continued growth is itself a manifestation of the forces of endogenous propagation. This occurs in the same way in which those forces moved the economy back to trend during the recovery, as exemplified in particular during the revival when prices were falling.

As a general matter, the resilient mechanisms that generate reversion-to-trend behavior appear to be rooted in the dynamics of an enterprise economy—the incentives, opportunities, and flexibilities in such a system. They are intrinsic to a market-based economy, such that a deviation from the equilibrium trend brings on as a matter of course economic responses that induce the economy toward its trend rate of movement. In other words, when the economy is below trend, there is what may be regarded as an endogenous propagation mechanism in the economy. The constituent particulars of it, the sources of it, are not however so easily observed, measured, or modeled.

This suggests a kind of black box, one in which there is no formally articulated mechanism generating the movement to trend. But that is not unique to the present case. That one must plead ignorant to likely, tractable adjustment responses that underlie adjustments to trend, that is, to those responses encapsulated in the endogenous propagation mechanism, is not unique to macroeconomics. In analyses of mean-reversion in the stock market, there similarly is no framework in which adjustment processes mitigating deviations of prices from their fundamental values are understood. The paradigmatic pricing model is that of efficient markets in which information relevant to a stock is quickly encapsulated in the stock's price. Hence, if there are forces leading to a rise in the stock above its fundamental value, there would be immediate selling, pushing the price down; thus, there could not be mean-reversion in the efficient markets framework. But then, if prices reflect bubbles, what is it that brings them down? In other words, there is in stock markets an absence of understanding of forces making for mean-reversion, similar to that in the economy.[20]

Illustrative of the absence of likely adjustment processes is the fact that none of the studies pointing to a return to trend suggests what any such mechanisms are, much less what any of their particulars might be. Neither DeLong and Summers nor Bernanke and Parkinson even hint at any likely mechanisms, nor of course does Cochrane. Theirs are econometric studies whose concern is with isolating empirical patterns, not with investigating rationales for the underlying behavior.

Though Friedman similarly disavows a formal underpinning for his empirical findings, he implicitly indicates that the robustness of the rebound from the sharpness of the previous decline may be due to the vigorousness of the growth of the money stock. Such an explanation, however, cannot hold in the present case because a rebound owing to increases in the quantity of money is an aggregate demand action, the effects of which raise rather than lower prices. Whatever the particular nature of the individual adjustment channels, they nonetheless are present and operative. How else to account for the observed tendency to move back to trend, particularly when the widely adopted aggregate demand approach cannot provide a satisfactory explanation?

This interpretation serves as a distinct historical lesson that complements DeLong and Summers's inquiry. It represents a historical case whose behavior exemplifies the process they identified; that is, the first two-plus-year period of revival adds well-grounded credibility to their empirical results. The conundrum posed by the revival's evolution of money, prices, and output can be understood in terms of their mean-reversion conclusion.

One of their principal conclusions was that "shocks to output are transitory," and so the economy's evolutions during the Depression "favor a model of mean reversion" (1988, 467–68). Because their study dealt with the time-series properties of output, they abstained from relating their findings to any historical episode. The interesting thing about the postdepression deflation period was that it constituted a case in point exemplifying mean-reversion, to which their results led. This movement toward trend was not the result of any aggregate demand policy impulse; it occurred as a result of the internal dynamics of an economy that was not operating at its trend capacity growth rate.

To the extent there is a framework holding promise for understanding adjustment paths intrinsic to the endogenous propagation mechanism, it appears to be in the realm of real business cycle theory (Prescott 1986a; Plosser 1989). In this, individuals are treated as optimizing agents reacting intra- and intertemporally to shocks, with technology shocks—a supply shock—being the most popular example.[21] The behavior of individuals gives rise to a particular rate of growth and to convergence to that trend. In addition, and this is the key focus of the theory, the intertemporal substitution among work effort, leisure, output, saving, and investment decisions generates cyclical movements that converge to the trend growth path.[22] Whether that theory is the key to understanding the mechanisms of endogenous propagation is not certain, but it appears to be a promising, leading line of inquiry.

The idea of adjustment to trend is largely a product of recent investigations of time-series properties of economic variables and of economic growth, though there were hints of the latter in the 1930s, particularly in the work on business cycles (Angell 1941). The notion of trend implies the tendency to operate neither systematically above nor below but at the trend value, with the economy having a self-correcting tendency in which there is a kind of built-in mechanism inducing economic actions that move the economy toward trend, what here is called endogenous propagation.[23]

Analytically, it is useful to think of two systems at work. One deals with factors influencing the trend growth rate. These are essentially exogenous to policy in the short run, though policy may and certainly is intended to affect them over the long haul. The other is concerned with the economy as it is below trend. It has within its purview various short-run adjustment avenues that give rise to endogenous propagation.[24]

There is strong historical precedent for the notion of "exogenous-like" forces affecting output. One case for which there are reasonably satisfactory data is the U.S. experience during the greenback period of 1867–79, the time between the return to normalcy after the Civil War

and the resumption of the gold standard. In this period, prices fell at a
3.5 percent annual rate. The stock of money—fiat greenback currency
plus deposits—increased 1.1 percent annually, and velocity fell 1 percent annually.[25] All the while, output increased reasonably rapidly, at
an annual rate of 3.6 percent.[26] Note that output rose while prices
declined. In addition, the fall in prices was due to the relative increase
in the demand for money, that is, to a decline in velocity. This is the
same behavior that can be seen in the revival from the late-1930s
depression.

An understandable, even natural, penchant is to inquire into developments making for such an increase in output, especially since it
occurred when prices were declining. The purpose is to seek a "cause,"
to make sense of observed changes. In this case, the growth in output
was apparently due to the existence of several "exogenous" factors, the
growth of population and perhaps the expansion of railroads. As Friedman and Schwartz put it, "there can be little doubt that [the 1867–79 sit-
uation] reflects primarily a rise in output" (1963, 34). The respective
evolutions of the demand and stock of money influenced prices, with
rising "exogenously determined" income increasing the demand for
money relative to its quantity.

A more striking pattern occurred from 1879 through 1897.[27] In 1879,
the United States returned to the gold standard. From then until 1897,
there were five cycles, including of course the famous banking panic of
1893. Both velocity and prices declined during this eighteen-year
period, the former at the remarkably large rate of almost 3 percent per
annum and the latter by a bit more than 1 percent annually. At the same
time, the money stock increased 6 percent annually while output rose
nearly 4 percent. In contrast to 1867 through 1879, there did not appear
to be any readily identifiable driving forces.

The anomalous behavior of prices and output led Friedman and
Schwartz to conclude that "generally declining or generally rising
prices had little impact on the rate of growth. . . . [T]he forces making
for economic growth over the course of several business cycles are
largely independent of the secular trend of prices" (1963, 93). For them,
the independent forces generating economic growth were fundamental
to determining the trend rate of growth, a rate that is virtually impossible to detect over a short span of time.

In the two and a quarter years of revival following the late-1930s
depression, there is little doubt that the United States was operating

well below trend. Neither aggregate demand nor supply shock explanations are satisfactory frameworks in which to understand the recovery of output while prices were falling.

The model that can explain the course of the revival has as a driving influence the endogenous propagation mechanisms; the movement toward trend is due neither to the behavior of the stock of money nor to a more expansionary fiscal policy due to the increasingly darker war clouds nor to any increasingly vigorous lending activity of banks. That is, there are no dominant, overarching demand shocks.

Similarly, there was not a fortuitous run of positive supply shocks pushing the economy toward trend while at the same time pushing prices down. The archetypical anecdotal accounts deal with demand influences, of which the most popular is that the revival was due to government expenditures relating to the war, both the buildup and the actual conflict, the notion that "World War II got us out of the Depression."[28] Typical of this sentiment is Thomas Hall and David Ferguson: "Therefore, the Great Depression was ended by an enormous stimulus to aggregate demand caused by a combination of rapid monetary growth beginning in 1938 and, later, the U.S. defense buildup and increased orders for war materiel from Great Britain" (1998, 155–56).[29]

What appears to have happened is that the economy moved of its own accord. This may be regarded as a sequential run of supply shocks, but only in the definitional sense of regarding endogenous propagation adjustments as such a sequence.

There are two parts to the resolution of how to explain strongly rising output when the stock of money is increasing at the same time that prices are falling. The first concentrates on velocity decreases stemming from an increased desire to hold money in excess of what was being supplied, which served to move prices down. The second is a movement of output back to trend, spawned by the endogenous propagation responses that come into play when the economy is not operating at trend. In other words, the forces of endogenous propagation are responsible for mean-reversion. In summary, there is heavier emphasis on the fall in velocity as the reason for the decline in prices in the face of rising output and greater emphasis on the return to trend as the driving element in the increase in output.

If this is correct, and it is difficult to arrive at an alternative framework, then it follows that analyses of business cycles should devote relatively more attention to the forces of endogenous propagation, difficult as they are to identify, and less to the traditional monetary, fiscal, and shocks approaches.

The two-plus-year experience following the May 1938 trough was exceptional in that it revealed the effects of the workings of the internal adjustment mechanisms of the economy. Those mechanisms were operative throughout the recovery; they did not suddenly make their appearance only in the late 1930s. It was however in that revival that the effects of their influence were to be seen. Conventional explanations of the course of the revival, that is, those based on aggregate demand impulses, were unable then to deal satisfactorily with its driving elements.

Prior to the revival, it was impossible to isolate the effects of the endogenous propagation mechanism. They were intertwined with other impulses, with commingling spanning a bit more than 75 percent of the 111 months of recovery. This left about a fourth of the time when its operation was prominently on display. In the months of commingling of effects, the money-driven recovery mechanism operated on output in the same direction as did the endogenous propagation impulse, so it was not possible to distinguish it, as could be done for the succession of monetary impulses. But it was there throughout the recovery.

To what extent was it a powerful force during the entire recovery? To what extent was it perhaps even the most influential? Unfortunately, the particular channels through which it worked were neither clear nor even well articulated in a scientifically satisfactory sense. Even if it were possible to identify its avenues, there would be considerable empirical difficulty in isolating their influence from that of the other forces, of which the monetary one appeared most important.

In an important sense, resorting to the forces of endogenous propagation is not very satisfying intellectually. People wish to know more than simply the existence of a process; they want to know how it works and how its various relations interact, hence the concern about modeling behavioral relations and causal connections. To the extent that a system is recursive, the attraction is even greater.

A key ingredient in the mechanism is productivity. This is almost definitional: with output climbing rapidly and unemployment falling slowly, any of the usual measures of productivity would show a rise.[30] The harder question deals with the factors that underlie the productivity increase. What are they? What is it that operates to induce rising productivity, to induce greater work effort? Is there an automaticity about it, and if so, why? It is here that there is a further absence of satisfactory understanding, much less information, about the influences.

To appeal to endogenous propagation without dealing specifically with any of those particular influences, to discuss it in general, almost platitudinous terms, certainly diminishes its appeal. But that does not mean that the notion is vacuous. There is, after all, considerable empirical evidence supporting the hypothesis of the tendency of the economy to rebound toward trend. The question has to do with the internal forces and the particular channels through which this occurs.

Another area of ignorance of the operation of economic mechanisms is the transmission of information. How is it that a good produced in one place, dependent on many suppliers elsewhere, somehow gets distributed in numerous markets to consumers willing to purchase in sufficient quantities and at high enough prices to warrant further production?[31] How can this hold for the millions of goods produced? What is the structure of such a system? What is it about the system that it continues to function continually, reasonably flawlessly?[32] How is it that changes in individual consumer preferences are made known to the many producers of that good and they in turn have their altered situation communicated to their several suppliers? To say it is a mystery is somewhat of an exaggeration; it nonetheless is not an overstatement to say that economists' specific knowledge of the varied channels is limited.

Answers to questions about the operation of the market system are not couched therefore in terms of close, reasoned, behavioral, causal models. Rather, such discussions employ expressions, indeed idioms, such as self-interest, incentives, individual freedom, signaling, "prices as information," and the like. Oftentimes, these many dimensions are subsumed by the famous Smithian epigram "led by an invisible hand" (*Wealth of Nations*, bk. 4, chap. 2).[33] Because economists do not have a well-articulated framework that takes account of the many avenues, or even many of the avenues, whereby the system operates so satisfactorily so much of the time in so many situations does not mean that it does not exist.[34]

So also for the mechanism of endogenous propagation; though one cannot set out a carefully articulated mechanism by which it operates does not mean that such a mechanism does not exist. As the foregoing indicates, it operates to move the economy back toward its trend rate of output, as seems clear from attempting to understand the economy's movements in the over two years of revival from the late-1930s depression.

Concluding Comments

The mounting evidence on the driving forces in the recovery centers on the growth of the money stock. There, however, are two difficulties with this reading. Since the basis for the growth was a rising monetary base due principally to gold inflows, the logical corollary of the monetary view of the recovery is that there would have been virtually no rebound had there been none of the brewing troubles and actual turmoil that occurred on the Continent. It is virtually inconceivable to take seriously the proposition that the United States would have languished at its 1933 levels through the seven-plus years leading to World War II had there been no such European difficulties.

Second, according to conventional frameworks, an expanding stock of money in the face of depressed economic activity results in increases in prices and output. Yet the experience following the late-1930s depression had the two moving in opposite directions for more than two years, as the money stock continued growing. For almost a quarter of the entire recovery, prices and output behaved "perversely."

One of the attractions of examining pathological cases is the challenge they pose. Part of the fascination of the 1930s is its abnormality, its obvious deviation from the realm of customary developments. In the case at hand, to understand why prices and output moved in different directions though the stock of money was increasing reasonably rapidly is a challenge, for this is an anomaly from the normal expectation of a positive short-run response to money stock changes. How then best to understand this?

The framework adopted here uses the quantity theory to fathom price movements. Falling prices are due to increases in the demand for money, owing to several factors attributable to the late-1930s depression. Among them are the likelihood that the depression was interpreted as (further) evidence of the inability of the system to recover. Acting in concert is the disposition to regard deflation as synonymous with depression. Yet another factor leading to an increase in the demand for money would be expectations of further price declines.

The present interpretation looks to mechanisms endogenous to the economy that propagate it toward its equilibrium trend path. The particular processes are not empirically observable. Their presence, however, can be inferred from the particular evolution of the economy in the two-plus years of revival from the late-1930s depression where their influences were highlighted. More generally, they operate whenever the economy is not at trend. The attraction of concentrating on the first years of the revival is that it is there that the influence of the mechanism of endogenous propagation could be observed, in that the traditional channels are unable to explain satisfactorily the observed, evolving developments.

CHAPTER 10

A Summing Up

A great deal has been written about the Great Depression, enough for a lifetime of reading. The dominant concern by far is the Great Contraction, the disastrous decline of 1929 into 1933, and that is not surprising. Its dramatic, radical departure from what was widely believed to be normal levels of economic performance was a dramatic shock; it therefore provided an exceptional opportunity for exploration and comment. Of prime concern were its causes and the reasons for the deep, extended unwinding of the economy. In this literature, bank failures, the stock market crash, sustained falling prices, the continued deterioration of the agricultural sector, the structure of the economy with particular emphasis on the business sector, and the gold standard were prominent themes. And as was the wont of economists and others, the research agenda became the motor for reform proposals, the intended effects of which were to return the economy to its normal ranges of operation.

A parallel thread, prominent among social historians, was the human toll, the plight of workers and families, and the growing anxieties, indeed despair, as the economy continued deteriorating and then seemed if not to languish at least not to rebound as rapidly as it had deteriorated, settling in to what appeared to be a permanent state of malaise.[1] Adding to the widespread despair and uncertainty was the sharp, deep depression four years into the recovery. For many, this reaffirmed doubts about the likelihood that the economy would ever attain its previous levels and that the prosperity that they had known would ever again be realized. With the recovery drawn out through the decade, the phrase *the Great Depression* applies to more than just the years of the Contraction.

In contrast to the exhaustive attention paid to the Contraction, discussion of the recovery receives much less, to the point where it pales in comparison. What has been written concentrates largely on the political stage, in particular on the programs of Roosevelt's New Deal, sometimes in contrast to the policies of his predecessor but mostly in terms of the particular ingredients making for a change of regime. The Hundred Days of the special session called the day after Roosevelt's inauguration, for instance, is a much-examined period, almost to the point of necessitating careful consideration of it as a de facto requirement for investigating the remainder of the recovery.

It is only in the last decade or so that serious, concerted attention has focused upon the economics of the recovery. That is the orientation of the present investigation with its look into monetary, fiscal, credit channel, and endogenous propagation forces. The credit channel is typically not viewed as an independent force, being taken as ancillary to the monetary impulse in the sense that it is not taken as of sufficient consequence to stimulate full recovery by itself.

One of the major findings of postwar research was that the recovery was evidently due to the expansion of the money stock. This result was quite robust. It came through in simple graphical examinations and in more complex econometric inquiries. It held for different measures of the quantity of money, for analyses based on data available in the recovery period, and for more satisfactory data available for postwar investigations.

The earliest systematic analysis identifying the role of the growing quantity of money was that of Friedman and Schwartz (1963). This was done largely in the narrative and graphical genre. Subsequently, other investigations used formal models and econometric tools. They similarly singled out the importance of the growth of the money stock as key to understanding the recovery. Each of these studies employed estimates of the 1930s money stock based on work by Friedman and Schwartz (1963, 1970).

That the behavior of the quantity of money was fundamental to the course of output and prices, including the detour that was the sharp depression of 1937–38, highlights the quantity theory of money as a framework for interpreting the recovery. In that decade, that theory was the only macroeconomic underpinning available on which to structure an inquiry.[2] Did economists living in those times use it to understand what was happening? One difficulty, a potentially severe one, was that there were no official money stock series.[3] The alternative to an official series was to construct a proxy, and several economists did that. Those data, however, were annual.

The present study constructs monthly series based on *M1* and *M2* definitions; the respective series are denoted as *M1FRB* and *M2FRB*. The data source is two separate tables in each issue of the *Federal Reserve Bulletin*. Since these were readily available in the 1930s, anyone at that time could similarly construct such series. Furthermore, these are essentially real-time data that can be compared against available other real-time data, notably the Index of Industrial Production (1923–25 = 100) and the Wholesale Price Index, which had a base of 100 in 1926.

As the Contraction continued, the increasingly popular approach to recovery was an activist "inflationist" program, rather than monetary expansion. Perhaps that was due to the understandable desire to "do something" rather than rely on the disguised, mysterious workings of the monetary mechanism. More likely, it was the result of a general belief that the American economy as it was known was a thing of the past and that a fundamental restructuring was in order. Accordingly, a drastic restructuring of the economy was taken as the appropriate route, not only to recovery but also to a new economy. This was based largely on an underconsumptionist explanation of the Contraction. The idea was "to prevent unfair competition and disastrous overproduction" wrought in part by "cut throat underselling by selfish competitors," hence the need for "fair competition" (Roosevelt 1938, 202). The vehicle was the NIRA and the Agricultural Adjustment Administration. On his signing of the former, Roosevelt stated:

> History probably will record the National Industrial Recovery Act as the most important and far-reaching legislation ever enacted by the American Congress. It represents a supreme effort to stabilize for all time the many factors which make for the prosperity of the nation and the preservation of American standards. Its goal is the assurance of a reasonable profit to industry and living wages for labor, with the elimination of the piratical methods and practices which have not only harassed honest business but also contributed to the ills of labor. (1938, 246)

Even discounting the understandable hyperbole associated with the signing ceremony, it represented a clear indication as to the direction for recovery. The approach reflected in large part the position of many, especially those in the economics profession (though not all were convinced, particularly as to the details).

It is instructive to note that the thrust of the times did not single out monetary expansion as an important recovery vehicle.[4] It was in a sense accidental that such expansion came about, being the product initially of the mid-April 1933 devaluation followed the next January by the formal abandonment of the gold standard.[5] The intent of devaluation was to raise prices, perhaps to their 1926 levels, the target of Irving Fisher's reflation campaigns, but at least to their pre-Contraction 1929 levels. Rising prices, reflation in the jargon of the times, were viewed as symptomatic of an improving economy and thus were regarded favorably. Deflation was identified as synonymous with depression.

The immediate effect of the devaluation was to increase the monetary base. This was a one-time effect. To maintain an increasing quantity of money required another fount through which to feed the base. The brewing troubles, the growing anxieties and uncertainties, in Europe proved to be just that. As it became increasingly clear that continental Europe was moving toward unsettled times, there was a flight of capital, taking the form of gold flows to the United States, the safe haven. It was that inflow of gold throughout the decade that allowed for the expansion of the base and the growing stock of money. The actual process through which the base increases translated into a growing stock of money involved principally bank purchases of U.S. government securities, as banks more than tripled their holdings of such. Government securities became the most important bank asset, rising from 30 to 53 percent of the earning assets of banks. Because the money stock changes derived from the devaluation and then from the inflow of gold, they were independent of the course of the economy; they were exogenous. There was no endogenous basis for those increases.

An increase in the quantity of money would be a macroeconomic demand shock. Its effect therefore would be to push up prices and output, especially when there is excess capacity.[6] Using the methods of the 1930s, the effects of increases in the quantity of money were seen to do exactly that. Prices and output rose when the money stock increased and fell when it declined, as in the late-1930s depression. This result held for the constructed *M1FRB* and *M2FRB* money series and also for the later more satisfactory Friedman and Schwartz data. Postwar investigations into the recovery similarly highlighted the importance of the growing money stock.

A widely held belief was that fiscal actions were important, if not most important, in stimulating recovery. This certainly was the case following the late-1930s depression, particularly the idea that it was federal government expenditures associated with World War II that returned the economy to trend. There was the *post hoc, ergo propter hoc* theme that linked the recovery to growing deficits, a position shared by some economists, Arthur Smithies (1946) being one of the most prominent. Later research, led by E. Cary Brown (1956), questioned fiscal policy's contribution, to the point of outright skepticism and even denial of its effects. The several empirical models in the present inquiry similarly found no quantitatively significant fiscal effects. To the extent that the deficits were monetized, as banks increasingly bought government securities with their increased reserves from the gold flow, fiscal policy was an accessory but not a prime motivator. To view fiscal policy in that way, however, would be to give to it a quite different meaning than is conventionally done.

As the economy improved, a good deal more slowly than it had deteriorated, the lending activity of banks came under scrutiny. Were they being too restrictive, thereby impeding the recovery? The notion was that there was a credit channel whereby bank actions impacted the economy. To that end, the federal regulatory authorities promulgated the "Uniform Agreement on Bank Supervisory Procedures," in which they agreed to alter examination procedures to gloss over asset and capital losses. The importance of the credit channel was further emphasized in the Contraction when Bernanke showed that the increased cost of credit intermediation reduced lending, adding further to the economy's deterioration.

This naturally suggested that the channel might have added to the forces making for recovery, in the symmetric sense that since it exacerbated the Contraction it may well have supplemented recovery forces. To appraise its role, a variety of evidence was examined, in particular tests of the influence of changes in real commercial and industrial loans on industrial production. That evidence failed to uncover any positive influence. There was no indication that the credit channel rekindled increased activity.

One of the enigmas in the 1930s is the absence of any satisfactory analysis of the recovery in terms of the extant macroeconomic theory, the quantity theory. It would seem to be a textbook experiment: an investigation of the linkage of prices and output to an exogenously changing money stock. Yet, for all the writings employing the quantity theory in the theoretical work in that decade, none uses such a framework explicitly to understand the recovery. What is especially puzzling is that several reported money stock estimates during that time show it rising after the Contraction's trough; yet none connects the recovery to the documented money increases.

Foremost among those compiling estimates exhibiting an increasing money stock were James Angell and Lauchlin Currie, though the latter's evidence covered only 1934, the first recovery year. Angell (1941), building on his mid-1930s work (1936), extended his estimates through 1939. Since his analyses led him consistently to view the money stock as responding to movements in income, it was not surprising that he did not argue that the rising quantity of money was crucial to the recovery. In fact, he simply did not comment on the then six-year recovery, nor did he say anything about the sharp depression that was clearly evident in his data.

The situation with Currie was different. By the time his 15 percent increase in the quantity of money for 1934 appeared, his assessment of the ingredients for recovery had evolved beyond emphasizing the role of the money stock. He now placed greater emphasis on the fiscal position of the federal government, as he in conjunction with Martin Krost produced a much-cited series entitled "Federal Income-Increasing Expenditures." Moreover, he came to view the quantity of money as endogenous, as witnessed by his enthusiasm for increasing reserve requirements with the Banking Act of 1935's newly granted authority to do so. His reading of the causes of the subsequent depression denied the role of the contraction of the money stock. It gave prime importance to the reduction in the net federal government income-increasing expenditures, owing jointly to the 1937 cessation of the Veterans' Bonus and the institution of Social Security taxes.

The picture that emerges of Irving Fisher was puzzling, to say the least. Here he was, the quintessential quantity theorist and a world-class empiricist who typically looked at evidence to test monetary stabilization hypotheses. Yet his interpretation of the Contraction diverged sharply from his decades-long research program. It now was largely impressionistic, and to a large extent autobiographical. It had debt-deflation as the cause, whatever the reason for the initial overindebtedness. Associated with borrowers' attempts to reduce their bank debts, there was a contraction of demand deposits—his deposit currency. Prices accordingly fell. Banks however did not respond to their enhanced reserve positions by acquiring additional assets. Their earning assets thus ratcheted down with their deposits. The stock of deposits was therefore endogenous. Furthermore, the economy was stuck in a liquidity trap, for which stamp scrip was his antidote.

Though he continued his monetary-oriented research into the last year of his life, he only commented in 1936 regarding the behavior of a monetary variable on the recovery. His subsequent research was devoted essentially to demonstrating the constancy of velocity. In those mid-1930s comments, he acknowledged that the post-1933 rebound was linked to the growth of deposits, but that was not the main theme. First, the growth of deposits was not brought about in what he regarded as the normal way, by borrowing at banks. Rather, it occurred because banks bought government securities, thereby casting doubt in his mind about the robustness of the money mechanism. Of more con-sequence, it was this seemingly anomalous situation in which deposits increased because of bank purchases of governments, rather than "the usual way," that was further ammunition in his campaign for 100 per-cent reserves. Coupled with the growing volume of excess reserves, this led him to take a positive view of the soon-to-be-implemented dou-bling of reserve requirements. At the same time, he expressed outright skepticism about the sufficiency of the increase, indicating that a dou-bling might well be inadequate.

Though he appeared agnostic as to the reasons for the excess reserves, the logic of the matter was that he believed that the excess was due to a shortage of borrowers, a failure of borrowers "to come forward." Had he thought that the growing excess reserves were due to bank caution, he would not have crusaded for higher reserve requirements.

The recovery that began in April 1933 ran to mid-spring 1937, with both prices and output increasing in line with the expanding stock of money, itself driven by the inflow of gold. At that point, the economy's four-year rebound came to an end as it entered a yearlong depression in which industrial production fell sharply, as did prices. That each fell was what would be expected when the money stock declined, as it did. The Treasury's gold sterilization program and the increased reserve requirements of the Federal Reserve were the proximate causes of the fall in the quantity of money.

That depression was important in a number of ways. It caught many by surprise, both its timing and its steepness, and thus cemented suspicions about the economic system's ability to return to full capacity. The market system as they knew it was caught in a permanent high-unemployment equilibrium trap, and thus an approach alternative to the traditional system was necessary. The depression, for instance, convinced Alvin Hansen that his earlier skepticism of Keynes was ill founded. It also convinced Roosevelt of the necessity of committing to fiscal policy as an instrument rather than an accident of government policy options.

The depression ended a year after it set in, as the quantity of money and output began increasing. Each increased sharply during the following years. Prices however continued to fall, declining until midsummer 1940, falling in all twenty-seven months as the economy moved rapidly toward trend.[7] During that same two and a quarter years, the quantity of money increased 36 percent and industrial production 58 percent. This indeed was an incongruity of the first order: for almost a fourth of the recovery, the economy experienced rising output and falling prices, along with an increasing money stock. Explanations that rely on aggregate demand stimuli offer no satisfactory rationalization. More to the point, no demand shock hypothesis is tenable because any one that has output rising cannot have prices falling.

How could it be that the course of the economy through four years of rebound and one year of decline behaved as though governed by the quantity theory of money, and then suddenly it deviated dramatically from the theory's dictates? What was happening?

The strong version of the theory has increases in the stock of money affecting only prices, most definitely in the long run. In the short run, both prices and output move as the demand shock resident in the altered money stock impacts the economy. Yet, here in the depression's revival, prices fell as the money stock increased. Adding further to the conundrum were the large and growing number of postwar analyses that held the growth of the money stock as the driving influence on the recovery. If the money growth hypothesis was the appropriate one, then prices should have risen.

A further irony is that the literature seems to have ignored this episode. Friedman and Schwartz, for instance, devote only two paragraphs to the postdepression revival, one of which deals with rates of monetary growth (1963, 545).

Likewise, Allan Meltzer, in his detailed reading of Federal Reserve documents and in his analysis of the revival, does not comment on the incongruity of the extended deflation in the face of rapid monetary and output growth, except to note the aggregate demand mechanism that "the principal force for recovery [from 1937–38] came from the decline in prices [for which no reasons are offered] that raised the real value of the money stock and, later from the rise in the nominal stock of money" (2003, 574).

Christina Romer (1999) identifies the fall in prices in 1939, but does not single it out for comment. This is all the more surprising because she earlier (1992) argues strongly for a money-driven recovery. Ironically, her framework for understanding why prices rose during the recovery does not employ the quantity of money as a consideration.[8] Kenneth Roose (1954) similarly does not acknowledge the incongruity, though this is more readily understandable because at the time he wrote there were no official data on the money stock, nor was the role of the quantity of money held to be of consequence.

One of the advantages of studying the Great Depression is that behavior and observations quite outside the norm come into view, and the probe into the factors underlying them produces insights that otherwise would likely never occur. On that count, the two and a quarter year period of deflation in the face of rapid monetary and output growth definitely qualifies as an "outlier" situation. Overlaying the conundrum of prices and output moving in opposite directions as the money stock increases is the problematic, controvertible basis of the money stock's growth.

With gold continuing to flow to the United States as a result of the growing uneasiness in Europe, the monetary base expanded and with it the stock of money. The behavior of the money stock was properly regarded as exogenous. It was the growing quantity of money as the engine of the recovery that had been identified so prominently in the literature. Presumably, therefore, had there been no gold inflow, had there been calmer times on the Continent, there would have been essentially no recovery. Still, that there would have been virtually no recovery for year after year after year from the Contraction's nadir through the remainder of the decade seems most implausible.

The resolution of the seeming paradox about the two and a quarter years of revival from the 1937–38 depression cannot rely on demand shocks. That is, monetary, fiscal, and credit channel impulses cannot be paramount. Instead, understanding the economy's postdepression evolution involves a combination of two forces. One is the role of increases in the demand for money relative to the rapidly expanding stock of money. The other, seemingly most unlikely given the "inadequate aggregate demand" orientation of analyses of the Depression, has forces inherent in the economy pushing it toward its trend value.[9] This is what here is called *endogenous propagation*, in the sense that forces endogenous to the economy interact to produce movements of the economy toward its trend rate of output.

There are several reasons underlying the relative increase in the demand for money, especially the sharpness of the depression conjuring up fears of the not so long past Contraction, and the depression "confirming" that the four-year recovery was transitory, thereby reinforcing uncertainties about the future and especially about the durability of any recovery. Still another factor is the depression's fall in prices increasing expectations of further deflation. There is also the understandable tendency in the 1930s to identify declining prices as synonymous with a deteriorating economy, a direct consequence of the 37 percent fall in prices from 1929 into 1933.[10] In a symmetrical fashion, there would be the propensity to associate improving economic circumstances with rising prices. Since prices fell in the depression, it would be understandable to translate that into an omen of future difficulties. The confluence of these would be a decline in velocity, which did fall, beginning at the start of the depression and continuing through the two and a quarter years of revival.

Identifying reasons why the demand for money increased during the revival was only part of the puzzle. Why did it not continue rising? What brought about the turnaround in velocity? Were there recognizable circumstances reversing its direction, ones that led to desires to hold smaller real money balances relative to real incomes?

A major consideration was the increasing recognition that the war in Europe, then almost a year old, would impact the United States. The signs were undisguised, and they signaled "an end to isolation." The shift from fear of continued depressed conditions to concern about a war and the "prosperity" it would bring would have moderated the increased demands for money relative to its growing stock, thereby reducing velocity.

The behavior of output during this extraordinary revival period is also a puzzle. It is understood here as the inherent tendency for output to return to its trend path, that is, the predisposition to revert back in an "exogenous-like" manner (sometimes characterized as mean-reversion). The idea is that the economy contains within itself mechanisms that endogenously propagate output movements toward trend. As a general matter, the resilient mechanisms generating such behavior are rooted in the dynamics of an enterprise economy. Among them are incentives, opportunities, signals, and flexibility, the effects of which increase productivity. These are intrinsic to the system, such that, as a matter of course, a deviation from the (equilibrium) trend path propagates economic responses inducing the economy back toward its trend growth path. The constituent particulars of it are not, however, so easily observed, measured, or modeled. For now, the leading theoretical candidate for understanding the phenomenon appears to be real business cycle theory, in which the actions of individual optimizing agents drive the economy toward its trend rate of output as well as determining what that rate is.[11] Whatever the particular adjustment impulses are and whatever the theoretical framework in which they occur, they nonetheless are present and operative.

There are several empirical studies that identified a tendency for the economy to rebound. Among them are the Cochrane (1988) investigation finding large transitory components in the growth of GNP and the DeLong and Summers (1988) study implying mean-reversion. In addition, there is the Bernanke and Parkinson employment adjustment model suggesting that "self-correcting tendencies of the 1930s economy were probably much stronger than is generally acknowledged" (1989, 210) and the "plucking model" of Friedman (1993) where output "snaps back" to trend from below. No adjustment avenues that may underlie the tendency to rebound are articulated, but there is little doubt that something in the nature of an endogenous propagation mechanism may have been at work. The interesting aspect of the present inquiry is that the postdepression revival is a concrete example where the forces of endogenous propagation can be seen at play.

Just as there was not the usual demand shock framework, there also was not a fortuitous run of positive supply shocks moving the economy toward trend while at the same time pushing prices down. Rather, the economy adjusted of its own accord. This may be regarded definitionally as a positive series of supply shocks, in the sense that price and output movements must be due to aggregate supply and demand changes.

In summary, there are two parts to the resolution of the puzzle of explaining strongly rising output when the stock of money was increasing and prices were falling. First, velocity decreases stemmed from the increased desire to hold money in excess of what was being supplied, which served to move prices down. Second, there is a movement of output back to trend, spawned by the endogenous propagation responses that come into play when the economy is not operating at trend, these forces giving rise to mean-reversion.

One of the difficulties with the endogenous propagation hypothesis is that the operation and processes inherent in it cannot be observed directly. There is a natural tendency to try to understand how things work, to look for cause and effect and so to eliminate that which is extraneous and retain that which is crucial.[12] To that end, modeling of structures, physical, social, and economic, is the method of choice. And so it is that approaches to understanding the recovery utilize the aggregate demand impulses of monetary and fiscal actions as the preferred vehicles. Since the forces of endogenous propagation, important as they may be, are neither readily observable nor therefore quantifiable, they can easily be overlooked. This is understandable; to rely on what seem to be mysterious elements is not intellectually appealing. It is easy to discount them in favor of articulated channels that are prominent in the literature. In place of forces inherent in the economy then, the results from examining traditional impulse mechanisms, with their associated data and empirical tests, mask the forces of endogenous propagation.

The revival from the 1937–38 depression highlighted the endogenous propagation forces. Before then, the influence of the growth of the money stock appeared as the dominant force in the recovery. Just as endogenous propagation was important in the revival, so it must also have been operative and important throughout the entire recovery, and not just in the approximate one-fourth of it in which it was clearly on parade.

In the literature, the robust finding had monetary growth as the major vehicle promoting recovery. There were many attempts to identify the principal recovery forces; time and again, it was growth of the quantity of money. The influence of endogenous propagation was not at all evident until the revival from the mid-1930s depression. It was only then it could be seen, when the monetary growth hypothesis foundered, as did any hypothesis built on demand shock foundations. That there was no outward manifestation of the endogenous propagation forces before the revival does not mean they were absent until then. They operated throughout the recovery. It was impossible to say how important they were, but they certainly must have been of major consequence, as attested by their important influence in the crucial revival period.

This does not imply that there was little merit to any of the traditional recovery mechanisms, nor that the role of the growth of the money stock was a mere chimera. The standard, normal propagation avenues, especially that of the money stock, may well have been operative. However, the finding of the existence of an endogenous propagation mechanism diminishes the relative importance assigned to the effects of aggregate demand policy actions. This emphasis on aggregate demand effects has come to dominate professional discourse in light of viewing the Depression decade as a problem of insufficiency of aggregate demand.

If this view is correct, then theoretical and especially empirical macroeconomic analyses of business cycles must devote relatively more attention to the forces of endogenous propagation toward trend, difficult as they are to identify and model satisfactorily, and less to the traditional approaches.

Notes

1. The narrative history in Watkins 1999 captures to an extent some of the same feelings evidenced in personal reminiscences and documented oral history. There is much in his third-person recounting to underscore the notion that the Great Depression was indeed the entire decade.

2. In the literature recounting the decade, there is a decided one-sidedness in the telling of individual chronicles, which overwhelmingly dwell on personal agonies. Conspicuous by their absence are discussions of those who fared well. Among them are those whose real incomes rose as prices fell, for example, the many factory workers who remained employed. Similarly, retailers who made inventory profits as a result of devaluation-induced rising prices are not heard from.

3. Herbert Hoover Presidential Library, West Branch, IA.

4. The idea of purchasing power insufficient to acquire the nation's available output—a glut of goods, as in the case of agricultural products—was a prominent theme. One particularly outspoken advocate of this was Rexford G. Tugwell, a member of Roosevelt's "Brains Trust" (1932, esp. 86–87).

5. As an example, consider the observation almost a half century afterward of a member of the fabled "Band of Brothers" company of the 101st Airborne Division: "There is not a day that has passed since that I do not thank Adolf Hitler for allowing me to be associated with the most talented and inspiring group of men that I have ever known" (Ambrose 1992, 20). Does anyone believe that the paratrooper held such sentiments as he parachuted into France before dawn on D Day?

6. These estimates come from Stanley Lebergott 1964, 512. In an important contribution, Michael Darby (1976) finds that the official (Bureau of Labor Statistics) unemployment rates failed to count workers on relief jobs, such as the WPA (Works Progress Administration), as employed. The effect of including such workers in the ranks of the employed results in lowering annual unemployment rates by 4 to 7 percentage points. Hence the drop in the unemployment rate between 1933 and 1941 is from 20 to 6 percent rather than from 25 to 10 percent.

7. In reminiscences about the attractiveness of socialism in the Depression

now at the end of the twentieth century, socialism either is not mentioned or is treated as a lighthearted diversion. This is another example of the difficulty of re-creating a historical event.

8. There were no published unemployment data at that time, and even today there are no monthly ones for the 1930s. The index of factory employment, a series that was available then, declined 43 percent. This exaggerated somewhat what now is known of the unemployment situation. On the basis of postwar estimates, the unemployment rate in 1933 stood at 25.2 percent of the civilian labor force (20.6 percent by Darby's estimates) and almost 50 percent higher—37.6 percent—for nonfarm employees (Lebergott 1964, 512).

9. Reference to real GNP fails to detect any recovery in 1932. Such data, however, were not then available. The extant data, readily accessible in the *Federal Reserve Bulletin,* on which one could track the economy in those times were monthly series on industrial production, wholesale prices, and indices of construction contracts awarded, freight-car loadings, factory payrolls, and factory employment. These similarly showed an upturn in late summer 1932, again to decline through March 1933.

10. The *Federal Reserve Bulletin* in the early 1920s reported wholesale prices but not industrial production. That series first appeared in the February 1927 issue, supplanting the Index of Production in Basic Industries series. Each monthly issue had an opening Review of the Month along with the series Condition of Retail Trade, from which useful information on the state of the economy could be gleaned. Unemployment jumped from 1.4 percent in 1919 to 5.2 and then to 11.7 percent in the next two years before receding to its 3.7 percent average for the remainder of the decade (Lebergott 1964, 512).

11. The data on industrial production reported in the 1930s tend to be more volatile than subsequently revised data. For instance, data from that decade indicate that industrial production increased 67 percent (364 percent annual rate!) between March and July 1933 whereas currently revised estimates show a 58 percent increase, each remarkably large.

12. Biographical details about him, along with a discussion of his analyses of the Contraction, are in Steindl 1995, 98, 105–10.

13. One occasionally finds references to the 1936–37 "Roosevelt" recession. See, for instance, Bernstein 1983, 1049.

CHAPTER 2

1. In August 1939, the Board began publishing a revised series that had a base of 1935–39 = 100. The data used in this study have been adjusted to the 1923–25 = 100 base, to maintain a consistent real-time series.

2. She finds "that the methods used to construct the historical series exaggerate cyclical fluctuations in industrial production" (Romer 1986b, 314). Similar sentiments hold for GNP and unemployment data.

3. A similar discussion underscoring the sharp output movements is in Garfield Cox 1936, 5–6. He concludes that October 1934 was the first month of

sustained recovery, since each previous advance was "wholly or largely canceled by the immediately succeeding decline" (1936, 6).

4. Use of the 1930s real-time industrial production index yields an estimated annual rate of recovery of 26 percent, this being another example of the greater amplitude of that series.

5. The thrust of the Roosevelt economic recovery program stressed raising prices as the key to recovery, hence the National Industrial Recovery Act (NIRA) and the Agricultural Adjustment Administration (AAA). On this, see William Barber 1996, 4–14, 26–32 and Ellis Hawley 1966.

6. The industrial production data are taken from Mitchell (1998, 421–22), who in turn used data from the *World Economic Report* of the League of Nations. Since the data extend beyond the breakup of the USSR, he entitles his series Russia/USSR. For ease of communication, Russia is used here instead of "the former Soviet Union."

7. An especially articulate proponent of planning and the consequent demise of the market system who looked admiringly at Russia—"the future is becoming visible in Russia"—was Rexford Tugwell (1932, 92).

8. The overstatement of the data may have been due also to systematic deception. Without doubt, it reflected the Austrian theme about the difficulty of economic calculation in a nonmarket economy (von Mises 1951, esp. 131–42).

9. In addition to substantive data revisions—for instance, real GNP increased 9.2 percent between 1929 and 1939 as contrasted with 1.3 percent in the earlier data—the price index was changed from the fixed weight implicit price deflator to a chained index.

10. The data have subsequently been revised, the effect being to modify slightly Higgs's conclusion. The current revision has real output declining 11.1 percent in 1946.

11. Quotations from auction yields show negative rates in the early 1940s. As Stephen Cecchetti (1988) has shown, such rates imply a price premium that reflects an imbedded option.

12. The data are monthly figures derived from reports of weekly reporting banks in 101 leading cities (Board of Governors 1943)

13. The data on loans include loans for purchasing and carrying securities. They would not be of consequence in moving real economic activity. In April 1933, loans for carrying securities were 43 percent of total loans. Subsequently they fell to 8 percent by June 1942. Rather than aggregate loans, it may well be that commercial and industrial loans are the vehicle that directly affects economic activity.

14. The series was first reported in the *Federal Reserve Bulletin* as of January 1929. At that time, excess reserves averaged a bit less than $50 million. At the Contraction's bottom, they were approximately ten times that level.

15. It also reflects other things, such as acceptances and Federal Reserve float, but these typically are minor.

16. The earliest use of the term *high-powered money* that I could find was in the revised edition of W. Randolph Burgess 1936, 5. Burgess thus seems to have invented the expression (Steindl 1995, 49 n. 9).

17. An analysis of the monetary models of others who advanced monetary-flavored views of the Great Contraction prior to Friedman and Schwartz's is presented in Steindl 1995.

18. A concise discussion of estimates of the money stock by various researchers, including the Federal Reserve, is Friedman and Schwartz 1970, 260–74.

19. Subsequently, they published an extended, revised series (1970, 24–34). These are systematically higher, by approximately 2 percent, for the M1 and M2 series they reported in 1963.

20. John Burbidge and Alan Harrison (1985, 53) constructed a series in much the same spirit. Theirs was a monthly M1 series based however on data in *Banking and Monetary Statistics* (1943). As far as I am aware, this is the only other postwar attempt to obtain a monthly money stock series for the entire recovery independent of Friedman and Schwartz 1963.

21. Visual inspection reveals several blips, the most noticeable being in April 1937 when the constructed M2 series jumped $771 million and then decreased $956 million the following month (annual rates of 24 percent increase and 23 percent decline).

22. The correlation between the 1963 and 1970 Friedman and Schwartz estimates is also 0.999; hence there is remarkable coherence among them.

23. One is *Historical Statistics of the United States* (1976) for which there are several series, one based on the administrative budget and another on the consolidated cash statement. A more satisfactory series is the U.S. Department of Commerce's National Income and Product Accounts (2001).

24. The apparent reason for the 1934 increase was the increased emergency expenditures, as well as those from the Trust Fund, each of which increased sharply in January and then decreased almost as sharply the following month (U.S. Treasury 1935, 306–13). The 1936 increase was linked to the Veterans' Bonus, the Adjusted Service Certificates of $1.6 billion (U.S. Treasury 1936, 345).

CHAPTER 3

1. The concentration on microeconomic restructuring remained prominent through the decade, as William Barber (1996) makes clear. See his discussion of the intellectual thrust of the late-1930s Temporary National Economic Committee (TNEC), which had as its raison d'être a systematic investigation into the concentration of economic power (1996, 115–17, 120–26).

2. As one of the leading political economists of the time saw things, the appropriate analogue of economic competition was armed conflict, viz., "War in industry is just as ruinous as war among nations; and equally strenuous measures are taken to prevent it. . . . [S]o long as nations and industries are organized for conflict, wars will follow" (Tugwell 1932, 75).

3. According to Paul Samuelson (1997, 157), and in correspondence with him, the term *macroeconomics* (then spelled *macro-economic*) first appeared in 1939, in Eric Lindahl 1939, 111, though Ragnar Frisch used *macro-dynamic* in the

Cassel *Festschrift* (1933, 181). Macroeconomics as a distinct area of inquiry by that name seems to have entered economists' lexicon only after the war.

4. A reading of the journals of the time indicates that the Institutionalist mode was the most widely employed approach. The policy prescriptions that issued from it stressed structural reform, that is, industrial reconstruction, what Barber called the Structuralist Agenda (1996, 26–32).

5. Among the profession's prominent non-Chicago economists whose names repeatedly appear in discussions of the quantity theory in the Depression are James W. Angell (Columbia), Lauchlin Currie (Federal Reserve Board, formerly at Harvard), Lionel D. Edie (formerly at Chicago), Irving Fisher (Yale), Arthur W. Marget (Minnesota), Harold L. Reed (Cornell), James H. Rogers (Yale), and Carl Snyder (New York Federal Reserve Bank). In addition, there is the Chicago group, some familiar—Henry C. Simons and Jacob Viner—others not—Paul H. Douglas and Aaron Director, to whom George Tavlas (1997) has directed particular attention. Lloyd Mints is not mentioned here because his writings on the 1930s only appeared in the mid-1940s.

6. Strict quantity theorists have the theory holding as a comparative statics equilibrium theory, so that an increase in the stock of money raises the price level in direct proportion but has no effect on output.

7. Clark Warburton, though presenting data on the stock of money through the Depression decade (1966, 147–50, 168–72), did not systematically investigate the recovery. His few observations on the recovery were directed at the interplay between bank regulation and monetary policy (1966, 317, 322–26). He also analyzed the reasons underlying the "extraordinarily large amounts of excess reserves" (1966, 63) in 1934 through 1940, noting that the Federal Reserve's "impinging on the quantity of reserves" was responsible for the 1937–38 "business depression" (1966, 315).

8. In fact, the increase in reserve requirements had widespread support. Among those favoring it were Irving Fisher (1936b, 106) and Arthur Marget (1937), as well as James Harvey Rogers and Winthrop Aldrich, the president of Chase National Bank of New York, this because of concern about "undesirable inflation" (*New York Times* 1936, 1).

9. *Banking and Monetary Statistics, 1914–1941* (Board of Governors 1943, 400) carries the footnote, "Since 1934 member bank borrowings at Federal Reserve Banks have been negligible."

10. With the financing requirements of the war, the System's purchases of securities increased, so that it held $2.6 billion in June 1942. Interestingly, their holdings of U.S. government securities were constant at $2,184 million from November 1940 through the following November.

11. This conclusion is also that of Christina Romer. "Since the . . . money multiplier fell during the recovery from the Great [Depression], the observed rise in [the quantity of money] must have been due to even larger increases in the stock of high-powered money [i.e., monetary base] during this period" (1992, 772).

12. On this and the interrelations between the Treasury and the Federal Reserve, see G. Griffith Johnson 1939.

13. The correlation between the base and Federal Reserve credit is slightly negative, –0.144.

14. The sterilization program was effectively ended then with the desterilization of $300 million of gold. It was formally modified the following February and officially ended in April 1938 (Johnson 1939, 133–60).

15. In this paper, Bernanke built on the work of Eshan U. Choudri and Levis A. Kochin (1980), who initially investigated the effect of choice of exchange rate regime on the economic experience of countries through 1933. They examined countries that either were never on the gold standard (Spain, which had a flexible exchange rate) or left early and floated for a time (Denmark, Finland, and Norway). As Bernanke acknowledged (1995, 11), others contributed to this literature. Barry Eichengreen and Jeffrey Sachs (1985) concentrated on the macroeconomic effects of devaluation, that is, their analysis was concerned with the post–gold standard period. Bernanke and Harold James (1991) expanded the list of countries and the variables under consideration, from which Bernanke (1995) further expanded the sample. The results were similar: the sooner a country abandoned the gold standard, the sooner it began to recover.

16. In this view, actions by the Federal Reserve to play by the gold standard's "rules of the game" would have as a consequence the decline in the money stock from 1929 into 1933. Elmus Wicker is among the earliest who argued that monetary policy in the Contraction was principally influenced by international considerations: "Domestic considerations were significant for the determination of monetary policy only when they happened to coincide or did not conflict with international considerations, namely the maintenance of gold convertibility of European currencies" (1965, 327). Others are Peter Temin (1989, 35) and David Wheelock (1991, 117).

17. There are two issues involved here. One is that the abandonment of the gold standard freed the hands of policymakers to pursue expansionary policies, whether monetary or fiscal. In this view, there is no preferred or even likely policy. This is the approach of Barry Eichengreen (1992). A second view is that the devaluation of the currency associated with abandoning the gold standard allowed for an immediate expansion of the money stock and then for continued increases. That is the position of Bernanke (1995).

18. The Federal Reserve's first official series, which appeared in *Banking Studies* (Board of Governors 1941), had annual data for 1890 through 1940. For the 1930s, its $M1$ estimates are in reasonably close agreement with Friedman and Schwartz's, differing by less than half of 1 percent. The $M2$ data, however, are substantially at variance, with the System data at times over 35 percent larger.

19. Currie's initial estimates (1933), which were annual as of June 30, went through 1932. His subsequent book (1934b) added another year, and the second edition a year later (1935) added data for 1934. Angell (1933), though not explicitly concerned with money estimates, presented (in a *Quarterly Journal of Economics* article immediately preceding Currie's) annual estimates of income velocity, which he preferred to label circular velocity, where the requisite money stock data were of the $M2$ type. In his book, annual estimates of the $M1$

(circulating money) and M_2 (total money) series and monthly estimates of the M_1 series were given (1936, 175–79). The details as well as the shortcomings of the techniques each used were discussed in Friedman and Schwartz 1970, 268–71.

20. His series, which at first glance appears to be an M_2 type, differs markedly from the Friedman and Schwartz money stock, amounting to almost 25 percent greater. His contrast with Currie has the money stock falling 24.6 percent from 1929 through 1933, whereas Currie's fell 24.2 rather than the 23.1 percent (due to rounding) he calculated (Lin 1937, 81).

21. As an example Stephen Foster in an article in *The New Republic* used an M_2-type series constructed from the *Bulletin* (1933, 39–40). He argued for increases in the money stock to promote the up to then unrecognized recovery.

22. As he pointed out, the term *deposit currency* was adopted from J. Laurence Laughlin, *The Principles of Money* (Fisher 1911, 51 n. 1).

23. With few exceptions, the relationship is positive when the revised industrial production series is used. This holds both for M_1FRB and M_1.

24. The subsequent revision of industrial production shows a 33 percent fall. The M_1 money stock declined 6 percent.

25. Fisher was principally concerned with equilibrium positions. The exception was the single chapter (chap. 4, on transitions) in which the interplay of real and nominal interest rates was central to the cycle.

26. The September price increase was the second largest monthly rise in the entire period, with a 100 percent (annual rate) rise in July 1933 the largest.

27. A perusal of Money and Banking textbooks published in the early 1940s indicates a similar absence of comment on falling prices in the face of a vigorous recovery. See, for instance, Harold L. Reed (1942), who was an active participant in the monetary debates of the early to mid-1930s, and Rollin G. Thomas (1942). Data on the stock of money were not available, and so it is not surprising that there was no acknowledgment of increases in it and falling prices.

28. The growth rates for M_1 and M_2 were 36 and 26 percent, respectively.

CHAPTER 4

1. Schumpeter seems to have recognized the recovery a bit earlier, although his discussion is devoid of explicit references to ongoing developments. He offers as his explanation for the "recovery" (his quotation marks) the confluence of Kondratieff, Juglar, and Kitchen cycles, whose combined joint negative movement in the summer of 1929 was the cause of the start of the Great Contraction (1935, 167–68).

2. He nonetheless was optimistic about the longer-term prospects for recovery.

3. In contrast to Sprague's doubts about the recovery, Willford I. King led a session the previous year on recovery measures in various nations. The general tenor was that recovery was definitely under way. As one participant put

it, "we have now reached the point in the recovery process at which it is necessary to add new persons to the pay rolls, instead of merely lengthening the working week" (1937, 225).

4. It may be that a concentrated focus on sectoral detail, such as Sprague's and Bernstein's, obscures seeing the broader macroeconomic movements.

5. In addition to the mainline economics journals such as the *American Economic Review, Economic Journal, Journal of Political Economy, Quarterly Journal of Economics*, and *Review of Economic Statistics*, other periodicals examined were the *Annals of the American Academy of Political and Social Science, Harvard Business Review, Journal of Farm Economics, New Republic, Political Science Quarterly, Social Research*, and *Yale Review*; in addition, articles in the *New York Times* relating to prominent economists were examined. In speeches reported by the *Times*, E. W. Kemmerer had a quantity theory framework in mind as he repeatedly argued against the inflationary potential arising from the administration's gold policy. Those speeches did not link gold to the behavior of the stock of money.

6. His model included a currency-deposit ratio, which he took as a parameter denoted k. This is the first instance I have found of what later became the conventional notation for the currency ratio.

7. Later, Rogers developed the concept of what he called the monetary base, and presented a chart of it. It consisted of sources and uses. On the sources side, he had gold, treasury currency, and Federal Reserve credit. His concept differed in minor respects from the current notion of the base (1937, 110–13).

8. The rapid growth of time deposits in those years (1922–28) was also the stimulus for D. R. French (1931). He however was content to examine the behavior of such deposits among different classes of financial institutions. He was not interested in the implication of time deposits for the measure of the money stock in that he did not relate their rapid growth to the movement of the economy, particularly to prices.

9. Allied with the issue of using bank data to "test" theoretical assertions, William Neiswanger (1933) sampled six banks over an eleven-year period to determine the actual extent of credit creation in an individual bank. He found that the actual ratio was about 3.5 for credit expansion *and* contraction.

10. The reference to him as a monetary economist, a term that became popular two decades after the war, derives from his referring to himself as such (1936, 127). An earlier use was Fisher's referring to James H. Rogers as one of the "ablest monetary economists in the world" (Steindl 1995, 153 n. 19).

11. In present parlance, circular velocity is known as income velocity, though Angell vehemently disagrees with that: "Some students have used the term 'income velocity' to describe the magnitude here called the 'circular velocity of money.' . . . The term 'income velocity,' however, seems to me to be inaccurately used here" (1936, 131 n. 1). It was Currie (1934a, 353–54) who took him to task for including time deposits in his velocity estimates (to whom Angell has reference in his "some students" assignation).

12. Due to the Bank Holiday, there were no data for March 1933.

13. David Laidler (1993, 1085 n. 18) employing a similar quote pointed out

that Clark Warburton disputed Angell's interpretation of his evidence. War-burton, in an extended footnote (over two pages!) discussing and lamenting "the unanimity with which economists have ignored" monetary considera-tions, argued that Angell's conclusion rested on his analysis of considering cur-rency and (circulating) deposits separately relative to various output indices (1966, 81, 82 n. 10). Had he examined those series relative to the circulating money series, he would not have concluded "contrary to his data" (1966, 82) that the money stock "never [moved] *before* the several broad indices of pro-duction" (Angell 1936, 60).

14. The formal model appears in Angell 1941, 79. It is quite similar to the multiplier-accelerator model.

15. Anticipations were the driving mechanism in his framework; it is changes in them that influence investment, spending, and the distribution of money holdings between "hoards and other uses" (1941, 6).

16. The details of his eventful life are covered in Sandilands (1990). A dis-cussion of his monetary analysis is in Steindl 1995, 61–78.

17. The changes amounted to correcting a few printing mistakes, adding another year of data, deleting the three penultimate paragraphs in the fifth chapter, and substituting in their place a chart. The effect was to leave the pag-ination unchanged between the two editions.

18. The presumption was that that amount of gold coin had been lost, since it was not surrendered when it became illegal to hold gold, a consequence of the Gold Reserve Act of 1934.

19. George Tavlas (1997, 169–70) points to Currie's reminiscences (1978, 541) as evidence that he abandoned the quantity theory by 1931, when he advo-cated deficit financing in his Harvard classes. Perhaps, but then why did he subsequently publish the monetary analyses for which he is known today? Laidler similarly dismisses the notion that Currie had abandoned the quantity theory in the early 1930s, pointing out that in 1935 he defended his analysis in Benjamin Anderson's attack on his book (Laidler 1999, 244 n. 35).

20. He also translated from German an article by Jacob Marschak, which appeared in the January 1934 issue of *Econometrica.*

21. Recall that at that time there were no official data on the quantity of money. Apparently, he did not attempt to garner any money data at that time. That was to change with the advent of the *Monetary History* project in 1948 (Hammond 1996, 48). The project's first published fruit explicitly using money stock data was Friedman (1952). In response to a letter in 2002 inquiring about my interpretation of that course, Friedman wrote, "As a staff member of the Bureau, I was of course closely involved with their particular business cycle procedure. Thus I am not surprised to find that in the course I taught on busi-ness cycles at Wisconsin, I did not put any special emphases on the quantity of money." His work at the Bureau dealt with "the problem of professional incomes and also the theory and measurement of national income."

22. There are no excess reserves data for March, the bank holiday month.

23. The archival resource JSTOR—Journal Storage—lists ninety-two articles that mention "excess reserves" from 1934 through 1942. Some simply mention

the term, but many deal with it as a phenomenon of concern, generally as indicative of the impotency of monetary policy.

24. Additional citations holding that the reserve requirement increases were not of consequence can be found in George Morrison 1966, 21–33 and Kenneth Roose 1954, 101–2.

25. He never used the term *liquidity trap,* nor did anyone else in the 1930s. The earliest use of the term was in 1940 by D. H. Robertson, in his essay "Mr. Keynes and the Rate of Interest" (Laidler 1999, 286). Nonetheless, Currie's analysis of the "excess reserve problem" can be interpreted and understood in that framework.

26. Kenneth Roose develops this position in great detail, using it as evidence that the Federal Reserve's actions were important contributors to the downturn (1954, 103–17). He does not examine, much less mention, the money stock in connection with his otherwise systematic, thorough investigation of the depression. Clark Warburton also pointed out that member bank withdrawals from the Chicago and New York City central reserve banks forced the latter to sell "approximately $1 billion of United States government obligations" (1966, 70) in order to maintain their excess reserve positions.

27. The fact that policy was viewed in terms of the bond market was the basis for Charles Whittlesey's proposal that the Federal Reserve adopt a new policy instrument: the *threat* of open market sales if banks are expanding "too freely," this based on banks' investments amounting to over two-thirds of their earning assets (1939, 158). In addition, symptomatic of the times, such a policy would be "especially significant at a time when we are accustomed to think of the effectiveness of traditional Federal Reserve policies as pretty much a thing of the past" (1939, 159).

28. In addition to Currie and Fisher, three others who may be mentioned are C. O. Hardy, though in a different context from that in which he is treated here, Willford I. King, and Carl Snyder.

29. In JSTOR, there are over 550 articles dealing with gold in the 1934 through 1942 period, of which about 200 appeared in the *American Economic Review,* many in connection with the Proceedings volumes of the annual meetings. The annual rate of publication did not abate greatly as the period came to a close; from 1939 through 42, just over 200 articles appeared.

30. In his jeremiad against the gold actions of the period, hence his plea for a "return to an international gold standard" (1938, 115), James Paris presents a handy chronology of important dates relating to gold, from the 1792 founding of the U.S. Mint through the April 1938 official cessation of the gold sterilization policy.

31. For a detailed account, see Friedman and Schwartz 1963, 506–8. See also Edward Simmons 1940, 325. The differential effect on the base owing to the 1937 gold sterilization program and the dampening influence of this on the money stock, coming as it did when reserve requirements were increased, is similarly discussed by Friedman and Schwartz (1963, 510).

32. This was not a unanimous opinion. George Harrison of the New York Bank "felt that the powers of the Board of Governors for credit control were

belittled in [a] report which at the same time tended to over-emphasize the credit control powers of the Treasury" (Friedman and Schwartz 1963, 533 n. 34).

1. This clearly was the case for Fisher (1911) since there was at that time no Federal Reserve System.

2. One way in which he obtained an estimate of V was to have Yale students keep detailed records for a month on their expenditures and cash balances (Fisher 1911, 379–82; Dimand 2000, 334).

3. These were essentially formula writing, accompanied by a somewhat more insightful version of the fulcrum charts from the *Purchasing Power of Money* (1911, 23, 48).

4. Coming on its heels, it is not surprising that large parts of the later effort are taken directly from the earlier book.

5. Fisher did not formally investigate an inflation-unemployment connection. Rather, he dealt with an employment series from W. L. Crum's research unit, the Harvard Committee on Economic Research (1926, 790 n. 2).

6. In an appendix, a sampling of Fisher's forecasts over the September 1929–October 1931 period is presented (Dominguez, Fair, and Shapiro 1988, 607). One can see here the absence of monetary data as an ingredient in forecasting prices and economic activity.

7. His zeal in attempting to stir the public comes through in the exaggerated tone that pervades the book. Among the "chief inciters to over-indebtedness" were "high-pressure salesmen" of financial firms whose efforts were in part responsible for "steadily and enormously [inflating] the deposit currency" (1932, 74). In fact, the data reported by Fisher show negligible rates of increase of net demand deposits.

8. Albert Hart in contrast was not so convinced of the importance of overindebtedness. Though he acknowledged that "rash lending [overindebtedness (?)] created a situation that was bound to collapse," he argued nonetheless that the Contraction brought about debt default and that regardless of the Contraction's seriousness "large sections of the debt structure were bound to give way . . . even without being pushed by a prior decline in business" (1938, 6–7). Hart was concerned with garnering evidence on the size of debt and not with an interpretation of its role. Accordingly, it was not surprising that he did not cite Fisher.

9. That the stock of currency, his M, was dictated by the demand for it, at least with the founding of the Federal Reserve, was not something he felt the need to address. He continued to assume that the central bank determined M, as when he commented that the wave of bank failures in late 1931 with its consequent increased demands for currency "more than defeated the [greater than 80 percent increase in] new issues of Federal Reserve notes" (1932, 103–4). Accordingly, the 1930–31 increase in currency was dismissed as a "misleading" notion of money in circulation because the "increased quantity of Federal

Reserve notes" was being hoarded and thus was "not circulating at all" (1932, 96). He reiterated the same point the following year, using virtually identical phrasing (1933b, 57 n. 8). That the System was accommodating an increase in the demand for currency was not something he acknowledged.

10. The mechanism he used was essentially a simple Phillips (1920) *Bank Credit* multiple deposit expansion framework with its emphasis on bank reserves (Fisher 1932, 37 n. 3). He later based the decline in deposit currency on a framework of his former student and now colleague James Harvey Rogers (1933a).

11. See also Fisher: "Almost all checking accounts . . . grow out of the business loans made by commercial banks. But in order to maintain these borrowed accounts, business men must have the confidence to borrow" (1933b, 22).

12. Though the notion of a monetary base was around at the time, Fisher did not use it in his studies. For him, the relevant policy variable was bank reserves.

13. Some details of the stamp scrip proposal were considered in the appendix entitled "Other Plans for Reflation and Stabilization" (Fisher 1932, 225–43). A fuller discussion of it would have to wait until the following year when in response to having "answered four or five hundred inquiries about it" (1933c, 1), he wrote a book in which he laid out the case for it. Keynes similarly was familiar with Gesell's "famous prescription of 'stamped' money" (1936, 357), though he had reservations about its feasibility as an antidote to the depression.

14. Subsequently, he offered the opinion, an ambivalent one, that the growing excess reserves resulted because banks "either would not use [such reserves] (because they were afraid to lend)" or "because . . . borrowers fail to come forward" (1936a, 104, 44).

15. As he explained in congressional testimony in mid-1932, increasing the price level was not inflation but reflation, which "means inflation which is justified by virtue of its counteracting recent great and rapid deflation" (Steindl 1995, 99).

16. He felt it necessary to point out that *money in circulation* was "a misleading term" because such money is "partly hoarded" (1932, 57 n. 8).

17. The third edition, published in 1945, was an exact reproduction of the second, except for the inclusion of a six-page "Addendum" that brought to date reactions to the proposal.

18. As this discussion makes clear, I was in error when I wrote earlier that there was no evidence that Fisher ever looked at money or deposit data during the recovery (Steindl 1997, 258).

19. On this, see note 14 in this chapter.

CHAPTER 6

1. The concept of net income-increasing expenditures plays a prominent role in Roose's assessment of fiscal policy (1954, 70–86). Among those who

relied heavily on the Currie-Krost series are Arthur Gayer (1938) and Henry Villard (1941). Villard's worksheet estimates were used by Gayer.

2. The bonus had been approved for World War I veterans for payment in 1945. Due to the exigencies of the upcoming election, bonds were issued to the veterans in June 1936. They could be sold immediately at par (Blum 1970, 124–32). Of the $1.7 billion of bonds issued, $1.4 billion was cashed and presumably spent within six months (Roose 1954, 73).

3. In addition to a large decline in expenditures owing to the one-time nature of the Veterans' Bonus, Alvin Hansen also finds that the bonus contributed to the depression through "maladjustments in the price structure caused by the great bulge in expenditures" (1938, 269).

4. His estimate that the value was negative implies that the federal government's net expenditures were income-*reducing*. This was clearly a cause for concern for him, in that he argued earlier "the case for government deficit spending" (1941, 92–113).

5. In addition to the undistributed corporate profits taxes in 1936, there was a year earlier a "soak the successful" package of inheritance and gift taxes, as well as increased marginal rates on "very great individual incomes" and corporate profits (Leuchtenburg 1963, 152).

6. An insightful discussion in the context of the general purview of industrial concentration in the 1930s can be found in the "New Deal Policy and the Recession of 1937" section of Ellis Hawley 1966.

7. The only exception to the sterilization program occurred on September 13, 1937, when the Treasury released $300 million from its inactive account by issuing gold certificates to the Federal Reserve, thereby increasing the monetary base in the form of bank reserves by that amount.

8. Hardy believed that the sizable volume of excess reserves was sufficient to accommodate the increases. Schumpeter dismissed the subsequent "minute increase" in interest rates as having any effect, and Slichter held that the increase would have little effect because firms relied on internal funding of investment needs.

9. "At the close of business" on August 15, reserve requirements were to be 50 percent higher. In January 1937, they were increased "another 50 percent . . . one-half of this second increase to become effective March 1 and the other half May 1, 1937" (Board of Governors, *Annual Report* 1936, 9). Requirements on demand deposits at Central Reserve City banks accordingly went from 13 percent to 19½ percent (August 15, 1936) to 22¾ percent (March 1, 1937) to 26 percent (May 1, 1937).

10. See, for instance, the discussion in George Morrison 1966, 26–27 as well as note 8 in chapter 3.

11. The Board of Governors estimated that the amount of excess reserves was sufficient to accommodate the increases and that they were widely distributed among banks. Increasing requirements would therefore leave monetary conditions easy; "it was not the intention of the Board to reverse the policy of monetary ease which has been pursued by the System since the beginning of

the depression" (Board of Governors, *Annual Report* 1936, 13). "The policy of maintaining easy money . . . continued to be in effect" (Board of Governors, *Annual Report* 1937, 2).

12. Clark Warburton seems to be the first to point this out (1966, 347–48), although the Board discussed it but decided it was not an issue of consequence (Friedman and Schwartz 1963, 525 n. 26).

13. In addition to reserve requirement increases and gold sterilization, an additional monetary measure taken was the doubling to 50 percent of margin requirements in early 1936.

14. This is the title of the lead article in the January 1940 *Federal Reserve Bulletin*.

15. The decline was almost continual until August 1939, when there was a two-month surge, followed by another ten months of falling prices. The sharp price increases were due to the start of the war in Europe.

16. "Despite the fairly good showing made in the recovery up to 1937, the fact is that neither before nor since has the administration pursued a really positive expansionist program. . . . For the most part, the federal government engaged in a salvaging program and not in a program of positive expansion" (1941, 84).

17. "There can be little or no doubt that the expansion of net expenditure in 1938 and 1939 played an important role in checking the recession and bringing about expansion" (1941, 341).

18. Roose is paraphrasing here James Meade's work in the *World Economic Survey, 1938/39* of the League of Nations.

19. For central reserve city banks, the requirement went from 26 to 22¾ percent on demand deposits. Reserve city banks had theirs reduced from 20 to 17½ percent, and country banks from 14 to 12 percent. The requirement against time deposits went from 6 to 5 percent.

20. On one occasion, the *Bulletin* presented a discussion and graph showing total deposits and currency, based on Call Report data (January 1940, 6–7).

21. To construct their money stock series, they relied on *Banking and Monetary Statistics, 1914–1941* (1943). This approach is markedly similar to the one used to construct *M1FRB*, the main difference being that the latter is real-time, that is, its component elements were as initially reported and not revised.

22. VAR frameworks deal not with the stock of money but with innovations—monetary surprises—in the quantity of it. For ease of exposition, the text refers to such innovations as the stock of money.

23. Wholesale prices rose to their July 1929 (immediate pre–Great Depression) level in February 1942.

24. The real rate is taken as the nominal rate on U.S. government bonds in May 1937. Thereafter it is calculated by subtracting from the bond rate the year-over-year rate of change of prices.

25. Real GNP declined 11 percent between 1937:2 and 1938:1. This 15 percent annual rate was larger than any yearly decline in the 1929–33 period. The data are from Nathan Balke and Robert Gordon 1986, 795.

26. Since prices declined the month before the depression began, the actual price decline was 15 percent through August 1939.

27. Due to a reclassification of business loans at the end of 1937, there is a break in the series; hence the behavior of such loans over the entire period is not comparable.

28. The *M1FRB* and *M2FRB* measures exhibited somewhat greater increases.

29. The gold sterilization policy contributed to the Depression, by reducing the base's growth in the face of increases in the demand for the base arising from increases in reserve requirements.

30. On this, see William Barber 1996 and Ellis Hawley 1966, 13–16, 283.

31. As has frequently been pointed out, the higher prices and wages owing to the NIRA were a one-time occurrence; they could not be held responsible for the general inflation of 1933 into 1937.

32. This simplest of her Phillips curve frameworks had prices falling each year until 1942; not only that, but in each of the nine years in which the model had prices falling, the model shows them declining more than actually occurred; and in 1942 they rose less. The correlation coefficient between her estimated inflation rates and the actual ones was 0.4.

33. Following the sharp depression of 1920–21, prices rose 12.5 percent in the fifteen months after December 1921. See also the evidence on the price increases following on the deep 1879 and 1891–96 depressions (Friedman and Schwartz 1963, 497–98).

34. The basis for this conclusion was a reduction in the growth-rate effect model's root mean squared error of almost two-thirds from that of the baseline modified Phillips curve model.

35. The impetus of unionization and NIRA on prices would have served to raise them inasmuch as average earnings rose 3.7 percent (7.3 percent after deduction for unemployment) in 1939. With the decline in prices, this translates into real increases of 5.4 and 9.1 percent (U.S. Bureau of the Census, *Historical Statistics* 1997, Series D 725–26).

36. The notion of the "struggle for Roosevelt's soul" comes from the debate between the fiscal expansionists and the structuralists, who continued to adhere to the view that the cause of the difficulties was monopoly power. The phrase comes from the title of a chapter by Herbert Stein—"The Struggle for the Soul of FDR, 1937–1939" (1969, 91–130).

37. The Firestone (1960) data have the deficit approximately doubling through the first year of the revival and then declining about 25 percent through the rest of the period of deflation.

38. The data are from the historical data appendix in Balke and Gordon 1986, 811–18.

39. This is the chapter title to his vivid description of the change in Americans' perceptions as the decade of the 1940s began. See especially pages 299–309.

40. The professional literature on mean-reversion is heavily concentrated on financial assets.

41. The substantial literature on unit roots is directly relevant here. The assumption in this is that there is no unit root in output, that there is a tendency for output to return to its trend value.

CHAPTER 7

1. Among the economists signing the document were Paul H. Douglas, Simeon E. Leland, H. A. Millis, H. C. Simons, and Jacob Viner.

2. Davis concentrates on the stimulus dimension of budget deficits. He downplays deficits as a means of increasing the stock of money, i.e., monetization, a position central to many Chicago plans.

3. See note 5 in the previous chapter.

4. The Supreme Court had declared the Agricultural Adjustment Act unconstitutional. That act had processing fees in it, and so that revenue source disappeared. Also, the Veterans' Bonus necessitated a search for increased revenue.

5. This is based on economics journals indexed in JSTOR. The growth tailed off to a bit less than 200 per five-year interval over the next fifteen years.

6. The formal underlying model is a Keynesian cross framework with multipliers depending on the propensity to consume out of national income and disposable income (Brown 1956, 859 n. 4). Multipliers so calculated have the most favorable impact on national output of a change in a fiscal variable.

7. That World War II showed the influence of fiscal policy was the major theme of J. R. Vernon 1994.

8. Brown's full employment surplus (as a percentage of potential GNP) is always less than Peppers's. In most years, Brown has a deficit whereas Peppers has a surplus (1973, 200).

9. His brief note was not offered as a comment on any specific analysis. It rather was presented mainly as a rebuttal to those who argued that fiscal policy was a "flat failure" (1963, 321).

10. Thomas Beard and W. Douglas McMillin used these data as they examined fiscal influences in the 1930s (1991; Raynold, Beard, and McMillin 1991).

11. There is a vast literature on Ricardian Equivalence and the conditions under which it is fully operative. The empirical evidence suggests that it is a force but is not fully operative. Fortunately, for present purposes, it is not necessary to resolve the issue.

12. When longer lags are considered, all but one of the deficit coefficients are statistically insignificant. The significant one is the second lag, and its sign is appropriately negative. That significant negative sign is present, however, only for lags of three through seven periods. After that, no DLNRBB coefficient is significant.

13. If instead, the change in the logarithm of receipts and expenditures is entered separately in this or the previous equation, the significance results are much the same. None of the receipt coefficients is significant, and only the second lagged expenditure coefficient is. The net effect of the joint influence of

receipts and expenditures is zero, as shown in each table. The money and interest rate coefficients have the same significance.

14. As the lags are increased to ten, the coefficients of DLNRBB are never significant. It is only when the lags go beyond ten that one and only one fiscal coefficient is significant, but then it is positive.

15. The interest inelasticity of investment was an important element in the appeal of fiscal policy, from theoretical and policy perspectives. The monetary transmission process in the developing Keynesian model stressed reducing interest rates. With low rates and interest-inelastic investment, monetary policy was not able to generate sufficient increases in investment. The policy perspective tended to look to direct action, and fiscal stimulus became the clear option.

CHAPTER 8

1. One difference between them is that Fisher regards debt deflation as the cause of the Contraction. Bernanke makes no such claim. For him, the credit channel represents a changing cost of credit intermediation. It reinforces movements originating elsewhere, such as a reduction in the stock of money.

2. Though the vast majority held a commercial-loan theory view, two who argued that banks restricted lending by raising their credit standards were Lionel D. Edie and James Harvey Rogers (Steindl 1995, 109–10, 126).

3. There were other factors increasing excess reserves. Clark Warburton discusses several considerations responsible for the "extraordinarily large amounts of excess reserves throughout the period from 1934 to 1940" (1966, 62). Among them are (1) "a renewed emphasis by supervisory authorities" on the traditional 10 percent capital-deposit ratio; (2) hints that the Federal Reserve was going to mandate "large increases in [reserve] requirements"; (3) "unusual sensitiveness of the banks to the riskiness and character of the assets they acquired . . . and the criticism to which they were subjected"; and (4) the belief of bankers that prudence dictated holding large excess reserves in light of being "unable to obtain discounts at the Federal Reserve banks" in the early 1930s (1966, 63).

4. Ben Bernanke and Mark Gertler argue that tests of the credit channel using credit aggregates are generally invalid in "normal" conditions because credit aggregates are endogenous. In "outlier" circumstances, such as the Great Depression, they may be relevant (1995, 43 n. 20). The recovery certainly qualifies as such. Though credit aggregates are endogenous, it nonetheless must be the case that if the credit channel is an influential mechanism, the behavior of such aggregates is an integral link in the relation of banks and firms. That would be particularly true in the 1930s, when commercial banks were the dominant supplier of credit to firms.

5. These comprise between 40 and 45 percent of total loans from 1929 through 1935. By 1940 through 1941, they are down to 10 percent.

6. The series relevant to the recovery aggregates agricultural loans with commercial and industrial loans. In January 1956 the Federal Reserve began

reporting agricultural loans separately. They averaged between 2 and 3 percent of commercial and industrial loans for the period through December 1970.

7. Conversations with Ben Bernanke and Charles Whiteman helped clear up some difficulties in replicating, particularly the notion of y_t being industrial production's growth "relative to trend"; this was estimated by the coefficient b in the regression $IIP = ae^{bt}$. Bernanke also supplied a disk containing an earlier attempt at reproducing his results by Masahiro Hori (1996). Susan Green and Charles Whiteman (1992) raised econometric reservations about Bernanke's results. Each of the three sets of replication estimates was in concordance with Bernanke's monetary model. Neither Hori nor I was successful in duplicating his second equation, the Lucas Supply Curve model. Green and Whiteman did not attempt to estimate it.

8. In their reassessment of Bernanke, Green and Whiteman (1992) point out that his money demand equation, which was not reported, similarly has low explanatory power. They then construct a monetary innovations variable based on an eight- rather than four-period lag.

9. The inclusion of additional lags continues to show that only the fourth lag of DLNRCI is significant, but negative.

10. The VAR results reported later incorporate six-month lags, with a twenty-four-month response period. Note that these are the same as employed by Ben Bernanke and Alan Blinder (1992).

11. Though Irving Fisher articulated the distinction between the two rates in 1896, it tended to be ignored until the late 1960s, when rising nominal rates stimulated a rediscovery of the Fisher mechanism. One reason for the shift of emphasis from the neoclassical view that the interest rate was a real rate was the widespread acceptance of the Keynesian model, which led economists to think in terms of the nominal rate. Associated with this emphasis perhaps was Keynes's deprecation of the importance of Fisher's distinction between the two rates (1936, 142).

CHAPTER 9

1. In a nonrandom survey of about three dozen economists, I asked how each would approach the general problem of trying to understand the forces promoting the recovery. Without exception, fiscal and monetary actions were cited as the things at which to look, with differences of emphasis as to the appropriate measures of those actions. The credit channel was not mentioned directly but the lending activity of banks was. I take this to be confirmation and corroboration of the statement in the text regarding the approach of economists. A few mentioned examining the effects of New Deal policies.

2. Technically, the National Socialist German Workers' Party—Die Nationalsozialistische Deutsche Arbeiterpartei (NSDAP).

3. This strong way of putting things is based on the ceteris paribus method. Quite likely, had there been no gold inflow, policies would have evolved differently. What they would have been is surely speculative.

4. While in general true, there may be some circumstances when the econ-

omy might be somewhat above trend, such as likely may have been the case during the war, but those times are the rarest of exceptions.

5. Proponents of real business cycle theory reject the separation of growth theory from business cycles, among whom are Edward Prescott (1986a, 10), who prefers to refer to business cycle phenomena rather than business cycles, and Charles Plosser (1989, 58–59). The latter, for instance, after considering a permanent increase in labor productivity, argues that the "transitory dynamics" in reaching "a new higher steady state level" is a case in point illustrating that "the real business cycle model . . . provides an integrated approach to the theory of growth and fluctuations" (1989, 60).

6. A useful introduction to mean-reversion in stock prices is Charles Engel and Charles Morris 1991.

7. There is an interesting asymmetry in the orientation of economists and finance researchers in their studies of mean-reversion. For the latter, such reversion relates mainly to adjustments *down* to fundamental values of stock, that is, the concern is about "bubbles." For economists mean-reversion consists of identifying adjustment *up* to trend.

8. The particular series was output per person of working age sixteen to sixty-five (1988, 474).

9. In large part her comments disputed their rejection of her previous findings that the postwar evidence exhibited no less volatility than the prewar years (1986a, 1986b).

10. In her study emphasizing the growing money stock, Romer rejects this assertion. After explicitly using their "substantial degree of mean reversion" quote (1992, 758), she later states "my findings appear to dispute studies that suggest that the recovery . . . was due to the self-corrective powers of the U.S. economy in the 1930s" (783).

11. The measure of unexpected inflation is the difference between actual and estimated inflation rates. In the empirical tests, increases in unexpected inflation increase employment, as expected from any of a number of theoretical models—ones encapsulating Phillips curve and Lucas supply functions, for instance.

12. Much the same graph appears in DeLong and Summers 1988, 476. An updated graph is shown as figure 9.2.

13. This if the one-time price shock due to the start of the war in Europe is set aside.

14. In fact, it actually fell a bit, even allowing for a large one-time increase in September–October 1939 (an annual rate of 94 percent based on the July–August average).

15. The figure is much the same as figure 3.5 with the exception that the present one adds the behavior of industrial production and uses the Friedman and Schwartz *M1* stock series, whereas the former graph was drawn in terms of prices and the constructed *M1FRB* series.

16. For some, the 1929–33 experience reaffirmed the lessons of the 1920–21 depression, when prices fell 44 percent and industrial production 28 percent between June 1920 and June 1921. Falling prices implied bad times.

17. This thesis is implicit in Peter Temin and Barry Wigmore 1990 in which the change of regime signaled by devaluation led to rising prices and the onset of recovery.

18. The trend is calculated by averaging the beginning and ending three years.

19. An attempt to come to grips with this is the introspective grappling by Robert Lucas (2002, 9–13), who reflects on the importance of learning-by-doing within a group as an element in human capital accumulation.

20. One attempt to describe a likely mean-reversion setting has a surprise dividend announcement pushing a stock's price up. Optimistic traders step in, pushing the price above its fundamental value. Traders who pay attention to fundamental values then begin selling, at which point the price direction is the net of two forces. The sellers eventually win, thereby generating the mean-reversion that moves the price down to its fundamental value (Engel and Morris 1991, 25). The difficulty with this view is that traders concerned with fundamentals would sell in sufficient amounts anytime a price was in excess of what the fundamentals dictated; hence there would not be any mean-reversion.

21. The term *shock* is a bit disproportionate to the intended initiating pressures. It connotes a one-time tremor of noticeable consequence, when in fact the intention is more to the effect of small disturbances to equilibria (Prescott 1986b, 29).

22. Two instructive discussions of real business cycles are Mark Rush (1987, 23–30) and Charles Plosser (1989, esp. 56–57, 59–60). A skeptic is Lawrence Summers who maintains, "My view is that real business cycle models . . . have nothing to do with the business cycle phenomena observed in the United States or other capitalist economies" (1986, 24). Also of interest is Prescott's response (1986b).

23. The substantial literature on unit roots is directly relevant here. It assumes that there is no unit root in output, that there is a tendency for output to return to its trend value.

24. It is useful to recall here the rejection of such taxonomy by real business cycle theorists, as stated in n. 5.

25. The data are from Friedman and Schwartz 1963, 32–33.

26. If the trough-to-trough business cycle of 1869 through 1879 is considered, velocity was approximately constant, falling through 1875 and then rising so that the annual rate of increase was 0.4 percent. Prices fell, and the stock of money and output increased (Friedman and Schwartz 1963, 37).

27. The NBER's monthly reference cycle series dates the trough in June 1897, though annual data has 1897 as the first year of expansion (Friedman and Schwartz 1963, 89 n. 1).

28. The importance of the war as critical to ending the Depression is a dominant theme in Randall Parker's interviews with economists on their Depression experiences (2002). Of the eleven economists interviewed, seven attribute the Depression's end to the war. None of the others venture an opinion, perhaps because they were not asked. Those citing the war as critical are Milton Friedman (Parker 2002, 50), Moses Abramovitz (68), Albert Hart (82), Charles

Kindleberger (100), James Tobin (138), Herbert Stein (178), and Victor Zarnowitz (193).

29. Friedman's explanation does not rely on the war's fiscal dimension as critical. He sees money-financed deficits as the vehicle responsible for ending the Depression. "Government spending for armament was financed by printing money. Indeed in a way you can say that what ended the Great Depression . . . was the application of the Simons/Knight/Viner/Douglas proposal for running a deficit and financing it by printing money" (Parker 2002, 50).

30. Productivity measured by output per man-hour rose 3, 4, and 3 percent respectively during 1938, 1939, and 1940; nonfarm output per man-hour during the same time rose 3, 4, and 4 percent (U.S. Bureau of the Census 1997, 162). Total unemployment fell 9 and 14 percent respectively in 1939 and 1940 (U.S. Bureau of the Census 1997, 135). The percentage fall in the unemployment rate was approximately one point greater.

31. Adding to the recondite process, few of those intermediate suppliers know how their products will be used.

32. There is a substantial literature that advocates economic planning attempts to emulate the operation of the market. In the postwar era, considerable efforts were made in many developing nations to implement such planning but the outcomes of the plans foundered, due in part to the inability to understand, even to approximate, the processes of the market.

33. The particular context for Smith's invisible hand is in the argument for free trade, in particular, the thesis that the actions of individuals acting in their own interest in a regime of free trade maximizes social welfare. Economists frequently, however, use the invisible hand metaphor as a shorthand summary of the workings of the market system.

34. The case of price adjustments in response to market excess supplies (or demands) is another example of a process that lacks for a fundamental understanding, particularly in the market for services. How is it that buyers and sellers come to adjust their particular supply and demand prices when no one knows that excesses exist? One prominent (artificial) solution is the Walrasian auctioneer and the associated *tâtonnement* process.

CHAPTER 10

1. There are numerous examples of such writings. One is the narrative history study of T. H. Watkins, whose approach relied heavily on individuals' accounts—anecdotes—to capture the decade's despair, an approach that had much in common with the personal stories relayed by Lorene Hickok to Harry Hopkins on her travels around the country (Watkins 1999, 176–78; Kennedy 1999, 160–62). Along the same line, David Kennedy nicely captures the hardships of families: "To borrow from Tolstoy, every unhappy family was unhappy in its own way" (1999, 164).

2. This is not to say that it was the reigning orientation of economists. That belongs to the institutionalist school.

3. The data in the table labeled "Money in Circulation" in the *Federal Reserve Bulletin*, which suggests a quantity of money series, actually is the Currency in Circulation series.

4. In discussions of economic and political policies, there is a predilection to look for underlying, systematic themes, a philosophy. This seems especially true of Roosevelt. What comes through, however, is the lack of a consistent, coherent mind-set. As Albert Romasco emphasizes, Roosevelt was interested in short-term results; he was a political animal; hence "without politics, there is little meaning to any New Deal policy" (as quoted in Bernstein 1983, 1048). Similarly, David Kennedy, quoting Raymond Moley, writes, "To look upon these policies as the result of a unified plan . . . was to believe that the accumulation of stuffed snakes, baseball pictures, school flags, old tennis shoes, carpenter's tools, geometry books, and chemistry sets in a boy's bedroom could have been put there by an interior decorator" (1999, 154).

5. Peter Temin (1989) and Barry Eichengreen (1992) argue that the gold standard was a restraint on expansionist policy. Accordingly, worldwide recovery commenced when countries cut their ties to gold and thus could undertake such policies. In their analyses, the abandonment of the gold standard represented a change of regime. Neither followed up by attributing the subsequent recovery to the growth of the quantity of money. In other words, the demise of the gold standard could be viewed as important in and of itself but also as the first step in an expansion of the money stock. The continued recovery would then have required additional, continuing sources of monetary expansion.

6. There is an implicit assumption that there are also frictions and rigidities so that even in the presence of fully rational expectations, output would respond to monetary shocks.

7. There was a one-time price spike in September–October 1939, a 41 percent annual rate, associated with anticipatory buying at the start of World War II in Europe.

8. This would seem to be an inversion of the usual processes of the quantity theory where in the long run prices are affected but not output. Her method has the money stock influencing output but not prices.

9. If the Depression were viewed as a problem of insufficient aggregate demand, the appropriate policy would be to employ traditional measures to boost the demand for output. Investigations into the recovery have, without exception, concentrated on just such actions.

10. For those old enough to remember, the 1920–21 experience of depression and deflation may also have been of consequence.

11. The argument in the text is not that the recovery can be understood from the point of view of real business cycle theory. Rather the suggestion is that the mechanism of endogenous propagation contains within itself much of the individual adjustment behavior stressed by that theory.

12. A rich example is the Keynesian model, particularly in its *ISLM* incarnation, which largely accounts for its widespread appeal. On this count, see David Laidler 1999.

References

Allen, Robert L. 1993. *Irving Fisher: A Biography.* Cambridge, MA: Blackwell.

Allen, William R. 1977. "Irving Fisher, F. D. R., and the Great Depression." *History of Political Economy* 9 (winter): 560–87.

Ambrose, Stephen E. 1992. *Band of Brothers: E Company, 506ʰ Regiment, 101ˢᵗ Airborne from Normandy to Hitler's Eagle's Nest.* New York: Simon and Schuster.

Angell, James W. 1933. "Money Prices and Production: Some Fundamental Concepts." *Quarterly Journal of Economics* 48 (November): 39–76.

———. 1934. "Gold, Banks, and the New Deal." *Political Science Quarterly* 49 (December): 481–505.

———. 1935. "The Federal Finances and the Banking System." *Journal of the American Statistical Association* 30 (March): 169–74.

———. 1936. *The Behavior of Money.* New York: McGraw-Hill.

———. 1940. "Round Table on Bank Deposits and the Business Cycle." *American Economic Review Proceedings* 30 (March): 80.

———. 1941. *Investment and Business Cycles.* New York: McGraw-Hill.

Angell, James W., and Karel F. Ficek. 1933a. "The Expansion of Bank Credit I." *Journal of Political Economy* 41 (February): 1–32.

———. 1933b. "The Expansion of Bank Credit II." *Journal of Political Economy* 41 (April): 152–92.

Balke, Nathan, and Robert J. Gordon. 1986. "Appendix B: Historical Data." In *The American Business Cycle,* ed. Robert J. Gordon, 781–850. Chicago: University of Chicago Press.

———. 1989. "The Estimation of Prewar Gross National Product: Methodology and New Evidence." *Journal of Political Economy* 97 (February): 38–92.

Bane, Frank, et al. 1933. *Balancing the Budget: Federal Fiscal Policy during Depression.* Public Policy Pamphlet no. 1. Chicago: University of Chicago Press.

Barber, William J. 1996. *Designs within Disorder: Franklin D. Roosevelt, the Economists, and the Shaping of American Economic Policy, 1933–1945.* Cambridge: Cambridge University Press.

Beard, Thomas R., and W. Douglas McMillin. 1991. "The Impact of Budget Deficits in the Interwar Period." *Journal of Macroeconomics* 13 (spring): 239–66.

Beckhart, Benjamin H. 1936. Review of W. Randolph Burgess, "The Reserve Banks and the Money Market." *Political Science Quarterly* 51 (December): 639–40.

Bell, Philip W. 1951. "Federal Reserve Policy and the 1937–38 Crisis and Depression: A Note." *Review of Economics and Statistics* 33 (November): 349–50.

Bernanke, Ben S. 1983. "Nonmonetary Effects of the Financial Crisis in the Propagation of the Great Depression." *American Economic Review* 73 (June): 257–76. Reprinted in Bernanke 2000, 41–69.

———. 1995. "The Macroeconomics of the Great Depression: A Comparative Approach." *Journal of Money, Credit, and Banking* 27 (February): 1–28. Reprinted in Bernanke 2000, 5–37.

———. 2000. *Essays on the Great Depression.* Princeton: Princeton University Press.

Bernanke, Ben S., and Alan Blinder. 1992. "The Federal Funds Rate and the Channels of Monetary Transmission." *American Economic Review* 82 (September): 901–21.

Bernanke, Ben S., and Mark Gertler. 1987. "Banking and Macroeconomic Equilibrium." In *New Approaches to Monetary Economics,* ed. W. Barnett and K. Singleton, 89–111. Cambridge: Cambridge University Press.

———. 1989. "Agency Costs, Net Worth, and Business Fluctuations." *American Economic Review* 79 (March): 14–31.

———. 1995. "Inside the Black Box: The Credit Channel of Monetary Policy Transmission." *Journal of Economic Perspectives* 9 (fall): 27–48.

Bernanke, Ben S., and Harold James. 1991. "The Gold Standard, Deflation, and Financial Crisis in the Great Depression." In *Financial Markets and Financial Crises,* ed. R. G. Hubbard. Chicago: University of Chicago Press. Reprinted in Bernanke, *Essays on the Great Depression,* 70–107. Princeton: Princeton University Press, 2000.

Bernanke, Ben S., and Martin Parkinson. 1989. "Unemployment, Inflation, and Wages in the American Depression: Are There Lessons for Europe?" *American Economic Review Papers and Proceedings* 79 (May): 210–14. Reprinted in Bernanke, *Essays on the Great Depression,* 247–54. Princeton: Princeton University Press, 2000.

Bernstein, Michael. 1983. Review of *The Politics of Recovery: Roosevelt's New Deal,* by Albert U. Romasco. *Journal of Economic History* 43 (December): 1048–49.

———. 1987. *The Great Depression.* Cambridge: Cambridge University Press.

Blum, John Morton. 1970. *Roosevelt and Morgenthau.* Boston: Houghton Mifflin.

Board of Governors of the Federal Reserve System. Various issues. *Annual Report.* Washington DC: Board of Governors.

———. 1941. *Banking Studies.* Washington, DC: Board of Governors.

———. 1943. *Banking and Monetary Statistics, 1914–1941.* Washington, DC: Board of Governors.

———. 1976. *Banking and Monetary Statistics, 1941–1970.* Washington, DC: Board of Governors.

———. 1985. *Industrial Production, 1985 Revision, Total Index and Major Groupings, 1977–100.* Washington, DC: Board of Governors.

———. Various issues. *Federal Reserve Bulletin.* Washington, DC: Board of Governors.

Bordo, Michael D., Claudia Goldin, and Eugene N. White. 1998. *The Defining Moment: The Great Depression and the American Economy in the Twentieth Century.* Chicago: University of Chicago Press.

Bowen, Howard. 1936. "Gold Maldistribution." *American Economic Review* 26 (December): 660–66.

Brookings Institution. 1936. *The Recovery Problem in the United States.* Washington, DC: Brookings Institution.

Brown, E. Cary. 1956. "Fiscal Policy in the 'Thirties': A Reappraisal." *American Economic Review* 46 (December): 857–79.

Burbidge, John, and Alan Harrison. 1985. "An Historical Decomposition of the Great Depression to Determine the Role of Money." *Journal of Monetary Economics* 16 (July): 45–54.

Burgess, W. Randolph. 1936. *The Reserve Banks and the Money Market.* Rev. ed. New York: Harper and Brothers.

Calomiris, Charles W., and David C. Wheelock. 1998. "Was the Great Depression a Watershed for American Monetary Policy?" In *The Defining Moment: The Great Depression and the American Economy in the Twentieth Century,* ed. Michael D. Bordo, Claudia Goldin, and Eugene N. White, 23–65. Chicago: University of Chicago Press.

Calomiris, Charles W., and Berry Wilson. 1998. "Bank Capital and Portfolio Management: The 1930s 'Capital Crunch' and Scramble to Shed Risk." Cambridge, MA: National Bureau of Economic Research Working Paper no. 6649.

Cassel, Gustav. 1933. *Economic Essays in Honour of Gustav Cassel.* London: George Allen and Unwin.

Cecchetti, Stephen G. 1988. "The Case of the Negative Nominal Interest Rates: New Estimates of the Term Structure of Interest Rates during the Great Depression." *Journal of Political Economy* 96 (December): 1111–41.

———. 1995. "Distinguishing Theories of the Monetary Transmission Mechanism." *Review,* Federal Reserve Bank of St. Louis, 77 (May/June): 83–97.

Chandler, Lester V. 1970. *America's Greatest Depression, 1929–1941.* New York: Harper and Row.

Choudri, Eshan U., and Levis A. Kochin. 1980. "The Exchange Rate and the International Transmission of Business Cycle Disturbances: Some Evidence from the Great Depression." *Journal of Money, Credit, and Banking* 12 (November): 564–74.

Cochrane, John H. 1988. "How Big is the Random Walk in GNP?" *Journal of Political Economy* 96 (October): 893–920.

Colander, David C., and Harry Landreth. 1996. *The Coming of Keynesianism to America.* Brookfield, VT: Edward Elgar.

Cole, Harold L., and Lee E. Ohanian. 1999. "The Great Depression from a Neoclassical Perspective." *Federal Reserve Bank of Minneapolis Quarterly Review* 23 (winter): 2–24.

Cox, Garfield V. 1936. "Some Distinguishing Characteristics of the Current Recovery." *American Economic Review Proceedings* 26 (March): 1–10.

Crawford, Arthur Whipple. 1940. *Monetary Management under the New Deal.* Washington, DC: American Council on Public Affairs.

Crum, W. L. 1933a. "Review of the First Quarter of 1933." *Review of Economic Statistics* 15 (May): 68–74.

———. 1933b. "Review of the Third Quarter of 1933." *Review of Economic Statistics* 15 (November): 184–91.

———. 1935a. "Review of the First Quarter of 1935." *Review of Economic Statistics* 17 (May): 34–41.

———. 1935b. "Review of the Third Quarter of 1935." *Review of Economic Statistics* 17 (November): 143–50.

———. 1936. "Review of the Year 1935." *Review of Economic Statistics* 18 (February): 42–51.

Currie, Lauchlin. 1933. "Money, Gold and Income." *Quarterly Journal of Economics* 48 (November): 77–95.

———. 1934a. "A Note on Income Velocities." *Quarterly Journal of Economics* 48 (February): 353–54.

———. 1934b. *The Supply and Control of Money in the United States.* Cambridge: Harvard University Press.

———. 1935. *The Supply and Control of Money in the United States.* 2d ed. Cambridge: Harvard University Press.

———. 1978. "Comments and Observations." *History of Political Economy* 10 (winter): 541–46.

———. 1980. "Causes of the Recession." *History of Political Economy* 12 (fall): 316–35.

Darby, Michael R. 1976. "Three-and-a-Half Million U.S. Employees Have Been Mislaid: Or an Explanation of Unemployment, 1934–1941." *Journal of Political Economy* 84 (February): 1–16.

Davis, J. Ronnie. 1971. *The New Economics and the Old Economists.* Ames: Iowa State University Press.

DeLong, J. Bradford, and Lawrence H. Summers. 1988. "How Does Macroeconomic Policy Affect Output?" *Brookings Papers on Economic Activity* 2: 433–80.

Dice, Charles A., and Philip Schaffner. 1939. "A Neglected Component of the Money Supply." *American Economic Review* 29 (September): 514–20.

Dimand, Robert W. 1994. "Irving Fisher's Debt-Deflation Theory of Great Depressions." *Review of Social Economy* 52 (spring): 92–107.

———. 2000. "Irving Fisher and the Quantity Theory of Money: The Last Phase." *Journal of the History of Economic Thought* 22 (fall): 329–48.

Dominguez, Kathryn M., Ray C. Fair, and Matthew D. Shapiro. 1988. "Forecasting the Depression: Harvard versus Yale." *American Economic Review* 78 (September): 595–612.

Eccles, Marriner S. 1951. *Beckoning Frontiers: Public and Personal Recollections.* New York: Alfred A. Knopf.

Eichengreen, Barry. 1992. *Golden Fetters: The Gold Standard and the Great Depression, 1919–1939.* New York: Oxford University Press.

Eichengreen, Barry, and Jeffrey Sachs. 1985. "Exchange Rates and Economic Recovery in the 1930s." *Journal of Economic History* 45 (December): 925–46.

Ellis, Howard S. 1938. "Mr. Lounsbury on Money." *American Economic Review* 29 (March): 102–3.

Engel, Charles, and Charles S. Morris. 1991. "Challenges to Stock Market Efficiency: Evidence from Mean Reversion Studies." Federal Reserve Bank of Kansas City *Economic Review* 76 (September/October): 21–35.

Fama, Eugene F., and Kenneth R. French. 1988. "Permanent and Temporary Components of Stock Prices." *Journal of Political Economy* 96 (April): 433–80.

Firestone, John M. 1960. *Federal Receipts and Expenditures during Business Cycles, 1879–1958.* Princeton: Princeton University Press.

Fisher, Allen G. B. 1935. "Does an Increase in Volume of Production Call for a Corresponding Increase in Volume of Money?" *American Economic Review* 25 (June): 197–211.

Fisher, Irving. 1911. *The Purchasing Power of Money.* New York: Macmillan. Reprint of 2d ed. (1922), New York: Augustus M. Kelley, 1971.

———. 1920. *Stabilizing the Dollar.* New York: Macmillan.

———. 1923. "The Business Cycle Largely a 'Dance of the Dollar.'" *Journal of the American Statistical Association* 18 (December): 1025–28.

———. 1925. "Our Unstable Dollar and the So-Called Business Cycle." *Journal of the American Statistical Association* 20 (June): 179–202.

———. 1926. "A Statistical Relation between Unemployment and Price Changes." *International Labour Review* 13 (no. 6): 785–92. Reprinted in Irving Fisher, "I Discovered the Phillips Curve." *Journal of Political Economy* 81 (March/April 1973): 496–502.

———. 1930. *Stock Market Crash—and After.* New York: Macmillan.

———. 1932. *Booms and Depressions.* New York: Adelphi.

———. 1933a. "The Debt-Deflation Theory of Great Depressions." *Econometrica* 1 (October): 337–57.

———. 1933b. *After Reflation, What?* New York: Adelphi.

———. 1933c. *Stamp Scrip.* New York: Adelphi.

———. 1936a. *100% Money.* 2d ed. New York: Adelphi.

———. 1936b. "The Depression, Its Causes and Cures." *Abstracts of Papers Presented at the Research Conference on Economics and Statistics Held by the Cowles Commission for Research in Economics,*104–7. Colorado College Publication, General Series no. 208, Study Series no. 21. Colorado College, Colorado Springs.

———. 1940. "The Velocity of Circulation of Money." *Report of Sixth Annual Research Conference on Economics and Statistics at Colorado Springs, 1940,* 55–58. Chicago: Cowles Commission for Economic Research, University of Chicago Press.

———. 1946. "Velocity of Circulation of Money." *Econometrica* 14 (April): 178–80.

———. 1947. "The Statistics of the Velocity of Circulation of Money." *Econometrica* 15 (April): 173–76.

Foster, Stephen M. 1933. "Money: Active and Static." *New Republic* 78 (August 23): 39–40.

French, D. R. 1931. "The Significance of Time Deposits in the Expansion of Bank Credit, 1922–28." *Journal of Political Economy* 39 (December): 759–82.

Friedman, Milton. 1940. Lecture Notes on Business Cycle course, University of Wisconsin, fall semester. Hoover Institution Archives, Milton Friedman Collection, Box 75, Folder 5.

———. 1952. "Price, Income, and Monetary Changes in Three Wartime Periods." *American Economic Review Proceedings* 42 (May): 612–25.

———. 1956. "The Quantity Theory of Money—A Restatement." In *Studies in the Quantity Theory of Money,* ed. Milton Friedman, 3–21. Chicago: University of Chicago Press.

———. 1993. "The 'Plucking Model' of Business Fluctuation Revisited." *Economic Inquiry* 31 (April): 171–77.

Friedman, Milton, and Anna J. Schwartz. 1963. *A Monetary History of the United States, 1867–1960.* Princeton: Princeton University Press.

———. 1970. *Monetary Statistics of the United States: Estimates, Sources, Methods.* New York: Columbia University Press.

Frost, Peter A. 1971. "Banks' Demand for Excess Reserves." *Journal of Political Economy* 79 (July/August): 805–25.

Gayer, Arthur D. 1938. "Fiscal Policies." *American Economic Review Proceedings* 28 (March): 90–112.

Green, Susan J., and Charles H. Whiteman. 1992. "A New Look at Old Evidence: On Nonmonetary Effects of the Financial Crisis in the Propagation of the Great Depression." University of Iowa, Department of Economics, April 30.

Hall, Thomas E., and J. David Ferguson. 1998. *The Great Depression.* Ann Arbor: University of Michigan Press.

Hammond, J. Daniel. 1996. *Theory and Measurement: Causality Issues in Milton Friedman's Monetary Economics.* Cambridge: Cambridge University Press.

Hansen, Alvin H. 1936. "Under-Employment Equilibrium." *Yale Review* 25 (June): 828–30.

———. 1938. *Full Recovery or Stagnation?* New York: W. W. Norton.

———. 1939. "Economic Progress and Declining Population Growth." *American Economic Review* 29 (March): 1–15.

———. 1941. *Fiscal Policy and Business Cycles.* New York: W. W. Norton.

———. 1963. "Was Fiscal Policy in the Thirties a Failure?" *Review of Economics and Statistics* 45 (August): 320–23.

Hardy, C. O. 1939. "An Appraisal of Factors ('Natural and Artificial') Which Stopped Short the Recovery Development in the United States." *American Economic Review Proceedings* 29 (March): 170–82.

———. 1941. "The Price Level and the Gold Problem: Retrospect and Prospect." *American Economic Review Proceedings* 30 (February): 18–29.

Hart, Albert Gailord. 1938. *Debts and Recovery: A Study of Changes in the Internal*

Debt Structure from 1929 to 1937 and a Program for the Future. New York: Twentieth Century Fund.

Hawley, Ellis W. 1966. *The New Deal and the Problem of Monopoly.* Princeton: Princeton University Press.

Higgs, Robert. 1992. "Wartime Prosperity: A Reassessment of the U.S. Economy in the 1940s." *Journal of Economic History* 52 (March): 41–60.

———. 1997. "Regime Uncertainty: Why the Great Depression Lasted So Long and Why Prosperity Resumed after the War." *Independent Review* 1 (spring): 561–90.

———. 1999. "From Central Planning to the Market: The American Transition, 1945–1947." *Journal of Economic History* 59 (September): 600–623.

Hori, Masahiro. 1996. "New Evidence on the Causes and Propagation of the Great Depression." Ph.D. diss., University of California, Berkeley.

Hubbard, Joseph B. 1940. "Easy Money: Doctrine and Results." *Harvard Business Review* 19 (autumn): 52–65.

Johnson, G. Griffith, Jr. 1939. *The Treasury and Monetary Policy, 1933–1938.* Cambridge: Harvard University Press.

Johnson, Louis, and Samuel H. Williamson. 2002. "The Annual Real and Nominal GDP for the United States, 1789–Present." Economic History Services. URL: <http://www.eh.net/hmit/gdp/met/gdp/> Accessed January 28, 2003.

Kashyap, Anil K., and Jeremy C. Stein. 1994. "Monetary Policy and Bank Lending." In *Monetary Policy,* ed. N. Gregory Mankiw, 221–56. Chicago: University of Chicago Press.

Kennedy, David M. 1999. *Freedom from Fear: The American People in Depression and War, 1929–1945.* New York: Oxford University Press.

Keynes, John Maynard. 1936. *The General Theory of Employment, Interest, and Money.* New York: Harcourt, Brace.

Kimmel, Lewis H. 1939. *The Availability of Bank Credit, 1933–1938.* Conference Board Studies no. 242. New York: National Industrial Conference Board.

Kindleberger, Charles P. 1973. *The World in Depression, 1929–1939.* London: Allen Lane, Penguin Press.

King, Willford I. 1937. "Indicia of Recovery." *American Economic Review, Proceedings* 27 (March): 225–28.

Kirkwood, John B. 1972. "The Great Depression: A Structural Analysis." *Journal of Money, Credit, and Banking* 4 (November): 811–37.

Knight, Frank H. 1933. "Memorandum on Banking Reform." March 16, President's Personal File 431, Franklin D. Roosevelt Library, Hyde Park, New York.

Krost, Martin. 1938. "The Measurement of the Net Contribution of the Federal Government to National Buying Power." Board of Governors of the Federal Reserve System, August 16, unpublished memorandum.

———. 1940. "Round Table on Bank Deposits and the Business Cycle." *American Economic Review Proceedings* 30 (March): 80–81.

Laidler, David. 1991. *The Golden Age of the Quantity Theory.* Princeton: Princeton University Press.

————. 1993. "Hawtrey, Harvard, and the Origins of the Chicago Tradition." *Journal of Political Economy* 101 (December): 1068–1103.

————. 1999. *Fabricating the Keynesian Revolution: Studies of the Inter-war Literature on Money, the Cycle, and Unemployment.* Cambridge: Cambridge University Press.

Lange, Oskar. 1939. "Is the American Economy Contracting?" *American Economic Review* 29 (September): 503–13.

Lebergott, Stanley. 1964. *Manpower in Economic Growth: The American Record since 1800.* New York: McGraw-Hill.

Lehmann, Fritz. 1939. "The Gold Problem." *Social Research* 7 (May): 125–50.

Lester, Richard A. 1937. "The Gold-Parity Depression in Norway and Denmark, 1925–28." *Journal of Political Economy* 45 (August): 433–65.

Leuchtenburg, William E. 1963. *Franklin D. Roosevelt and the New Deal, 1932–1940.* New York: Harper and Row.

Lewis, W. Arthur. 1949. *Economic Survey, 1919–1939.* London: George Allen and Unwin.

Lin, Lin. 1937. "Are Time Deposits Money?" *American Economic Review* 27 (March): 76–86.

Lindahl, Erik. 1939. *Studies on the Theory of Money and Capital.* London: George Allen and Unwin.

Lounsbury, Raymond H. 1937. "What Is Money?" *American Economic Review* 27 (December): 765–67.

Lucas, Robert E. 2002. *Lectures on Economic Growth.* Cambridge: Harvard University Press.

Marget, Arthur W. 1937. *Inflation: Inevitable or Avoidable?* No. 15, Day and Hour Series of the University of Minnesota. Minneapolis: University of Minnesota Press.

Means, Gardiner C. 1946. "Discussion." *American Economic Review Papers and Proceedings* 36 (May): 32–35.

Mehrling, Perry G. 1997. *The Money Interest and the Public Interest: American Monetary Thought, 1920–1970.* Cambridge: Harvard University Press.

Meltzer, Allan H. 2003. *A History of the Federal Reserve.* Vol. 1, *1913–1951.* Chicago: University of Chicago Press.

Miron, Jeffrey A., Christina D. Romer, and David N. Weil. 1994. "Historical Perspectives on the Monetary Transmission Mechanism." In *Monetary Policy,* ed. N. Gregory Mankiw, 263–300. Chicago: University of Chicago Press.

Mishkin, Frederic S. 1995. "Symposium on the Monetary Transmission Mechanism." *Journal of Economic Perspectives* 9 (autumn): 3–10.

Mitchell, B. K. 1998. *International Historical Statistics: Europe, 1750–1993.* New York: Stockton Press.

Mitchell, Wesley Clair. 1927. *Business Cycles: The Problem and Its Setting.* New York: National Bureau of Economic Research.

Morrison, George R. 1966. *Liquidity Preferences of Commercial Banks.* Chicago: University of Chicago Press.

Neiswanger, W. A. 1933. "The Expansion of Bank Credit." *American Economic Review* 23 (June): 245–63.

Nelson, Charles R., and Charles I. Plosser. 1982. "Trends and Random Walks in Macroeconomic Time Series." *Journal of Monetary Economics* 10 (September): 139–62.

New York Times. 1933. "President Starts Recovery Program, Signs Bank, Rail and Industry Bills; Wheat Growers Will Get $150,000,000." June 16, 1.

———. 1935. "Fisher Backs View Recovery Is Near." May 24, 38.

———. 1936. "Bankers Warn of a Credit Boom." April 3, 1.

Palyi, Melchior. 1938. "Present Federal Reserve Policies." *Journal of Farm Economics* 20 (February): 302–9.

———. 1939. "Should Interbank Balances Be Abolished?" *Journal of Political Economy* 47 (October): 678–91.

Paris, James Daniel. 1938. *Monetary Policies of the United States, 1932–1938*. New York: Columbia University Press.

Parker, Randall E. 2002. *Reflections on the Great Depression*. Northampton, MA: Edward Elgar.

Peek, Joe, and Eric S. Rosengren. 1995. *Is Bank Lending Important for the Transmission of Monetary Policy?* Federal Reserve Bank of Boston, Conference Series no. 39.

Peppers, Larry C. 1973. "Full-Employment Surplus Analysis and Structural Change: The 1930s." *Explorations in Economic History* 19 (winter): 197–210.

Phillips, Chester A. 1920. *Bank Credit*. New York: Macmillan.

Phillips, Ronnie J. 1995. *The Chicago Plan and New Deal Banking Reform*. Armonk, NY: M. E. Sharpe.

Plosser, Charles I. 1989. "Understanding Real Business Cycles." *Journal of Economic Perspectives* 3 (summer): 51–77.

Poterba, James M., and Lawrence H. Summers. 1988. "Mean Reversion in Stock Prices." *Journal of Financial Economics* 22 (October): 27–59.

Prescott, Edward C. 1986a. "Theory Ahead of Business Cycle Measurement." *Federal Reserve Bank of Minneapolis Quarterly Review* 10 (fall): 9–22.

———. 1986b. "Response to a Skeptic." *Federal Reserve Bank of Minneapolis Quarterly Review* 10 (fall): 28–33.

Ramey, Valerie. 1993. "How Important Is the Credit Channel in the Transmission of Monetary Policy?" *Carnegie-Rochester Conference Series on Public Policy* 39 (December): 1–45.

Raynold, Prosper, W. Douglas McMillin, and Thomas R. Beard. 1991. "The Impact of Federal Government Expenditures in the 1930s." *Southern Economic Journal* 58 (July): 15–28.

Reed, Harold L. 1942. *Money, Currency and Banking*, New York: McGraw-Hill.

Rockoff, Hugh. 1984. *Drastic Measures: A History of Wage and Price Controls in the United States*. Cambridge: Cambridge University Press.

Rogers, James H. 1932. "Gold, International Credits and Depression." *Journal of the American Statistical Association* 27 (September): 239–50.

———. 1933a. "The Absorption of Bank Credit." *Econometrica* 1 (January): 63–70.

———. 1933b. "Federal Reserve Policy in World Monetary Chaos." *American Economic Review Supplement* 23 (March): 119–29.

———. 1937. "Monetary Initiative in a Traditional World." In *The Lessons of Monetary Experience*, ed. Arthur D. Gayer, 99–116. New York: Farrar and Rinehart.

———. 1938. *Capitalism in Crisis*. New Haven: Yale University Press.

Romer, Christina D. 1986a. "Spurious Volatility in Historical Unemployment Data." *Journal of Political Economy* 94 (February): 1–32.

———. 1986b. "Is the Stabilization of the Postwar Economy a Figment of the Data?" *American Economic Review* 76 (June): 314–34.

———. 1988. "Comment on DeLong and Summers 'How Does Macroeconomic Policy Affect Output?'" *Brookings Papers on Economic Activity* (2): 485–90.

———. 1992. "What Ended the Great Depression?" *Journal of Economic History* 52 (December): 757–84.

———. 1999. "Why Did Prices Rise in the 1930s?" *Journal of Economic History* 59 (March): 167–99.

Romer, Christina D., and David H. Romer. 1990. "New Evidence on the Monetary Transmission Mechanism." *Brookings Papers on Economic Activity* (1): 149–213.

———. 1993. "Credit Channel or Credit Actions? An Interpretation of the Postwar Transmission Mechanism." In *Changing Capital Markets: Implications for Monetary Policy*, 71–116. Kansas City: Federal Reserve Bank of Kansas City.

Roose, Kenneth D. 1954. *The Economics of Recession and Revival*. New Haven: Yale University Press.

Roosevelt, Franklin D. 1938. *The Public Papers and Addresses of Franklin D. Roosevelt*. Vol. 2, *1933: The Year of Crisis*. New York: Random House.

Rush, Mark. 1987. "Real Business Cycles." *Economic Review*, Federal Reserve Bank of Kansas City 72 (February): 20–32.

Samuelson, Paul A. 1942. "Fiscal Policy and Income Determination." *Quarterly Journal of Economics* 56 (August): 575–605.

———. 1997. "Credo of a Lucky Textbook Writer." *Journal of Economic Perspectives* 11 (spring): 153–60.

Sandilands, Roger J. 1990. *The Life and Political Economy of Lauchlin Currie: New Dealer, Presidential Adviser, and Development Economist*. Durham, NC: Duke University Press.

Sargent, Thomas J. 1986. "The Ends of Four Big Inflations." In *Rational Expectations and Inflation*, ed. Robert E. Hall, 40–109. New York: Harper and Row.

Schumpeter, Joseph A. 1935. "A Theorist's Comment on the Current Business Cycle." *Journal of the American Statistical Association* 30 (March): 167–68.

———. 1939. *Business Cycles*. New York: McGraw-Hill.

Simmons, Edward C. 1940. "Treasury Deposits and Excess Reserves." *Journal of Political Economy* 48 (June): 325–43.

Simons, Henry C. 1934. "A Positive Program for Laissez Faire: Some Proposals for a Liberal Economic Policy." Public Policy Pamphlet no. 15. Reprinted in Simons, *Economic Policy for a Free Society*, 40–77. Chicago: University of Chicago Press, 1948.

———. 1948. *Economic Policy for a Free Society*. Chicago: University of Chicago Press.

Simonson, Donald G., and George H. Hempel. 1993. "Banking Lessons from the Past: The 1938 Regulatory Agreement Interpreted." *Journal of Financial Services Research* 7 (September): 249–67.

Slichter, Sumner H. 1936. "The Adjustment to Instability." *American Economic Review Proceedings* 26 (March): 196–213.

———. 1938. "The Downturn of 1937." *Review of Economic Statistics* 20 (August): 97–110.

Smithies, Arthur. 1946. "The American Economy in the Thirties." *American Economic Review Papers and Proceedings* 36 (May): 11–27.

Sprague, O. M. W. 1938. "The Recovery Problem in the United States." *American Economic Review, Supplement* 28 (March): 1–7.

Stein, Herbert. 1969. *The Fiscal Revolution in America.* Chicago: University of Chicago Press.

Steindl, Frank G. 1995. *Monetary Interpretations of the Great Depression.* Ann Arbor: University of Michigan Press.

———. 1997. "Was Fisher a Practicing Quantity Theorist?" *Journal of the History of Economic Thought* 19 (fall): 241–60.

———. 1998. "The Decline of a Paradigm: The Quantity Theory and Recovery in the 1930s." *Journal of Macroeconomics* 20 (fall): 821–41.

———. 2000. "Does the Fed Abhor Inflation?" *Cato Journal* 20 (winter): 215–21.

Summers, Lawrence H. 1986. "Some Skeptical Observations on Real Business Cycle Theory." *Federal Reserve Bank of Minneapolis Quarterly Review* 10 (fall): 23–27.

Tavlas, George S. 1997. "Chicago, Harvard, and the Doctrinal Foundations of Monetary Economics." *Journal of Political Economy* 105 (February): 153–77.

Temin, Peter. 1989. *Lessons from the Great Depression.* Cambridge: MIT Press.

Temin, Peter, and Barrie A. Wigmore. 1990. "The End of One Big Deflation." *Explorations in Economic History* 27 (4): 483–502.

Terkel, Studs. 1970. *Hard Times.* New York: Pantheon Books.

Thomas, Rollin G. 1942. *Our Modern Banking and Monetary System.* New York: Prentice-Hall.

Thorp, Willard L. 1934. "The History of Recovery." *American Economic Review Supplement* 24 (March): 1–9.

Towle, Lawrence W. 1935. "Time Deposits and Price Stability, 1922–28." *American Economic Review* 25 (December): 653–60.

Tugwell, Rexford G. 1932. "The Principle of Planning and the Institution of Laissez Faire." *American Economic Review Proceedings* 22 (March): 75–92.

U.S. Bureau of the Census. 1997. *Historical Statistics of the United States: Bicentennial Edition.* Cambridge: Cambridge University Press.

U.S. Department of Commerce. 2001. *National Income and Product Accounts of the United States, 1929–97.* Washington, DC: Government Printing Office.

U. S. Office of the Comptroller of the Currency. 1934. *Annual Report.* Washington, DC: Government Printing Office.

———. 1937. *Annual Report.* Washington, DC: Government Printing Office.

U.S. Treasury Department. 1935. *Annual Report of the Secretary of the Treasury for the Fiscal Year Ended June 30 1934.* Washington, DC: Government Printing Office.

———. 1936. *Annual Report of the Secretary of the Treasury for the Fiscal Year Ended June 30 1935.* Washington, DC: Government Printing Office.

Vernon, J. R. 1994. "World War II Fiscal Policies and the End of the Great Depression." *Journal of Economic History* 54 (December): 850–68.

Villard, Henry H. 1937. "The Federal Reserve System's Monetary Policy in 1931 and 1932." *Journal of Political Economy* 45 (December): 721–39.

———. 1941. *Deficit Spending and the National Income.* New York: Farrar and Rinehart.

von Mises, Ludwig. 1951. *Socialism: An Economic and Sociological Analysis.* New Haven: Yale University Press.

Warburton, Clark. 1966. *Depression, Inflation, and Monetary Policy: Selected Papers, 1945–1953.* Baltimore: Johns Hopkins University Press.

Watkins, T. H. 1999. *The Hungry Years: A Narrative History of the Great Depression in America.* New York: Henry Holt.

Weinstein, Michael M. 1980. *Recovery and Redistribution under the NIRA.* Amsterdam: North-Holland.

Wheelock, David C. 1991. *The Strategy and Consistency of Federal Reserve Monetary Policy, 1924–1933.* Cambridge: Cambridge University Press.

Whittlesey, C. R. 1939. "A New Instrument of Central Bank Policy." *Quarterly Journal of Economics* 54 (November): 158–60.

Wicker, Elmus R. 1965. "Federal Reserve Monetary Policy, 1922–33: A Reinterpretation." *Journal of Political Economy* 44 (June): 119–38.

Index